TESTIMONIALS

Read what powerful entrepreneurial women have to say about Dr. Patty Ann's *Not Tonight Dear, I've Got a Business to Run!*

"Dr. Patty Ann rolls up her sleeves to tackle what just may be the last frontier for women who yearn to create wildly successful businesses while keeping their marriage and family life intact! This is a brilliantly written and practical jewel of a book that every entrepreneur and woman business owner should read and take to heart!"

> Barbara Corcoran
> Founder—The Corcoran Group
> Best-selling author of *Shark Tales*

"This ground breaking book is a MUST read for female entrepreneurs and business owners seeking proven strategies and tools for building a successful, money-making business without having to sacrifice happiness in your marriage, family and other important relationships in your life. Relationship and Business Skills all in the same book—BRILLIANT and unprecedented!"

> Liz Lange
> Liz Lange Maternity, CEO and Founder

"The reality is: we can't keep our business and personal lives separate...and that's exactly why this book is so special. I've read a ton of books on entrepreneurship—but I've never read one written by a psychologist and relationship expert who's also an entrepreneur. There's incredible value in that unique perspective. I hadn't realized the odds against being a happily married entrepreneur: ½ of all marriages end in divorce + 9 out of 10 small businesses fail Congratulations on picking up this book—read it and you will have the tools to create an awesome life for yourself and your family."

> Susan Wilson, CEO
> The Judgment Group
> Fundher.com

"Superb! This book is a reality check for small business owners who are struggling to do it all—and who are putting their romantic relationship last. Dr. Patty Ann tells it like it really is. She's done her homework in writing a thoroughly researched, highly practical book that goes so far below the surface you might just wonder if she's been eavesdropping in your bedroom. With advice that's both profound and pragmatic, this book should be required reading within the first year of owning a business!"

Angelique Rewers, ABC, APR
The Corporate Agent

"I thoroughly enjoyed this book. It offers practical advice and forces you to ask all the right questions to ensure both a successful marriage and a successful business if you are thinking about starting and running your own business. The advice is down to earth and written with a warm, personal style. It includes great tips and exercises to cover all the important considerations.

"I particularly related to the chapter on risk assessment, which is useful both in your personal and family relationships, as well as in professional and work matters. I thought the questions and checklists in this section and the section on ones attitudes about money management, extremely well done.

"The lessons to be learned from reading this book cover all aspects of family life and provide wonderful insights on the importance of healthy communications and how to have healthy communications and conflict resolution with your spouse and family. The stories that are used to illuminate major points are very well done. They explore and address real feelings, offer sound advice without preaching, and truly enhance the point without overdoing it.

"I highly recommend this book as a "must read" for anyone considering becoming an entrepreneur. It will help you face the tough questions that you and your family must address before starting on the journey. It will help you really assess both the challenges and opportunities that you will face and give you very practical solutions on how to face them together, thus giving you a much better chance of both personal and professional success."

Juanita T. James
President & CEO
Fairfield County Community Foundation

Dr.
Patty Ann

NOT TONIGHT DEAR, I'VE GOT A BUSINESS TO RUN!

Enrich Your Marriage While Prospering In Your Business

Dr. Patty Ann Tublin

To Becci,
Wishing you
Success and love
Dr. Patty Ann

Copyright © 2012 Dr. Patty Ann Tublin, PsyD, MSW, MSW, MA, RN

Printed in the United States of America

ISBN 978-1467513-98-2

Library of Congress Control Number: TX-7-515-516

Distributed by Vervante Corporation www.vervante.com

This book is dedicated to my husband,

Mitch—the love of my life

&

our children: John, Bryan, Neil & Eileen

who radiate the very essence of love

Patty / Ann

ACKNOWLEDGEMENTS

As is true for most accomplishments, this book would not have been made possible without the love and support of so many people, some of whom I will mention now and others who insist on anonymity. First and foremost I would like to thank my husband Mitch, who supported me through every iteration and metamorphosis of this book and its publication. Without your unconditional love and support this book would have surely remained a "one day I am going to write a book" pipe dream! Thanks for being the wind beneath my wings!

Next I want to acknowledge all the clients and couples I have worked with over the years. Thank you for the blessing and privilege of allowing me to become an intricate part of your intimate lives. You have touched my heart and taught me more than you can imagine.

An incredibly heartfelt thanks goes out to two amazing women (you know who you are), who re-directed the course of this book in untold ways and helped make it a reality.

My profound thanks to Joan Neuschelar who, upon having read the initial version of this book told me it was about as exciting as watching paint dry. For better or worse, I have heeded your suggestion by adding a splash of color and more of my unbridled personality into this book.

Although I must apologize to his wife Rose for this, I begrudgingly thank Shawn Gibbs for his unsolicited advice and wisdom spewed forth on that rainy day on the "yacht" in Annapolis, Maryland—it's not true what "they" say about you Shawn! You charted a whole new course for this book—who would have thought?

Thanks to Pam and Al Irvine—who at any random moment could look out their window to find me lying in *their* pool—on *their* lounge chair—drinking and eating *their* refreshments as I de-stressed from the writing of this book! Remember guys—the blue pool chair that reclines in the water without spilling my drink is my favorite.

To my children: John, Bryan, Neil & Eileen—you have taught me more about life and love than you will ever know! Daddy & I have been truly blessed with the miracle of your lives! I do not tell you often enough how much I love you and how very proud I am of you.

My final acknowledgement goes out to my mom, Carole Ann Twomey. A woman of strength and courage who, widowed at 36 years old, spent her adult life working and raising 5 kids—never having the "luxury" of pursuing an entrepreneurial dream. You continue to be an inspiration to your children and grandchildren and you exemplify the concept of strength through adversity. You taught and demonstrated everything I needed to know to write this book: love of family, the value of education, hard work, commitment, resilience and perseverance. And I hate to admit you were right. If I hadn't gotten thrown out of Girl Scouts I might have learned to cook and sew—it would have come in handy!

Patty / Ann

TABLE OF CONTENTS

FOREWORD

When Dr. Patty Ann asked me to write the foreword for her upcoming book, I was flattered. It's an honor. Having now read the book—I'm looking at my marked up copy, with notes to myself all over the place, and I'm wishing that this busy entrepreneurial wife and mother had Dr. Patty Ann's counsel long before now. I needed this information more than any other woman on the planet, and I'm betting that most women who read this book will feel the same way!

I do believe entrepreneurship is much like one of those life experiences where the first high is so amazing, you end up spending the rest of your life in a futile attempt to feel that high again. So I'll confess right now, "My name is Susan Wilson and I'm addicted to entrepreneurship."

Entrepreneurship has impacted my personal relationships in a huge way. I wish I had this book long ago, when I signed the legal documents to become a founding member of my first startup in a hospital bed after giving birth to my second son. Within a few weeks, we created liveprint.com, raised $2 million in venture capital, did a strategic deal with the copy giant, Kinko's, raised another $10 million in venture capital as the company was rebranded kinkos.com (a separate entity from Kinko's that we intended to take public), and then the dotcom bubble burst. So we sold the company to Kinko's in 2000 for $100 million. Oh, and did I mention that I started all of this from a hospital bed after giving birth to my son? Yeah, it had a bit of an impact on his early months with Mom.

How about the start up that brought me to fire my husband? Think I could have used this book then? My second startup, The Judgment Group (TJG), earned me a spot on the *Fortune* Top Ten Female Entrepreneur List along with lifetime membership in Ernst & Young's Winning Women Program. That's the good news. But I had to fire my husband who was working with me, and by the way, during this time I gave birth to our third son. Giving birth to sons seems to be good luck when it comes to starting a company.

I didn't intend to sacrifice or make choices between my personal and professional roles, and I don't normally live with regrets, but I tell you what, I regret that I didn't have this book to read when I needed it over the past decade of the entrepreneurial rollercoaster ride.

I've read a ton of books on entrepreneurship but I've never read one written by a psychologist who's also an entrepreneur. There's incredible value in that unique perspective. I love that Dr. Patty Ann uses stories to share her wisdom. Somehow it makes the message more relatable and palatable.

An eternal optimist, I am absolutely a glass half-full girl. I happen to be a Certified Public Accountant and I truly consider myself a numbers girl. But until Dr. Patty Ann married up two key statistics, I hadn't realized the odds against being a happily married entrepreneur:

1/2 of all marriages end in divorce + 9 out of 10 small businesses fail

I haven't always fought fair with my husband or kids or even my parents—a revelation that jumped out at me while reading this book. I've manipulated my way to get what I wanted because I believed what I was doing was best for everyone. I thought I was doing something good but ultimately I was chipping away at my soul. And that's a tough lesson to learn at 41 years of age.

The reality is: *we can't keep our business and personal lives separate…* and that's exactly why this book is so special.

Congratulations on picking up this book. It happened for a reason. Figure out what it is, and create an awesome life for yourself and your family.

Susan Wilson, CEO

The Judgment Group

My About.Me Profile

PROLOGUE

By Dr. Patty Ann Tublin

If you are an entrepreneur, or you are married to one, you know that owning your own business carries with it a unique set of joys and challenges.

As a married entrepreneurial woman with four children, it has been my burning desire to write this book since giving birth to my oldest children, identical twin boys, John and Bryan. Once I became a Mom, I immediately began trying to figure out how in the world I was ever going to create a successful, meaningful career while raising my kids, (who were very premature and sick at birth), without losing the happiness in my marriage—or my mind! Two years after the birth of my twins, I gave birth to my third son Neil; four years later, just when I thought life couldn't get any crazier or more hectic, my daughter Eileen was born.

Those early years of my young family's life—caring for four children born six years apart, growing a private psychotherapy practice, being married to a husband with a corporate career, and caring for the family dog—were filled with days and nights when I literally did not have time to go to the bathroom alone or think one solitary thought. Forget about finding the time or energy to write a book; it was a cause for celebration when I was able to drink three sips of coffee—while it was still hot—without someone screaming: "Mom, where are you? I need you—NOW!!"

For the breadth of my career as a relationship and communication expert and therapist, which now spans over two decades, I have revisited, and been consistently asked by other women: "how can we be successful in our careers without sacrificing happiness in our marriage and family life?" *Women desperately want and need to know the answer to this question.*

For me, and I would imagine the readers of this book, the answer to this question has been found in entrepreneurship—owning your own business, or working for yourself, where you create the rules you work and play by. It is my personal experience and belief that entrepreneurship provides women with a much greater chance of creating business success that enhances our marriage and family life, so we are not faced with the false choice of a successful career or happy marriage and family life. The flexibility of entrepreneurship, which allows for the scheduling of our own work hours along with the freedom to work where we want, on the projects we want, with whom we want, is irreplaceable for an entrepreneurial woman and mom like myself. For all these benefits and advantages however, there is the flip side of entrepreneurship and owning your own business. The following dilemma I experienced years ago clearly illustrates the challenges of entrepreneurship and it is still etched in my mind as if it were yesterday. I bet you'll relate:

> *A winter snowstorm crippled the North East, canceling school for my young children, my husband was stranded in an airport away on a business trip, and the babysitter for my infant daughter was snowed in. The first client of the day in my practice was an extremely driven executive. I knew full well he would have never thought to cancel our regularly scheduled appointment, blizzard or no blizzard—and just as importantly, he would have every expectation that I would be in my office available to him. If I were working for someone else, I would have called the office, asked them to re-schedule this client—and my entire day because I would not be coming in. However this was my private practice and it was my responsibility and problem to solve. The buck stopped with me! My friends still tease me about the frantic early morning phone calls I made desperate for someone to watch my kids. They jokingly tell my husband they thought I was going to have a heart attack, I sounded so stressed that wintry morning.*

My point is for all the positive aspects of owning your own business, there are also many challenges and difficulties you don't have to deal with when working for someone else. When I elected to be there for my client, despite the challenges in childcare that this raised for me, I was still empowered, because I was making the decision to deliver for my client. If I worked for someone else, and I had to go through all these shenanigans, I would have been full of resentment and fear—will I be fired if I can't pull this off? Instead, I was full of adrenalin and self-empowerment and determination, and when I met with this client, in the middle of a blizzard, with my kids safely cared for, I remember feeling, *whew, I did it, and this feels good*, and also feeling, *wow, that was really tough! But at least, if I had to go through that, it was for my own business, and not to make someone else rich.*

Whether you have children or not, female entrepreneurship brings its own set of struggles for women who are multi-tasking at what feels like the speed of light. I would be shocked to discover that the only thing you are doing as you read this book now, is reading this book.

Nonetheless, entrepreneurship is the path I have gladly chosen and if I were to do it all over again—I would not hesitate for a moment to walk down this same road. That being said, it would have been really nice to have had the information available to me that is within this book, but raising four kids, taking care of my marriage, expanding my work from a private practice to include professional speaking, seminars and workshops for entrepreneurial groups and corporations, the question remained: "How am I ever going to find a way to write this book?"

And then it suddenly dawned on me! I already had a lot of written material relevant for my book created in preparation for the workshops, seminars and speaking engagements I hold around the world.

With dogged determination, which has always been one of my character traits (so much so I can be a royal pain in the neck) this book began to come to life. I awoke in the early morning hours, long before my family or the sun came up and using my speaking material as a very rudimentary blueprint, I expanded my writings—which actually transcended my original material and this book became a reality.

I am so excited to share with my clients, and women I may never meet, real practical solutions to the problems that are keeping them from creating the meaningful, happy life they want to enjoy. Throughout the years, as my work evolved, I met even more women, in both the entrepreneurial and corporate world—from those running seven-figure businesses to those struggling to make ends meet—who were feeling pressured and/or frazzled to make a false choice between a successful business or a happy marriage and family life.

If you are struggling with creating this meaningful life, please do not despair. It *is* possible to have business success that does not cost us our marriage—but it does require some creative work and proven strategies that must not be ignored. Take the time to do the exercises in this book and practice implementing its proven strategies. Read about the real life examples provided that illustrates how a marriage is capable of coming back from the brink of divorce and despair to happiness and commitment. Engage in honest discussions with your partner about the challenges you face and learn the art of problem solving with effective communication skills and conflict resolution techniques.

Regardless of the size or scope of your work, this book speaks to entrepreneurial women and business owners across the board. Whether you hold an MBA from an Ivy League university or a high school diploma, this book contains invaluable information and strategies for you. The creation of a business that complements, rather than competes against our marriage and family life is an evergreen issue for all working women. Although this book has been written for entrepreneurial women, it is relevant for corporate women who also feel pressured to make the same false choice between a successful career and a happy and meaningful marriage and family life.

It is your life to live. Don't let anyone tell you how to live it. As entrepreneurial women, we know success is not truly measured by the "bottom line" of our business but by the quality of our interpersonal relationships. Our marriage and children hold the most sacred place in our hearts. With careful deliberation and planning, you can reconcile your marriage and career, and create success and happiness on your own terms.

Dr. Patty Ann Tublin

HOW TO GET THE MOST VALUE OUT OF THIS BOOK

We are all busy women. We're lucky if we can fit in the time for a hair cut, or a trip to the gym, or a cup of coffee with a good friend. It's a luxury to read a book cover to cover. Most of us pick up a good book from time to time, reading what we can finish before the next responsibility calls us away. I understand. I'm there too. I have a stack of books in my office I'm in the middle of reading, and I know the feeling of wishing that I could just slow down the world for a few minutes so I can catch up. In fact I just purchased a Kindle in the hopes of technology assisting me to find more time to read.

So, I get it. You don't have the time, really, to read this book. And yet, you bought it because you are in pain in your marriage, or because you want to prevent getting into pain. And you know that if you don't invest some time into figuring out how to reconcile the responsibilities of work and family, your marriage could go off in a ditch.

So this is what I suggest.

If you can't resist going first to the chapter topic that is calling your name, just do it, go there first.

But then return to the beginning, because a lot of research and thought went into this book and although it's tempting to skip around, I take you through a process that is much more effective, and powerful, if you begin at the beginning, and walk through it step by step until you reach the end of the book.

Throughout the book there are exercises for you and your spouse to complete, to enhance understanding and dialogue of complex issues that have likely arisen in your relationship, and if they haven't, they will.

Yes, it's tempting to skip forward past those exercises – who needs more work?

Take it from me, I have invested years of my life learning and working as a relationship expert, I see the aftermath of couples who choose not to invest essential time into talking about hot topics before they get too hot to handle.

Consider this book a lot cheaper than marriage counseling and/or a divorce attorney! Now I am making this as easy as possible for you. (Almost) every exercise in this book is available for you to download as a PDF. You are provided with links to quizzes and other resources outside of this book. This is all available for you both so make use of it all.

Make a date night with your spouse and read it together. Get together with a girlfriend and talk it over with her. Scribble notes all over this book, or use a journal. Whatever you do, use it. Because I didn't write this book so that it will sit on your bookshelf looking brand new. I hope that your copy becomes dog-eared and worn out from use, and that you feel that you got exactly what you needed when you needed it, and before you were in trouble. And even better, I hope this book is shared with your spouse/intimate partner, who needs this book too.

Invest in yourself, and in your marriage. You are worth it.

Dr. Patty Ann Tublin

PART 1

CREATING
A FAMILY
PLAN

Not Tonight Dear, I've Got a Business to Run!

I

FAMILY PLANNING— I'M NOT JUST TALKING BIRTH CONTROL!

Considering Family Issues When Choosing Entrepreneurship

> When I decided to buy the sporting goods store, my husband, David, said he was all for it. But then he started giving me all sorts of grief when I had to work long hours and when we couldn't take our normal vacations anymore. I wish I had known how he really felt before I bought the store.
>
> *David and Jill, a couple in their mid-fifties*

After twenty-seven years of marriage, David and Jill found themselves on different paths. Jill dreamed of several prosperous stores and David longed for a comfortable early retirement with his wife. If they had discussed the questions necessary for entrepreneurs to create a mutual family plan, then they might have discussed their differences before investing their savings in the sporting goods store.

You've heard the gruesome statistics. Over half of all marriages will end in divorce. (Believe me, I know—my practice is full of couples on the brink of divorce if we don't do something fast to quiet the raging fire.) Add to that the fact that statistically, the chances of succeeding in a small business are about one in ten, and in all marriages, you can bet that during some time in their marriage, one or both of the spouses is apt to say to one another: "Honey, I've been laid off," or, "Sweetheart, what do you think if I quit my job and invest in an Internet business instead," or, "Dear, I have bad news—that idiot boss of mine fired me!," or "Sugar, let's go into business together, what do you think?!"

If you are considering becoming an entrepreneur by either starting your own business, or purchasing a business with your spouse or significant other, or you are already committed to entrepreneurship as a lifestyle, you've probably bought this book to help you beat the odds against divorce and business failure. Business experts stress the importance of creating a thorough strategic business plan before starting a new business. Women entrepreneurs and small business owners understand that we now need to learn how to prepare a family plan as well. Why? *Women do not want success in business to come at the expense of happiness in their marriage and family life and relationships.* Women have created a sense of urgency for a family plan as we embrace entrepreneurship at twice the rate of men while populating more seats than men in graduate professional programs such as medicine and law. Women want, and actually demand, a life that creates financial and personal success. Entrepreneurship is the answer to this burning desire and the question to: "How do I create a life I love?" A well thought out family plan makes certain our business and relationship goals are in synch, supporting rather than being at odds with each other. The old paradigm of keeping your business and personal life totally separate from each other doesn't work for entrepreneurial and self-employed women (and it never really worked all that great for men either). Today's women seek to reconcile and blend their professional and personal lives—something which is made simultaneously easier and more difficult thanks to modern technology.

Eleanor Roosevelt said: "The future belongs to those who believe in the beauty of their dreams." Women in today's modern world are better-educated and more driven for professional success than ever before. They are no longer bound by stereotypes with the new image of women represented quite well by the old commercial words: "We can bring home the bacon and fry it up in a pan and never let you forget you're a man". To do this we need a paradigm shift, one that acknowledges how our business success is influenced by success in our intimate and personal relationships.

This chapter provides the tools necessary for creating a family plan that meets the unique needs of every couple and family, not a one size fits all plan. For female entrepreneurs our goal is to create a thriving, profitable business while maintaining a romantic, loving relationship and fulfilling family life. Current research suggests people in happy relationships are more successful in business. Therefore, creating a family plan is as imperative to your entrepreneurial success as is your business plan.

WHY CREATE A FAMILY PLAN?

When you live with people who are important to you, business decisions are no longer entirely yours to make. What you do for a living, and how you shape your workday, affects all who live with you, or rely on you, each day. News flash: your business is not just about you!

The most common mistake married entrepreneurs make is to rush into business decisions without careful thought and discussion of how their business dreams will involve and affect their family. Consider several reasons why this happens:

- *Blind enthusiasm:* The entrepreneur, so excited about the prospect of a new business, doesn't want to consider any possible negative resistance.

- *Running away:* The entrepreneur is rebounding from sudden job loss, job dissatisfaction, worries about finances, or the failure of another business. The need to move quickly into a new alternative takes precedence over careful planning.

- *Egocentricity:* The entrepreneur assumes that his or her spouse and family will make the necessary adjustments to support him or her. For most couples, this is just not happening.

- *Fear or inability to communicate:* The entrepreneur isn't accustomed to discussing openly with a spouse issues that will affect their relationship and lifestyle. Act first, talk later (only if necessary), is this entrepreneur's motto. This is not recommended for any aspect of your relationship, and certainly not one that has financial ramifications.

- *Blissful naivete:* The entrepreneur is completely unaware of how the prospective business will affect marriage and family life. He or she can't imagine potential concerns and questions until they actually arise.

The most common mistake partners of entrepreneurs make is to offer unconditional support from the beginning—in concept—without thinking through the implications of such a lifestyle change. It is easy to be the head cheerleader early on in the game, but when your team is not doing so well it is more difficult to hold up the pom-poms. Support wanes when the actual hardships of self-employment rub up against their fantasy. Consider several reasons why this happens:

- *Well-intended support:* They want to champion their partner's dreams. They don't want to throw cold water on their mate's enthusiasm.

- *Starstruck:* They share their partner's romantic vision for great prosperity and an improved relationship and family life. They are as excited as their partners about the entrepreneurial opportunity ahead.

- *Lack of knowledge or awareness:* They don't really understand the demands of entrepreneurship or self-employment and how their partner's self-employment will affect their life.

- *Fear or inability to communicate:* They feel great reservations but are afraid to voice their opinion. They don't want their partners to think less of them, be angry with them, or feel unsupported by them.

- *It's better than nothing:* Their partner's job loss or lack of meaningful work frightens them. They are anxious for their spouses to find their right livelihood or to earn some income, even if family sacrifices may be necessary.

- *They weren't asked:* Though their partner's worklife affects them, their partners don't invite their involvement in the planning process or ask for their opinion. This may be okay if the business takes off, but watch out for fireworks in the relationship if it doesn't.

Some entrepreneurial naiveté is par for the course. Self-employment always involves risk and unknowns. To muster the courage required to start a business, entrepreneurs and their spouses must view their entrepreneurial prospects with a certain amount of romantic illusion. It is not unlike getting married or raising a child. Ask any honest parent if they were truly prepared for parenthood and they will resoundingly tell you "no way". Having said that, most will admit it is the hardest job they will ever love. Most parents secretly hold the fantasy that they are going to parent differently than everyone else, "differently" being the code word for "better". This fantasy goes out the window when reality rears its ugly head.

I remember my client, the new mom who insisted her infant son would *"never"* and she would emphasize the word *"never"*, play with toy guns. A few years later, I ran into this mom, now with two boy toddlers in the grocery store. The boys were shooting each other with fake guns in the grocery store aisles, playing special operations forces U. S. Navy SEALs. When inquiring about what happened to her edict about her boys *never* playing with toy guns, this mom just threw her hands up in the air and said: "Oh yeah, I gave up on that a few years ago; it was just too exhausting and unrealistic. I have to pick my battles."

Combining marriage and business; however, doesn't have to be a battlefield. Without a family plan, when the romantic illusion of your business dies, and its death impacts your marriage, your marriage may very well become a battlefield. Creating a family plan should avert these battles by preparing for the realities of entrepreneurship grounded in shared visions and goals for your business, marriage and family.

When we make a deep personal commitment to a relationship, "for better or worse," we know on some level that those worse days will come, yet we secretly hope they won't. We focus initially on positive dreams for the future and the deep love we feel for our partners. Imagine if we had a crystal ball and on our wedding day we could see some of our worst days ahead. If we knew what was ahead we might think we need our heads examined to sign up for this commitment of a lifetime. We might actually change our minds and check out of the relationship all together. Rosy-colored, romantic illusion encourages us to embark on an unpredictable difficult journey. Although we might be better off not knowing the exact trials and tribulations that await us, we still need some contingency plans in place for when unforeseen problems arise.

The family plan is a map as well as a compass for your entrepreneurial adventure. Creating a family plan will not eliminate your romantic vision or throw cold water on your entrepreneurial dreams. It will, however, ensure that you are at least traveling with your partner on the same path, in the right general direction. Thoroughly discussing your business dreams and planning with your family will help you choose the entrepreneurial path with the most potential for satisfying your long-term individual, couple, and family goals.

Before you choose to commit to your spouse for a lifetime, you ask and answer at least some basic questions. Do you want children? Where do you want to live? What religion will you observe? How much money and sex do you need to be happy? Though aware of differences, when the answers to enough basic questions are in sync with each other, you are able to envision building a life together. The same goes for business. This chapter provides discussion points so that you can involve your partner as early in the business planning process as possible. You can construct a family plan in any format that suits you, written or verbal, formal or casual, as long as it answers your most important couple/family questions and concerns.

FIFTY QUESTIONS TO ASK YOURSELF AND YOUR SIGNIFICANT OTHER WHEN CREATING A FAMILY PLAN

Think of creating a family plan for your business venture as the equivalent of those late-night discussions you enjoyed with your partner when you were first dating. Remember when you shared your dreams with each other in detail, when you wanted to know everything about each other? You would visualize how your life would look and feel after you took the plunge to live together, how you would share your living space, where you would live, even questions as simple as who would get the bigger closet (even though we all know the woman gets the bigger closet, always)!

When you meet your life partner, you answer questions big and small in order to merge your lives. The longer you are with your mate, the less likely you may be to communicate with each other like you did during those early dating times of all night conversations. Yet, the consideration of self-employment alternatives deserve that kind of soul searching discussion between you and your significant other, regardless of how long you have been together. Setting aside private time from your busy lives to answer the following questions about any self-employment alternative that either or both of you are considering will save you much heartache and financial woe down the road. As John Wooden, the legendary UCLA basketball coach said: "failing to prepare is preparing to fail".

Individually, in preparation for a serious discussion with your spouse/significant other, review the questions I've prepared for you here, derived from my research and understanding of what successful entrepreneurial couples consider as they are delving into a new entrepreneurial venture that will surely affect their family life:

DISCOVERY EXERCISE ONE: CONSIDERING FAMILY ISSUES

Completion time: 60-120 minutes

If you are exploring a particular self-employment option, set aside at least an hour or two with your spouse to consider the answers to the following questions. Answering these questions will help you evaluate how well a self-employment option suits you, your spouse, and your family.

Important Note: These fifty questions are designed to launch you and your partner into initial discussion of some of the larger issues related to self-employment. These questions are a good start toward thinking about family plan issues, but not all the questions to be considered. The chapters that follow in this book will lead you into discussion of family plan issues in more depth and enable you to prepare a more thorough family plan.

You may wish to write down your answers to these questions in a journal or to discuss them with your mate.

FINANCIAL CONSIDERATIONS

Initial Investment

1. How much initial capital will be necessary?
2. Will you need to borrow capital to invest?
3. What proportion of your total assets will you need to invest?
4. What major purchases are required?

Ongoing Investment

5. How much cash is required monthly to support the business?

Length of Time Before Positive Cash Flow

6. What is the learning curve in this business? How much time will it take before you can expect to be profitable?

Income Projections

7. What are reasonable expectations for positive cash flow in three, six, and nine months, one year, two years, five years?

Transition Options

8. Can you test the waters while keeping your current job?
9. Can you work the business part-time?
10. How long will the initial purchase or setup process take?

Insurance and Taxes

11. How will insurance needs for your family be cared for? What are the tax implications of the business?

Perceived Risk

12. Considering the norm in the industry, what are the likely odds for success?
13. What do you risk if the business fails?

TIME CONSIDERATIONS

Total Time

14. How much time every day and week is required to operate the business successfully?

Working Schedule

15. What will your working hours be?
16. Are there seasonal, daily, or monthly cycles to the business?

Vacations, Weekends, and Holidays

17. Will the business allow for vacation time—how much?
18. Will the business require weekend work or working on holidays?

TRAVEL CONSIDERATIONS

Travel Required

19. Will your business require any travel?
20. Will travel be local, national, or international?
21. Will the travel require overnight absence from home—for how long at a stretch? How much of an issue will that be for your spouse and/or children?
22. How long will the daily commute be? How will that impact your family life?

HOME OFFICE CONSIDERATIONS

Home Office

23. Will you work out of the home? Full-time or part-time?
24. What are the zoning regulations in your town?
25. How conducive is your home and family to a home office?
26. Does the business have to be located in any particular place? How does that mesh with the current location of your home?

PERSONAL CONSIDERATIONS

Right Livelihood

27. How does the business fit in with your natural personal inclination, what you love to do and do well at, your skills and abilities?
28. How excited are you about the product or service you will be delivering?
29. How will this business option help you achieve your business and family goals?
30. How does this business option integrate with your values?

Perceived Emotional Stress

31. How stressful for you would this business choice be? Are there aspects of the business you expect to find difficult?

32. How demanding will the working schedule be? Will you have to sacrifice anything important to your physical, emotional, and spiritual health in order to succeed in this business?

RELATIONSHIP CONSIDERATIONS

Spouse or Partner Involvement

33. To what extent will your spouse or partner be involved in the business operations?

34. To what extent will your spouse or partner be involved in the initial decision-making and setup process?

35. How supportive is your spouse or partner about this business option?

36. To what extent does this business option require your spouse's cooperation or support to succeed?

Couple Goals

37. How does this business option support your short- and long-term goals as a couple?

38. How is this business option synchronous with your mission and values as a couple?

Synergy

39. How does this business option mesh with your partner's work and livelihood? Is it synergistic, harmonious, and complementary? How will it conflict?

Relationship Maintenance

40. How much intimate time will you be able to devote to your partner?

41. Will you be working together? If so, what relationship issues are you concerned about?

42. How will this business option improve, solidify, or sustain your relationship?

43. How could this business option jeopardize or deteriorate your relationship?

CHILDREN CONSIDERATIONS (if applicable)

Family Support

44. What kind of family support do you need to be successful?
45. Will the children help in the business? How and when?

Family Needs

46. How will this business option allow you to care for your family needs?
47. How will this business option interfere with caring for your children or other family members' daily needs?

Long-Term Family Goals

48. Do you hope to pass the business along to your children?
49. How does the business support long-term financial goals for your children?
50. Will this business option prevent you from being able to meet your short- or long-term goals for your children?

CONSIDERING THE FAMILY PROS AND CONS OF SELF-EMPLOYMENT ALTERNATIVES

A business plan provides the framework for discussing and planning business activities and outcomes; it cannot prevent all business problems from happening. A family plan functions the same way. Your answers to the preceding questions will not eliminate challenges to your relationship and family. Every choice has its unique consequences, both benefits *and* hardships. The question at hand is not, "How can we avoid all stress?" but rather, "What kind of stress am I and my family willing to bear?" "How can we best prepare to manage this stress?"

Entrepreneurial couples report common positive and negative family experiences with a variety of entrepreneurial and self-employment options. Consider the following summary as warning signs, as sharing good news of coming attractions, and not as predictions of how your individual choice of business will turn out.

Starting Your Own Manufacturing Business

The good news is:

- You can take a timely idea, turn it into a finished product, and make a fortune.

- You can develop a company to be sold or passed along to children.

- You can build a company of several hundred or thousands of employees and have a critical impact on their life by handsomely rewarding their work. Your employees can become a part of your extended family.

- You can work with your spouse as a full partner. If your skills are very different from each other, and your work complements each other, all the better.

The bad news is:

- Changes in the economy, competition, or other external factors can suddenly put you out of business.

- You may have to travel extensively from home.

- The risk may be higher, and the financial investment greater, than you or your spouse had bargained on taking.

- You may find yourself working harder and longer hours than you ever worked before and family/relationship time may suffer.

- You may not want the headache or liability of managing other employees.

Starting a Service, Professional, or Commission Sales Business

The good news is:

- Depending on your service, you may be able to work anywhere in the country

- Start-up investment can be relatively low.

- You may be able to work out of your home.

- You can work flexible hours, depending on who your clients are and how much income you want to earn.

- You may never have to manage an employee other than yourself.

The bad news is:

- It can be a lot harder to get paying clients than you expected.

- Income is limited by what you can do with your time, unless you partner with someone or add staff. Your potential earnings is limited.

- You'll have to cope with your fair share of rejection.

- As a sole proprietor, you'll need to do tasks you may not be very good at, or like to do, unless you partner with someone who complements your strengths.

- You can come up with a powerful idea and a useful product, and still not be able to get the product to market or make a profit—even after years of work.

Buying a Franchise

The good news is:

- You are buying a product or service with a proven track record, so the chances of success are higher.

- You will receive training and support from your franchisor so you're not alone.

- The learning curve is reduced, since you are provided with the systems to follow.

- You can sell the franchise when you are ready to move on.

- Some franchises are ideally suited for working with your spouse and family.

The bad news is:

- You'll have to give up some control to your franchisor.

- The working hours of some franchises, particularly retail ones, can be exhausting.

- The initial capital investment can be sizable.

- The process for being selected as a franchisee can be time-consuming and very competitive.

- You'll probably have all the headaches associated with hiring and managing staff.

- You will be limited by your franchisor in your individual creativity and innovation.

Buying an Existing Business

The good news is:

- You will receive a good sense of the cash flow you can expect from the beginning.

- You may be able to purchase good will and reputation in the community.

- You can be profiting from day one if you buy the right business.

- The seller may be willing to extend purchase terms that lower the initial capital required.

- You can turn the right kind of business into a family business.

The bad news is:

- It can be as difficult to find a good business to buy as it is to find the right marriage partner.

- You may need to spend sizable dollars renovating or improving the business.

- Depending on the business, the working hours can be extremely demanding.

- You may discover negative aspects about the business after you have bought it.

- Selling a business can be a difficult, time-consuming process, if you decide you want to sell.

Patty / Ann

CONCLUSION

Since you purchased this book you are cognizant, at least on some level, of the necessity to create both a family plan and a business plan when embarking upon an entrepreneurial journey. Your relationships with your spouse and children are directly impacted when you take on the challenges of entrepreneurship and/or self-employment. Unanticipated financial, time and emotional stressors will influence your relationship with your spouse and children and jeopardize your chance for entrepreneurial success if you fail to create a family plan which anticipates the most likely challenges of self-employment. Married entrepreneurial wives and mothers do not have to sacrifice success in business in order to be happily married, and an effective parent!

If you would like the 50 questions listed here in this chapter to have on your computer, or to print out, go to www.relationshiptoolbox.com/familyplan.

II

THERE'S MORE THAN ONE RIGHT WAY TO DO IT!

Supporting and Partnering on the Entrepreneurial Journey

We'd kill each other if my spouse and I tried to run the same business together.

We can't relate to couples who hardly see each other all week. We spend twenty-four hours a day together and we love it.

We could never handle the risk of both of us being self-employed.

Which of these statements applies to you? What works well for one married couple may be disastrous for another. Every marriage and business is unique, and each couple has to search for the right path for them.

Some couples move through all combinations of marriage and entrepreneurship as life circumstances change. Other couples plant themselves squarely in one model for their entire marriage.

Similarly, when it comes to couples and entrepreneurship, some couples will settle into a comfortable routine, with each spouse finding their niche and sticking with it, and other couples will change their approach to entrepreneurship several times over their married life.

The question isn't which model of entrepreneurship is less stressful. The question is what *kinds* of stress do *you* choose to take on? What outcomes would *you* find the most rewarding? What type of stress is worth taking on for you and your relationship?

Let's begin by looking at three different models for combining entrepreneurship and relationship:

1. *Full partnership:* Full and equal partners in the same business. For example, Kyle and Alexis run a chain of franchise stores together.
2. *Dual entrepreneurship:* Each individual operates his or her own separate business. For example, Adrian is self-employed as a desktop publisher, and Joe is a chiropractor.
3. *Spousal support:* One spouse supports the entrepreneurial efforts of the other but does not work as a full partner in the entrepreneur's business. For example, Elaine works a salaried job and takes care of the children. Her husband, Robert, founded and heads up an engineering firm.

What can you expect in each of these scenarios? This chapter contains the lion's share of information needed to help you decide what type of entrepreneurial business model works best for you and your unique relationship and family goals. What are the primary challenges and rewards of each, and how can you tell which one is best for you and your marriage? This section walks you through each model with three assessment tests designed to predict your chances for success in each of the three. It is chock full of exercises and questions that business owners often neglect to ask, or don't know they should ask as they begin an entrepreneurial journey, one which impacts our partner and family as much as it impacts ourselves. You'll also find recommended strategies for solving common problems that entrepreneurial couples like you have successfully faced, taken from my research with entrepreneurial couples and clinical experience as a relationship expert helping troubled couples survive and thrive during entrepreneurial careers.

Let's begin by looking at the first model, full partnership. Whether you are currently working with your partner, considering the possibility, or curious about what it takes to make this model work *successfully,* read the next section. Caution: Many couples find this entrepreneurial model difficult for their relationship; the section below will help you decide with your eyes wide open if this model suits you and your partner.

Patty / Ann

BUSINESS OWNERSHIP MODEL ONE: FULL PARTNERSHIP

Full partners may have started the business together, or one spouse may join the first spouse after the launch of the business.

Both individuals are equally dedicated to the business, although their roles may be very different from each other.

Some examples:

- Co-owners of a restaurant

- Professional speaker and office manager

- President and vice president of a manufacturing company

- Partners in a computer consulting company

- Joint upline in a multilevel marketing organization

Are You Cut Out for Working with Your Spouse as a Business Partner?

A *preference* for the *lifestyle* benefits of full partnership does not necessarily mean that this arrangement *suits* your partnership. Many happy couples readily admit they would prefer death by a thousand cuts rather than work with their partner. The choice, however, is for each couple to decide what works best for them. There is no right or wrong model and one is not better than another. The key is to be cognizant of the different models and understand the ramifications it has for your relationship.

Evan and Carole opened up a franchise ice cream store 15 years into their marriage when Evan decided to quit practicing law. Prior to this time, Carole found herself pursuing a part-time job. Carole was extremely extroverted and loved volunteering with her home being "the" meeting place for the many organizations she chaired. Neither partner realized how Carole's innate capacity for giving and her inability to say "no" would bode disastrous for their entrepreneurial business. This couple could not predict how often and how many of Carole's friends would visit the ice cream shoppe seeking Carole's advice on school and/or community projects. While Carole interacted with her friends, Evan was left to work the counter alone. Evan became angry and resentful of Carole "wasting" time socializing instead of working. When Evan approached Carole with this anger and resentment, Carole was devastated and this couple sought my help. Their marriage was hanging on a thread as their commitment and emotional connection faltered. Carole and Evan were unprepared for the reality of how their business would compromise their leisure time and how their personal attributes would become a professional liability.

The following assessment test will help you evaluate whether becoming full business partners will strengthen your marriage and your business. Created from my research and interviews with successful couples in full partnership, this test highlights those elements found in solid, rewarding business and marriage partnerships or missing from those partnerships that failed.

No test is entirely predictive. You may beat the odds and create an outstanding business partnership, even with a low score on this test. Or, you can score high on this test, but then stumble through particular challenges, resulting in a counterproductive partnership.

Patty / Ann

DISCOVERY EXERCISE ONE:
ASSESSMENT TEST FOR JOINT PARTNERS

Important: Take the test separately from your spouse. Then get together to share the results.

Place the appropriate number next to each question, and then total your score.

> 1 = That doesn't describe us at all.
>
> 2 = That describes us somewhat.
>
> 3 = That describes us frequently.
>
> 4 = That describes us completely.

☐ We have worked successfully on joint projects many times in our marriage. We enjoy the process and get good results.

☐ We value each other's opinion and respect and admire each other's skill. If I were looking to hire a business partner, I would consider myself lucky to acquire my spouse's talents.

☐ I can freely express my opinions to my spouse, even if we disagree. My spouse listens to what I have to say and respects my involvement. We have learned that the best decision is one that considers both of our points of view.

☐ We understand that no one is perfect. If one of us makes a mistake, the other is generally forgiving. We apologize to each other when it's appropriate.

☐ We consider ourselves equal business partners in ability, dedication, and contribution. Since we have complementary skills, we're stronger as a team than we are separately.

☐ Our motivations for starting the business are similar or in harmony with each other. We hold the same values and want the same results from our business.

☐ We always knew we would go into business together, ever since we got together. We talked about it even when we were dating. We were just waiting until the right time in our life to follow our dream.

☐ Spending more time together strengthens our marriage. I can spend hours with my spouse without feeling bored or irritated.

☐ When conflict arises, we don't let problems and resentments build between us. We communicate anger and criticism productively, taking responsibility for our own part of the problem.

☐ Neither of us needs to be in control all the time. We can share responsibilities and delegate when appropriate. We aren't competitive with each other or jealous of each other's success. Neither of us has difficulty sharing the credit for our success.

☐ We cope well with stress, individually and as a couple. We don't lose our sense of humor for long, and we keep perspective in the difficult times. We've come through hard times with an even stronger relationship.

☐ We know what our expectations of each other are, both at work and at home. We agree on how to divide household, child-care duties, and business responsibilities. Both of us are willing to pitch in and do tasks we don't like to do, just because they have to get done.

☐ If we need to find a compromise, we are flexible and willing to discuss the issue until we find a solution that satisfies both of us. Neither of us has to be right all the time. We enjoy collaborating with each other, and willingly sacrifice total control for the benefits of our team approach.

☐ We have complete trust in each other to make sound and well-reasoned business decisions. We don't feel threatened by any personal relationships that may form as a result of our business.

☐ Our commitment to a lifelong marriage is complete and total. We will seek outside help if necessary to prevent our relationship from deteriorating. We wouldn't continue working together in business if it meant sacrificing our marriage.

☐ We both have compatible tolerance for financial risk. We have discussed where our comfort zone is for financial risk. We commit to not going beyond the safety level of either of us.

☐ Before we even considered working together in business, we had a great relationship. We believe that the foundation of our marriage is strong enough to withstand the pressures of starting a business together. We look forward to how working together as business partners could strengthen our relationship.

☐ Both of us prefer a lifestyle that closely meshes together our business, relationship, and family life.

SCORE

56-72: Destined for Success. Your foundation is strong. Success as full partners is likely, as long as you keep doing the things that work so well for you. You'll still experience challenges along the way, but the rewards could be enormous.

37-55: It Could Go Either Way. The potential for success or trouble depends on how you respond to the aspects of working together that challenge you and your partnership. If you capitalize on your strengths and work hard to improve your individual and couple weaknesses, you could strengthen your marriage as well as your business if you go into partnership together.

18-36: Look Out! Trouble Ahead. Be forewarned of the potential risks of partnering together in business. Work to strengthen your marriage before you risk a full business partnership. Seek the advice or counsel of an objective third party before embarking on this journey.

Which of the Following Couples Can You Most Relate To?

Robert and Nancy began an online coaching business together. Robert was a detailed-oriented person and a "numbers" guy. He took care of all financial costs and aspects of the business and Nancy was the actual coach—or as she liked to refer to herself she was the "creative genius." Nancy came up with programs, products and other ideas for the business. Robert assessed Nancy's ideas and made them happen from an operational and financial perspective. Two of the biggest relationship assets this couple brought to their coaching business was their ability to work together predicated upon effective communication skills and an inherent trust and respect for the other's opinion. As you would expect, Robert and Nancy scored a very high 68, well within the destined for success range of the Assessment test for joint ventures described above.

Susan and Douglas opened a restaurant together. Douglas was raised in a family that owned and operated a successful restaurant business. Douglas was very comfortable surrounded by the noise, chaos, fast pace and interpersonal challenges a customer-owned business lends itself to. Susan grew up in a traditional family where dad worked in the corporate world and mom stayed at home. She describes her childhood as being a well-oiled machine—organized, structured and predictable. Susan's closet reflected her hyper-organized tendencies and need for control. Her clothes and shoes were systematically color-coded and everything was in its designated place. Douglas was just the opposite, in fact, he would tell you he was a bit of a slob. His closet had pants, socks and underwear strewn across the floor and the inside of his car looked like a tornado hit it with empty coffee cups, water bottles and candy wrappers everywhere. Susan would never ride in his car because the mess gave her angst just thinking about it.

Douglas' strength was his ability to roll with the punches and go with the flow. He was a natural people-person who made everyone feel immediately at ease in his presence. His innate people skills were honed during a childhood spent comfortably surrounded by the boisterous noise and unpredictable nature of a restaurant business. He was your classic "guys guy."

This couple scored 47, well within the mid-range of the Assessment test. Douglas and Susan had a 50/50 chance of their marriage surviving and/or thriving while they ran their restaurant together. This couple would need to very clearly define and compartmentalize their duties and responsibilities. Based on their individual strengths, Susan could be in charge of inventory, ordering, etc. Douglas should be the "face" of the restaurant—greeting and socializing with customers, while being the "go to" guy to handle customer and staffing problems. Compartmentalizing their jobs would allow Susan and Douglas to utilize the strengths of their personalities to run a smooth and efficient restaurant business while avoiding the inherent conflicts of their organizational differences. Based upon their score of 47—Susan and Douglas would be successful running their restaurant if they were to "divide and conquer" responsibilities.

Vinnie owned a roofing company and his wife Theresa was the bookkeeper. Vinnie was a headstrong male who felt he was always right. He grew up in a home where his father dominated his mother and his siblings. Vinnie incorporated this authoritative style into his own marriage. Theresa was the peacekeeper in the marriage, a role she learned all to well while mediating the fights she witnessed between her parents as a child. Theresa dealt with Vinnie's headstrong ways by selectively telling him only things she knew he would agree with. This relationship experienced a tremendous amount of mistrust and poor communication. Differences of opinion were ridiculed and conflicts were rarely resolved—if even discussed. It is no surprise this couple scored a very low 22 on the Assessment test described earlier. Their inability to effectively communicate, respect differences of opinion and resolve any conflict unfortunately, led this couple into divorce proceedings, with a failed business as well.

Patty / Ann

FIVE PRIMARY CHALLENGES
OF FULL PARTNERS

Challenge One:
Financial Risk

Let's review the common challenges and rewards of full partnership.

"Putting all your eggs in one basket" is an apt phrase for one of the primary drawbacks of the full partner model. Investing all your money, time, and effort as a couple into one endeavor can reap substantial rewards. If the venture fails, however, you may lose everything in your bank account, as well as your relationship. There is no other job or business in the household to fall back on if the venture doesn't work. You may forgo pension, life insurance and disability benefits, subsidized health insurance, and paid vacations. You may pay a premium to maintain those benefits as business owners.

Financial risk for full partners extends beyond the money lost if the business fails. It also permeates such common life events as buying a house or medical insurance. Prior to the financial collapse of Wall Street, many mortgage companies disdain applications submitted by business owners. Until your business is profitable and has been established for several years, borrowing money to purchase a home, a car, or any other major purchase may be impossible or very expensive. Mortgage brokers charge a premium for mortgages that carry titles like "Nonverifiable income."

> When we decided to go into business together, our greatest worry was how we could get medical insurance to cover Karen. At that time, no insurance plans for the self-employed would cover a preexisting condition like cancer. We had to squirrel away enough money in our savings account to pay for her treatments out of pocket. If she needs any type of intensive cancer treatment in the future, it could bankrupt us.
>
> *Franchise owner*

A potential solution: You may not be able to predict all trouble spots, but you can prepare for some of the bigger known issues. Create a contingency plan for paying the bills if the business isn't profitable in your projected time frame. Full partnership may be your model of choice, but if one or both of you think that the financial risk is too great, then you must be open to taking another path temporarily. Flexibility and respecting your partner's needs is critical.

Challenge Two:
Relationship Tension

Full business partnership puts such complex relationship issues as shared power, joint decision making, and managing differences in work style under the microscope. You may fear or even experience some of these common challenges:

Loss of sexual attraction: Do you compartmentalize your life? Is there room in your vision for a sexy business partner? Not for some.

When John and his wife, Barbara, began a consulting firm together, John no longer viewed his wife as a sexual partner. Barbara's role as a business partner took over his perception of her as his wife, and his libido was completely lost. John had difficulty transitioning from business partner to husband. He lost all sense of boundaries and talked about work-related issues with his wife incessantly. His failure to relate to Barbara as his wife and not his business partner grew exponentially with time.

A potential solution: John and Barbara needed to establish boundaries between their professional roles and personal relationship. John and Barbara sought my relationship expertise and we focused their work on creating distinct boundaries in three main areas of their lives: space, time and roles. They created a dedicated office within their home and removed work paraphernalia from all other areas. They established work hours and strictly adhered to them. They wrote up a job description giving John and Barbara equal status and clearly defined roles and responsibilities without any overlap. Following a very short time after implementing these clear parameters, John was able to differentiate between Barbara's role as wife and her role as his business partner. The bedroom re-emerged as a place for personal conversation and the expression of intimacy. Strong boundaries established around their work and personal roles allowed their romantic relationship to flourish once again.

Different work styles: The power of your complementary skills can become a source of conflict as you learn how to accept your workstyle differences. Learning to celebrate and embrace your complementary characteristics, rather than negatively judging your partner, will be one of your greatest challenges as a couple. Every couple must learn how to manage their differences. When you work with your spouse, this can become a daily issue:

> *"She's the detail person, I'm the big picture guy. She enjoys dealing with the customers and I prefer to focus on business operations. She works best late at night after the kids are asleep, and I work best first thing in the morning. She needs daily business meetings and frequent communication with me and I'm happier if we just meet weekly. We're so different, and the tension between us becomes palpable; especially when business finances become tight. Then she gets angry and inpatient with my "big picture" orientation and blames me because I don't like to pay attention to the details."*

A potential solution: These differing work styles can create tension between a couple that becomes a relationship dealbreaker. One way to diffuse these tensions is to have a contingency plan in place for dealing with potential business crises before they explode. Have an "escape plan" in place long before one is ever needed. For example, "Every Wednesday at 1:00 P.M., we will hold a team meeting if revenue drops below a mutually agreed upon number."

Negative judgment: Beyond accepting your differences in work style, you may also witness a side of your spouse's personality you hadn't seen before you began working together. Living with your spouse is one thing—working with them is quite another. If your spouse works at an outside job, you may never know that she gets snappy with her employees or that he spends two hours a day on personal calls. When you work together, you expose yourself to unattractive work habits in your partner that you will need to accept. Talk with your partner frequently about how your relationship is faring. Staying current will help you manage any challenges that come your way. In my practice, I listen to many jealous couples whose buttons are pushed when one or both of them acts in a way that appears threatening to the marriage:

> The first time I watched my wife flirt with a male customer to get an order, I flipped my lid. I calmed down when I realized she had landed our biggest account yet. Later on, when we had some private time, I told my wife how I felt watching her flirt with that customer. She reassured me that I had nothing to worry about. It was just a sales technique to her.
>
> *Magazine publisher*

A potential solution: Research shows attractive people make more money than unattractive ones. We build relationships predicated upon conscious and unconscious connections and signals. Most women know there is a world of difference between using your appearance to connect and being sexually inappropriate. This situation can become complicated in a business partnership which includes a jealous spouse. To avoid the difficulty encountered by the couple in the above example, remind a potentially jealous partner prior to a business and/or sales meetings that the greatest asset we bring to "closing the deal" is who we are as a person—in total, which includes our physical appearance. Remind your partner that business people often (not always) choose to do business with people they like. How do we determine if we like someone? People universally like others to whom they can relate to—by connecting with them based on intelligence, personality, shared interests and yes, physical attractiveness—defined uniquely by everyone since beauty is in the eyes of the beholder.

Don't kid yourself, appearances count and can be an invaluable asset for opening doors and closing deals. This might be a controversial fact but it is true nonetheless! The value of physical appearance in the workplace is exemplified by *Dress for Success* books, workshops and image consultants. Sales people state there is very little difference between many competing products in their sales market. The person who makes the sale is, quite frankly, the one whom is best-liked and how you appear influences how well you are regarded.

Challenge Three:
Loss of Personal and Family Time

Most small businesses, especially in the startup and growth stages, require an all-consuming commitment of time and energy. You may have to sacrifice personal space and time with the children and each other. Although this is not recommended, working partners may go several years without taking any vacation. This is often the reality of this entrepreneurial model. If you choose a retail or service business, you need to be there for the customers and clients until you can afford to hire someone who you can confidently trust to back you up in your absence and keep their hand out of your cash register.

> After three years of working together I demanded that my husband and I take at least two weeks of vacation to travel where there are no booked gigs, no potential clients, and no tax deductions!
> *Professional speaker*

The likelihood of bringing work home will also crowd your personal time. If your business partner is available to you 24 hours a day, you may not wait until the office opens the next day to discuss a hot new idea. Children may suffer from neglect as their parents become consumed in the business, and even dinner conversations circle around business. Safeguard and build strong boundaries between work and personal life; non-existent boundaries are a red flag that romance could be in jeopardy.

If you and your partner operate a retail business outside the house, the freedom you sought as entrepreneurs may elude you. You can find yourselves chained to the retail location for ten to fourteen hours a day, six or seven days a week. You may be too cash poor in the early stages to hire a manager or assistant to relieve you, requiring both of you to practically move into the store.

Consider a couple who started an independent Japanese bookstore open seven days a week. They were each in the store 14 hours a day. The only holiday they closed was Christmas, so this couple took one day off work a year. Luckily they loved their work and working together, but that kind of schedule could strain even the best of marriages.

The loss of personal space can also impede your physical, emotional, and spiritual well-being. You may commute with your partner to the office, lunch with your colleagues, and devote yourself to your family's needs in the evening. You may feel too guilty or pressured to take time out for exercise, meditation, reading a book or magazine, or talking to a friend. If you do, then your partner may resent you. When you drop off to bed exhausted, the last thing you want to do is talk to your partner, never mind having sex with him or her.

A potential solution: The key is to set boundaries around personal, relationship, and family time when you need it. Get creative. If you wait until the "right time," it may never happen. Drive to work in separate cars. Schedule an exercise class or yoga class twice a week. Plan a "no business talk allowed" Saturday night date. Read Chapter 7, "Keeping it Hot, Intimate, & Fun" and pick out a few suggestions. Treat creating balance like an important problem to solve and you will find unique solutions that work for you both.

Challenge Four:
Preserving Your Individual Identity

When co-creating a business, you may struggle to maintain individual identity within the couple partnership. When you operate as one unit at work and at home, there is a pervasive element of "we-ness" in every aspect of your life. When the world thinks of you as "Joe and Jane" you may yearn to develop an aspect of your life entirely your own. As parents, we dislike being referred to only as Jamie's mom; in our marriage we don't like others perceiving us as being glued to our partner's hip either. Losing one's individuality is a very slippery slope towards waking up a few years down the road wondering what ever happened to the woman I use to be?

A potential solution: The desire for autonomy within a committed relationship is natural, healthy and an absolute necessity, especially if you are in business with your partner. Find activities outside the business that you can enjoy by yourself. Segregate an aspect of your joint business that is yours alone. A woman who has worked with her husband for years in the publishing and speaking business recently started a coaching practice that is an offshoot of their business together. Her coaching practice doesn't involve her husband at all. Similarly, I maintain a private practice office outside my home because I crave my independence and need to have some work space totally separate from the work environment I share with my husband in our home. I love working from home with my husband but I'm adamant about keeping my own individual identity, both personally and professionally. My independence allows me to maintain a separate identity as a professional and a woman without diminishing my commitment to my marriage or collaborative work with my husband.

Challenge Five:
Dividing Up the Work So that it Suits Both of You

Imagine you and your partner share a mutual love for exotic parrots. A business opportunity selling parrots might be a perfect match for both of you. But what if one of you loves parrots and the other merely tolerates their screeching and constant stream of bird poop? You may still go into business together if working together suits your lifestyle choice. Couples don't always start a business that perfectly suits the career aspirations and passions of both individuals in the relationship.

The challenge comes if each partner doesn't find an aspect of the business personally exciting or fulfilling. A nurse gave up her nursing career to assist her husband in running a UPS franchise. After two years, they sold the profitable business and the wife planned to return to her nursing career. Although she loved working with her husband, she missed her profession.

You may have different goals and desires related to the business. You might have stumbled upon your own business when your corporate position was eliminated and you were offered the opportunity to use your considerable talent as a human resource executive and work as a consultant for your former employee. Your husband might be more determined to grow this consulting business into a seven-figure empire. What motivates you to work every day may be different from your spouse. Perhaps your partner dreams of selling the company for a big profit but you would be happier with a business that didn't demand as much time and effort, even if the profit potential is less. You may dream of opening up a chain of stores and building an empire, but your partner prefers to limit the number of employees and locations. Idealistically, you and your partner will always be on the same wavelength. Realistically, as the business progresses and your family circumstances change, your business motivations will fluctuate, depending on your family concerns, financial needs and goals, health, age, spiritual values, and other interests.

A potential solution: If you miss your former profession, then consider remaining in a part-time job or working as a volunteer to maintain your connection. Look for creative ways that your current business can meet the same needs or interface with similar customers. Expand into a new business service that uses your former skills. Break out of the box and look for ways to fulfill the work aspirations of each partner.

Expanding to Include Your Spouse

If you evolved into a full partnership, you will meet with different issues than couples who began their business together. Often one spouse works a straight job until the business is profitable enough to allow that spouse to quit the job and join the family business. One spouse may join the other spouse's business after losing a job, rather than searching for new employment. Here are some examples:

> I used to run a department and make my own decisions. Suddenly my wife was my boss. She said she wanted me as her business partner, but what she really wanted was an employee who would do what she ordered.
> *West Coast businessman*

> My business was my baby. When my husband joined me in the company, it was hard for me to begin sharing the credit for our success. I wanted him to do the work, but I wanted to keep all the credit.
> *Midwest entrepreneur*

The most important step you can take toward dealing with this challenge is to communicate about it openly with your spouse. Discuss regularly how each spouse is experiencing the evolution to full partnership. Acknowledge the effort each is making toward contributing to a successful transition. Above all, be patient! It can take a year or more to evolve into a true partnership. Recognize this transition as a process that does not magically fall into place over night.

This transition is very much akin to the evolution that a newlywed couple makes in their first year of marriage. Forming a true marital partnership doesn't happen right away. As the relationship evolves, differences of opinion and values emerge. It is critical for newlyweds to openly and honestly discuss, in a timely manner, potential conflicts. Newlyweds require verbal and non-verbal communication skills to learn exactly what to say and how to say it so their partner receives the message with clarity and with love—and not animosity. Similarly, effective communication skills are tantamount to the success of your marriage and your entrepreneurial partnership.

Losing Your Escape Valve

Where do you go to complain when you're having a bad day at work? Often your partner. What if your spouse had the same miserable day, is part of the problem, or is too busy working to be available? When you work full-time with your intimate partner, you may miss the best friend who used to be available to you with an objective ear and unconditional loving support. Your spouse, now business partner, may move immediately into problem solving, reacting defensively, or judging you for the problem.

A potential solution: Create outside support systems available to you when you have an emotional need your spouse can't fill. Be clear with your partner if all you want to do is vent, and if you aren't looking for a solution, say so. Similar to your marriage, your business partner, who also happens to be your spouse, cannot possibly provide all the emotional support you need all the time in running your business.

Significant Rewards of Full Partnership

We've discussed many challenges of husbands and wives co-creating or eventually running a business together. Now, let's look at the rewards that you are probably experiencing, or hope to be enjoying, if you move into this model of entrepreneurial partnership with your spouse.

Greater Intimacy

Working toward a common goal: United by a shared purpose and vision, your business partnership can expand and solidify your personal relationship. For some couples, co-creating a business provides the same satisfaction as raising a family.

> Since my partner and I are unable to raise kids together, when our bed and breakfast opened its doors for the first time to the public, we felt as if we had given birth after a long year of labor!
> *Bed and breakfast owner*

Sharing a business with your spouse gives you more in common to discuss and experience. You understand each other's work intimately and your social life can evolve around shared friends and colleagues. When you experience business success, you celebrate together; when you confront business hardship, you fight it as a united team.

Tom and Grace owned and operated a PR agency which experienced financial difficulty due to the recent loss of a major client. Every morning Tom and Grace would openly and honestly critique their business. The couple's high level of intimacy allowed their relationship to survive some harsh, yet fair criticisms of each other. Tom found it difficult to slow down. Although he was a brilliant marketer, he was often overwhelmed doing everything himself. Grace appreciated that time was money and realized the need for a more fluid and transparent work system. Not only would a systematized business make their work more efficient, it would free Tom up from the minutia of details and allow him to focus on his marketing genius—the foundation needed to gain new clients.

A potential solution: The challenge of creating greater intimacy is best achieved by improving intimate communication between one another. It also helps a lot if each individual is open to constructive criticism so that they can draw closer by resolving issues. Grace effectively communicated to Tom how his lack of systematization wasted his time and cost them money. Tom respected the acumen Grace brought to the business and was able to implement Grace's suggestion that they bring in an outside contractor to systematize their business. This provided Tom the critical time he needed to allow his marketing brilliance to shine through. The intimacy between this couple allowed for an honest exchange of constructive criticism needed to win new clients.

Quicker Resolutions of Challenges

When you work with your intimate partner, you get to know all aspects of each other. You work to resolve your most troublesome relationship issues, so that you can work together effectively. The average overworked couple at the beginning of the 21st century spends only a few hours a week with each other. By substantially increasing your time together and communicating frequently, you can advance your relationship to entirely new levels.

> We're so tied together personally and in business, it forces us to deal with issues sooner and keeps us reassessing our life goals.
> *Chiropractor*

Improved Sex Life

Contrary to the individuals who lose their sexual attraction for their spouse and business partner, some individuals report that their sexual energy improves dramatically after going into business together. When you work together, there can be more time available for sex. Couples may celebrate business success or take a spontaneous break from a hard day's work by making love in the office. This element of romance and forbidden lust adds some juice to their marriages as well as their businesses!

> When my wife started working in my office after thirty years
> of marriage, I discovered she was not just the mother of my
> kids and a good hostess to my business associates; she was
> also a brilliant sexy woman, filled with creative energy and
> drive. I fell in love with her in a whole new way.
> *Professional Salesman*

Couples who thrive as working partners love to spend time together
and appreciate having a best friend as their business partner and spouse.
They welcome the challenges to their relationship as an opportunity for
personal growth. They have fun together, and their respect and love for
each other deepen the longer they work together.

It's Better for Business

Complementary skills: The greatest challenge to your relationship
also offers the greatest opportunity for strengthening your business. No
entrepreneur is an expert in sales, marketing, operations, finance, and
human resources. If you start a manufacturing company because you
have a great product idea, chances are you won't excel in ordering office
supplies or writing policy manuals. You will need a staff to care for the
details for you. Often your mate possesses just the work style that
anchors and balances you, with job skills that strengthen your business.

> My husband is the creative one, always coming up with crazy
> ideas. I'm the perfect office manager since I'm very
> methodical, organized, and detail-oriented. George has
> learned not to make any commitments to anyone until he
> checks with me. Even if he doesn't always like what I say,
> he's learned to listen to me. Nine times out of ten, I'm right!
> *Office manager for training team*

Immediate feedback: Full partners relish taking advantage of a
creative spark, whenever and wherever it may occur. A 24-hour-a-day
business partnership can be extremely productive and fun.

> If I have a brilliant idea at 3:00 A.M. I don't have to wait until the staff meeting tomorrow to discuss it with someone. My business partner is sleeping right next to me.
> *Partner in an employment agency*

Family Rewards

Child- and elder-care flexibility: When one of the kids gets sick, your spouse is likely to be more empathic and forgiving than a boss if you need to be with your child. The traditional workplace has no interest in meeting the needs of your children or personal life. Many work environments are unforgiving, ostensibly or covertly, towards working women (and men for that matter) who take time off to care for their children. (This is one of the many reasons women are choosing the entrepreneurial path at twice the rate of men.) When a baby is born or adopted, you can devise a schedule that works for you as a couple, rather than fitting into the constraints of your job's maternity or paternity policy. You can schedule time to be present when the children are home from school, when a school assembly begs your presence, or when after-school transportation is necessary.

In family crises where one of you must remain home for an extended time, your business might suffer; but you have more flexibility than if you were working in a traditional job. Many corporations remain unfriendly to workers who take legislatively mandated leave from their job to take care of ill family members, often pushing workers off the fast-track. Some working couples who own a business together, on the other hand, bring their young children to the job, from the time they are born. As the children get older, they can pitch in, learning valuable lessons about business and family teamwork and the effort required to earn money for groceries and school clothes. The role model of a successful full partnership may influence your children's career and marriage choices as adults.

The Evil You Know...

The evil you know may be better than the one you don't. When you choose a business partner who is not your intimate partner, you don't always know what you're getting and how trustworthy the new partner will be. If your spouse sleeps late in the morning, or argues stubbornly, then you can decide if those traits will prohibit a successful business partnership. A new business partner may have an obnoxious trait or two, but you won't know until you've already signed your partnership agreement.

Your Partner Accepts the Sacrifices

Starting a business can demand tremendous sacrifices by your spouse and family. If you jointly commit to a business, your partner is more likely to accept the hardships. (This is predicated upon the basic business tenant for change. Research shows that when workers have an input into change, they are more likely to become positive change agents and be more cooperative, increasing the chance of success.) If you unite in front of the children, then they will less likely resist changes as well. One couple I interviewed decided to relocate from two corporate jobs and a Midwest upper-class lifestyle to a dairy farm in the South, because they wanted to spend more time together and with their children. It was a mutual decision, or it would probably have never worked.

I caution against starting a business that demands enormous life changes from your spouse if your spouse is not ready or capable of making the change. All changes are stressful, but few situations could prove more stressful for a couple than leaving behind a comfortable lifestyle for the financial and emotional uncertainty of starting an entrepreneurial business. Raising children who will experience the pinch of a tightened cash flow makes it all the more difficult and imperative that this couple demonstrate support for each other and the business decision they have mutually agreed upon. Commitment to each other as a couple is as vital to the success of the business as it is to their relationship and family life; otherwise this couple would be in danger of the children dividing and conquering, pitting one spouse against the other.

The Seesaw

Full partners bring each other's mood up and are cheerleaders in hard times. Usually one partner is feeling more optimistic at any one time than the other. Like a seesaw, as one partner goes down, the other goes up to return the partnership to balance. In most partnerships, the roles of the optimist and pessimist shift. When one partner feels burdened, the other one gladly, albeit unknowingly, picks up the load.

Partners who operate as a team weather stormy business challenges better and remain afloat instead of drifting apart in rough seas.

> Our business slows down every summer. I always panic that we're going to go out of business. My wife calmly reminds me that we've made it through every summer for the past eight years, and we will again.
>
> *Retail store owner*

All Efforts Benefit the Family

Dual career couples often work 90 to 180 hours a week between their two careers. If a company employs one or both of you, much of your service is going toward increasing corporate profits. Entrepreneurial couples value knowing that their joint effort contributes directly to their own material wealth and to their children's inheritance.

BUSINESS OWNERSHIP MODEL TWO: DUAL ENTREPRENEURSHIP

Dual entrepreneurship is defined as two people in a committed relationship with each other, where each individual is responsible for running his or her own (separate) business. Here are some examples:

- Dentist married to a professional speaker

- Writer in committed relationship with president of a manufacturing company

- Sales trainer and public relations specialist

- Franchise consultant and graphic designer

You can combine dual entrepreneurship and marriage in four different ways:

1. Each individual establishes a business before entering the relationship. The businesses remain entirely separate. Personal and business money is not merged and each individual maintains sole control over the operation of his or her own business. This couple are dual entrepreneurs from their first day as a married couple.

2. When the relationship begins, one individual has a business and the other works in a company or at home raising children. At some point in the relationship, the second individual decides to start a business, placing the couple into the dual-entrepreneurship model later on in their marriage, rather than when they first meet.

3. Both individuals are self-employed or run businesses in the *same industry* or type of business. They choose not to work together as full partners because they do not wish to give up full control or because they feel the full-partner model would strain their marriage. They may consider themselves "side-by-side" business partners, because different from model number one, where each individual may run a business that has nothing

to do with the other, in this model, the individuals share a lot in common, working within the same industry—but they choose not to combine their individual businesses into one business.

4. Both individuals are self-employed in businesses that provide synergy, like a shared office suite, client referrals, combined travel, or joint projects. The public views them as two distinct businesses or practices, but by sharing space, clients, and often sitting next to one another on a plane, the individuals may think of themselves as joint partners, even if they keep some aspects of their businesses separate.

Is Your Relationship Cut Out for Managing Two Separate Businesses?

The following assessment test will evaluate whether your intimate relationship is well suited for dual entrepreneurship. Created from interviews with successful couples and my observations of the couples I've seen in my private practice, the elements in this test were frequently present in solid, rewarding dual-entrepreneur marriages or absent in those marriages not favorably inclined toward this model.

Patty / Ann

DISCOVERY EXERCISE TWO: ASSESSMENT TEST FOR DUAL ENTREPRENEURS

Take the test separately from your spouse. Or else do the test yourself and verbally quiz your spouse. Then get together to share the results.

1 = That doesn't describe us at all.

2 = That describes us somewhat.

3 = That describes us frequently.

4 = That describes us completely.

Place the appropriate number next to each question, and then total your score.

☐ We both had established separate businesses before we got together as a couple.
or
My spouse already has his or her established business. I have passions of my own I'd like to pursue with my own business.

☐ My spouse and I are both strong-willed. We each need to be the boss of our own business. It would never work to share control and decision-making.

☐ We love each other, but we would find it too suffocating and boring to be together all day and evening. Sharing the experiences we gain from our own separate businesses enhances our marriage.

☐ My partner and I have very different interests. It would be hard for us to find one business that excites us equally.

☐ We wouldn't be willing to take the financial risk of full partnership in one business. With two separate businesses, at least if one of the businesses fails, we have the other business to fall back on.

☐ We have very different work styles and approaches. We would fight too much if we ever tried to work together.

☐ Our kids are independent enough to handle the absence caused by both of our businesses.
or
One or both of our businesses are well suited for being available for the children.
or
We have the hired help necessary to take care of our children when we both need to be away for business.
or
We don't have any children at home.

☐ We prepared for the financial risk of two businesses, rather than suffer the drawbacks of one of us working in a nine-to-five job.

☐ We have enough emotional and physical energy to devote ourselves to two separate businesses and still have energy available for our relationship and family.

☐ I like it when my spouse travels for his or her business. Our brief separation adds some spark to our marriage and helps keep the romance alive. I enjoy my time apart from my spouse and don't find it a threat to our marriage.
or
My spouse and I both travel for our businesses. We can coordinate our travel schedules to be together at times while on business.
or
Neither my spouse nor I travel overnight for business.

☐ There is synergy between our businesses. We generate business referrals and advice for each other. My business is stronger because of my spouse's business knowledge and connections.

☐ We have the best of both worlds. We each have the freedom of entrepreneurship, and the benefits of a business partner to collaborate with when we choose to ask for advice. We don't have the hassles of a formal business partner to share decisions with.

☐ Healthy competition between us motivates me to work harder at my business. When my spouse is successful in his or her business, it inspires me to generate the same level of success in my business.

or

My spouse's cynicism regarding my ability to succeed in my own business challenges me. I take the attitude, "I'll show him or her!"

☐ We cope well with stress, both individually and as a couple. We don't lose our sense of humor for long, and we keep perspective in the difficult times. Our relationship has come through hard times even stronger.

☐ We acknowledge the potential stress of managing two businesses within our marriage. We will seek outside help if necessary to prevent our relationship from deteriorating. We will consider other work options if this one threatens our relationship.

SCORE

48-60: Dual Entrepreneurship Suits You. This model of combining entrepreneurship with your significant relationship either ideally suits you or is the only viable option that makes sense at this time, given your business interests. You are likely to try hard to make this lifestyle work.

29-47: Dual Entrepreneurship Could Be Difficult. The potential is there for success or trouble, depending on how you respond to the challenges of combining two businesses with your marriage. Be prepared for some bumps along the road. With effort and open communication you have the potential for two successful businesses and a thriving relationship at the same time.

15-28: There May Be Better Options for You. Your low score on this test indicates there are other models for combining marriage and entrepreneurship that may make more sense for you as a couple. Working together as full partners, or limiting entrepreneurial activity to just one of you, might be more suitable right now. Review other options available to you before pursuing this avenue.

BUSINESS OWNERSHIP MODEL THREE: SUPPORTIVE SPOUSE

Now that we've discussed two popular modes of business ownership combined with marriage – full partners, and dual entrepreneurs, there is a third model we don't want to miss. There are millions of unsung heroes working every day to support the entrepreneurial dreams of their spouse or significant other. Their contribution may be apparent or entirely hidden from public view. Regardless, the business could not thrive, or perhaps even function, without their support. They are very much impacted by their significant other's entrepreneurial adventures, and often, immersed in the lifestyle that accompanies it.

Spousal support can take many forms:

- My husband takes care of the children and the house so that I can concentrate fully on my business.

- My husband does my business books and pays my taxes.

- My life partner works at the store nights and weekends, above and beyond his regular full-time job.

- My girlfriend has been an emotional anchor during the worst of business times. I would have given up without her support.

- We're using my wife's inheritance to live off, since my company isn't bringing in any income. She's agreed to cut back on her spending, to live within our new budget.

- My husband is working a traditional job with medical benefits for the family so that I can start my own business. He'd love to quit his job too, but he sticks it out because we depend on his income and benefits. (Although we know these benefits and other corporate perks are rapidly fading from the corporate world).

A supportive spouse is an intimate partner who provides the emotional, financial, or practical support that enables the other partner to be successfully self-employed in business. Supportive spouses may work part-time as an employee in their partners' business or offer advice and consult for the business, but they are not full working partners in the business. Every intimate partner of an entrepreneur is a supportive spouse to some extent, even if he or she also falls into the model of full partner or dual entrepreneur. Much of the guidance in this section could apply to the other marital models for business ownership equally well.

Are You Cut Out for the Role of Supportive Spouse or Partner?

The following assessment test evaluates whether you have the emotional makeup and the kind of marriage that will help you thrive as the supportive spouse or intimate partner to an entrepreneur. Created from my research regarding successful couples, the elements in this test were frequently present in solid, rewarding supportive spouse partnerships or absent from those relationships that struggled or failed when a business was involved. When I see couples in my private practice, it is those couples who are in a true partnership, operating as a team, who score very high on this assessment test. These couples survive and thrive because they provide unconditional love and support for each other. They know the relationship wins when the entrepreneurial business succeeds. Couples who operate from a competitive model will most likely see their relationship suffer. Competitive couples are often critical and judgmental of each other and lack healthy communication and conflict resolution skills. They view their relationship through a competitive lens of winner vs. loser.

DISCOVERY EXERCISE THREE: ASSESSMENT TEST FOR SUPPORTIVE SPOUSES

Take the assessment test below if you are the intimate partner of a small business owner or entrepreneur, or you may become one. Place the appropriate number next to each question, and then total your score.

1 = That doesn't describe me at all.

2 = That somewhat describes me.

3 = That describes me most of the time.

4 = That describes me completely.

☐ I am fully behind the entrepreneurial pursuits of my partner. I support my partner's choice of business and efforts to be successful without reservation.

☐ We financially prepared for my partner to buy a business or be self-employed. I can handle the financial risk without being too distressed by financial worries.

☐ I'm eager to help my partner be successful in the business, but I have no desire to be his or her full business partner at this time.

☐ I may work in my partner's business on a part-time basis, take care of the children while he or she is working, be available for emotional support and practical advice, and/or work a straight job with steady salary and benefits to reduce our financial risk. My partner and I view these contributions as essential to his or her success and I feel valued.

☐ My partner regularly expresses appreciation for my contribution and tells other people about it as well. My partner rarely takes me for granted.

☐ I am doing what I want to do with my time. I'm not playing the role of supportive spouse only because I have to right now—I genuinely prefer this arrangement to any other.

☐ I don't resent the amount of time and energy my partner has to give the business, even if my partner isn't as available to me or our family. I know the short-term sacrifice is ultimately for our family's long-term benefit.

☐ I like being asked for my advice, but I don't need to have control over my partner's decision-making in the business. If my partner made a business decision I disagreed with, I could express my feelings and opinions and then let it go. What my partner does with the business is up to him or her.

☐ I have the energy and strength to handle the multitude of responsibilities that fall on my shoulders, while my partner is busy with the business.

☐ People help me to support my partner. I have a support system of friends, family, and coworkers to rely on when my partner is physically or emotionally unavailable.

☐ My partner gives me full authority within my areas of responsibility and respects my abilities. That might include work I do in the business, or household and child care responsibilities.

☐ I may be "behind the scenes" of my partner's business and not getting any public credit for my contribution. It's enough for me to know that my partner couldn't pursue a dream or achieve business success without my help.

☐ My partner shares with me as much information about the progress and daily happenings in the business as I care to know.

☐ My spouse and I make the time weekly for personal space and intimate relationship time so that I am reenergized to meet my partner's needs.

☐ When we met, I knew that my partner would be an entrepreneur. I prepared from the beginning of our relationship to brace myself for this journey and to be a supportive spouse.

☐ The pattern we have in our marriage now is very similar to what I experienced growing up in my family. It's a role that is very familiar and comfortable to me.

SCORE

51-64: Well Suited for Supportive Spouse Role. You appear to be the perfect candidate for the supportive spouse role. Your partner is lucky to have you behind the scenes, or by his or her side, and he or she knows it! You'll have your hard days, as anyone would, but you won't spend too much time wishing you were doing something else with your life.

35-50: Some Aspects of This Role Could Be Challenging. The potential is there for success or trouble, depending on how you respond to the aspects of being a supportive spouse that challenge you and your partnership. It will make a big difference if your partner gives you the recognition and appreciation that you deserve. Make sure you create support systems that will help you take care of yourself.

16-34: You'll Need All the Support You Can Get! Maybe you have no other choice right now, so you're going to make the best of it. You may want to support your partner's entrepreneurial dream even if it will be difficult for you. Regardless of your motivation, you are stepping way out of your comfort zone, and you will find the role distressing at times. Get coaching or counseling if you need it, and communicate your feelings and needs to your spouse when you're struggling. If you don't think you're up to the challenge, negotiate another arrangement with your spouse.

Primary Challenges for Supportive Spouses

This section will offer you solid marital advice that will help any marriage get stronger, not just marriages in the supportive spouse business ownership model. Let's take several issues that arise in supportive spouse marriages:

I Do a Lot of the Work, but I Don't Get Any of the Credit

If you need public recognition for your contribution to the success of the business, then you'll find the supportive spouse role difficult. Appreciation from your spouse may be your only recognition. The supportive spouse of a fast-track entrepreneur shared this analogy:

> It's as if my husband is in the army and I help prepare him for battle every day. I wouldn't want to be on the fighting lines with him. I'd rather be on the sidelines making sure he has the right ammunition, and enough food and water. I know he couldn't win the battle without my help, and that's enough for me.
>
> *Supportive spouse of manufacturing company owner*

Joan and Mark came into counseling with Joan feeling short-changed in their marriage. Mark was an entrepreneur who spent many evenings being wined and dined while Joan felt trapped at home cooking, cleaning and taking care of their two young children. When Joan attended social functions with her husband she felt invisible; people treated her spouse as if he were some kind of hero while practically ignoring her.

Joan felt unrecognized and unappreciated by her husband. She felt her husband took her support for his career for granted. She willingly took care of the house and kids so he could be laser-focused on his career and she resented not getting some acknowledgement for it. Mark was in disbelief when he heard Joan express these sentiments and immediately thanked her and told her he sincerely appreciated her unconditional support for his career. Joan told him it was the first time he had ever thanked her and she needed to hear it. She supported his career; she just wanted to be shown a little appreciation for her contribution to his success.

Supportive spouses need to find satisfaction in the work itself or share in their spouse's long-term vision for how the business's success will positively affect their marriage and family. To be happy, they must feel as if they are working with their spouse as a teammate, toward a mutual goal, and receive regular expressions of spousal appreciation.

Little Control Over Business Decisions that May Affect You

If you trust your mate completely to make business decisions on your behalf, and you have no desire to shape directly the direction of the business, then this challenge may not apply to you. If, on the other hand, you need control over events that will change your destiny, then you'd better fasten your seat belts for a challenging ride!

When you are a supportive spouse, rather than a full business partner, you can advise, criticize, or question your spouse's business decisions, but you do not have the authority to insist that your opinion be regarded. (Unless you and your spouse have an agreement that you must approve certain financial investments or changes in business operations that would affect you significantly.)

Gail found this aspect of being a supportive spouse very painful during the beginning years of their marriage. When her husband, George, started his consulting business and struggled with the usual startup difficulties, with all of the accompanying financial stress, Gail had very strong opinions about what he should and shouldn't do to improve the situation. Since his business success had a direct impact on the quality of her life, watching silently while he made some decisions that she wouldn't make was really tough. Since she was not his business partner, she could frequently register her opinion, but she had no control over his actions. She was in an untenable situation—unable to fix a problem that was affecting her. Ideally, Gail and George would have figured out how to communicate about hot issues with Gail's input and feelings taken into consideration. Ultimately, George ended up closing down his business start-up after just one year of operation, but they both learned a lot about that experience. If George were ever to start his own business again, this couple would be much better prepared to incorporate Gail's opinions into the process.

I was in a similar situation when my husband, Mitch, left a successful corporate career to start his own business. Having always had my own business, health benefits and other financial perks for the family always came from my husband's corporate job. The thought of losing those benefits along with a substantial salary and bonus structure was very frightening. I was supposed to be the entrepreneur, not my husband! Confident in my husband's proven intelligence, work ethic, self-confidence and commitment to take care of our family, I was able to trust his leap of faith into the entrepreneurial world. I was frightened, but was armed with the knowledge that he had always provided well for our family and had always provided unwavering emotional support for the attainment of my dreams and goals.

Supportive spouses struggle with this challenge most often if any of the following conditions is present:

- The business isn't doing as well as projected, directly affecting your quality of life.

- You haven't been married long enough to trust your partner's business abilities completely.

- You think you know more about how to solve your spouse's business problems than your spouse does.

- You are controlling by nature and find it difficult to let your spouse do his or her own thing, especially when it affects you.

- You are financially risk-averse, and the prospect of an inconsistent revenue stream is scary.

When the supportive spouse worries about finances or is anxious about having some control over the entrepreneur's business, the entrepreneur may suffer as well. The woman below shared her negative experience when she started a consulting business after losing her job and decided to try consulting instead of looking for a traditional job.

> My husband constantly interrogated me about how many billable hours I was doing each month. All he seemed to care about was how much money I was making. He didn't want to hear how difficult it was for me to get clients.
> *Consultant*

An entrepreneur already fighting the demons of self-doubt and fear may be unable to cope with an unsupportive "supportive spouse." If you are in the supporting role, you might increase your understanding of the business in some ways, especially if you form your opinion in a vacuum and aren't fully educated about the issues that your spouse is dealing with on a daily basis. It might be helpful to ask your spouse to help you understand the rationales behind each decision.

You might also distance yourself from the business, ask fewer questions, be less nosy. Catch yourself if you are asking, "How are things going?" when what you really mean is, "Are things going the way I think they should?" Your spouse will more than likely know the question you are *really* asking. If you start to interview your spouse like a boss, then you need to keep your questions to yourself and look for evidence in your marriage that your spouse can make wise decisions, even if you don't agree with them. Establish clear ground rules with your spouse regarding when you have the right to influence, and even provide permission for, business decisions. Then learn to leave your spouse alone when he or she isn't asking for or appreciating your advice. Remember to act as a spouse, not a business partner. That said, also know that sometimes, your spouse is so angry, fearful, resentful, etc. about your business and its impact, there isn't really any information you can give him or her that will stop them from asking incessant questions, and insisting on more information. In that case, recognize that this pattern is indicative of someone who is really frightened and needs reassurance. You will need to discover what the unspoken question that is not being asked really is. When people are fearful they often express their fear through negativity. You will need to explore what they really need from you—it is likely that it isn't more information, but probably, more boundaries—a promise not to overspend, or a promise to close the business down if it goes too far into debt, or even something as simple as a commitment to come home for dinner more often because your spouse is lonely!

Time for Connection Is Scarce

When you spend the workday apart from your spouse, you have limited time for connection and conversation. You may have some private time in the early morning, at the end of the workday, or before bed if you are on the same schedule. With children, intimate time becomes even rarer. You are operating in separate universes for most of the day. Although you may touch base during the day to share an update or two, it will never be possible to capture the subtle nuances and details of each day.

> My husband travels at least two weeks a month. I'm home with our three children full-time. He's great about calling me from the road, but sometimes I just feel angry after he calls. He gets to check in and then hang up leaving all the difficulties for me to handle.
> *Female supportive spouse*

The distance that can develop between business owners and their supportive spouses can range from mild and somewhat sad to severe and threatening to the marriage. Traveling away from home, working separate shifts, or working in jobs or businesses that are entirely different from each other increases the challenge. Maximize your opportunities for real sharing and connection no matter how short they may be. If your partner is willing to listen, talk to him or her about the small nuances of your worklife. The use of modern technology offers many ways to stay in touch, especially when one partner is traveling, if face-to-face conversations are limited or impossible.

Don't just portray an overall picture with no detail. ("My boss is a jerk"; "The customers are driving me crazy.") Attend business functions together whenever possible. Try to take a page out of each other's book. Take an afternoon off with the kids and give your stay-at-home partner a break. Help your business owner partner with a work project. Listen with real interest to your partner's concerns and stories of the day, even if they sound alien to you and you do not really understand the details of what you are being told. Research shows what your spouse probably wants from you more than anything is a best friend who will lend a sympathetic ear.

This advice applies to both the supportive spouse and the business owner, both of whom can easily get trapped in the busy demands of the workday and family life, and neglect the basic communication with one another that ensures thriving, instead of fighting, in the midst of turbulent times. True intimacy between individuals is created day in and out with thousands of conversations that range from what seems like the mundane, to what is actually life-altering. Being there for one another in the really big moments is a lot easier when you have supported one another every day with even the simplest of questions: "How was your day, dear?" and then taking the time to really listen to their response.

At the End of the Day, I Want Space and She Wants Connection

Abigail recalls the tension of her first year of marriage, now almost two decades ago: "When my husband, Sammy started working in a corporate job, and I was working at home self-employed, we had difficulty finding a level of intimacy that met both of our needs.

Sammy arrives home from work burned out from being with people all day long. His corporate job leaves him no personal space, so he has little desire for intimate connection with me when he comes home after a long workday. If he has any opportunity for free time later in the evening, he craves either sleep or being by himself."

Abigail's experience with Sammy is typical for partnerships where one individual is working mostly alone and the other is interacting with people all day. Similar issues reported to me in my interviews were:

- I'm on the road most of the month, eating out at restaurants. When I come home, all I want is a home-cooked meal. My wife has been home with the kids and she's dying to get out to a restaurant.

- I travel so frequently, I don't want to go away from home for a vacation. My husband, who works a corporate job, is eager to get away from the same old routine as often as he can.

- I miss my kids when I'm working all day, so when I'm home on weekends I want to be with them. My wife has been with them all week, and she needs a break. She'd rather be alone with me.

- My husband wants to spend most of our evening time entertaining clients. I miss having just a private date with him every now and then.

John Gray elaborates on male/female differences in the need for space and connection in his book, *Men Are from Mars, Women Are from Venus.* Generally, if a man gets even fifteen minutes of the private space he needs, he can be much more open for connection. When a woman has the opportunity for just ten minutes of talking, if she's really being listened to, it can be enough to satisfy her. Small shifts can make a big difference. Occasionally, instead of compromising, give your partner exactly what he or she needs. Every marriage has to consider the different needs of each partner, just as you consider the business needs of your clients. If you want everything your way, all the time, don't get married or have children. It's easier to have complete control when you are single and childless! The supportive spouse model often requires meeting each other halfway.

The Supportive Spouse Grows Unsupportive

You can provide the emotional, financial, or practical support that enables your partner to be in business successfully and still feel unsupportive to your entrepreneurial partner's business.

Tilly supported their family financially, and helped her husband Kevin in his business marginally, while he was starting his business. When Kevin's business failed to meet income projections in its first year and they discovered how difficult it was for him to find clients, her emotional support for the business began to wane. Over time, she came to hate his business and what it was doing to their relationship, bank account, and Kevin's sense of self-worth. As she became more unsupportive about this particular business venture, she began to resent her role of supportive spouse.

Another entrepreneur like Kevin decided to get an objective point of view:

> "My wife and I hired a consultant to take an objective look at the business. The consultant came back with bad news—I needed to overhaul my business completely if I wanted to turn it around. It was easier for me to hear that from him than from my wife."
> *Watch Repair Store Owner*

One of the hardest things you may have to do as a supportive spouse is to pull the plug on your support or deliver an ultimatum to your partner. If the business is draining your financial resources, negatively impacting your family life, endangering your partner's health or your own, you may reach a point where you no longer can support your partner's business.

You can pull your support away (both passively and actively) in a number of ways:

- Refuse to support the family with your paycheck.
- Set limits on your willingness to single-parent your children.
- Refuse to listen to complaints about the business anymore.
- Refuse to allow joint money to be invested any further into the business.

- Give an ultimatum—the business must be profitable within a designated time, or else ...

- Quit your part-time and unpaid assistance to the business.

Coping with the Entrepreneur's Mood Swings

Your entrepreneurial partner will probably experience moods of elation, despair, anxiety, and discouragement. From time to time, you'll be drawn in, like an insect caught in a spider's web.

> When my husband got hit with a lawsuit, he was hardly ever home. When he was home, he was either grouchy, depressed, or sleeping. I tried to cheer him up, but there wasn't anything I could really do for him except wait for him to recover.
>
> *Female supportive spouse*

In the supportive spouse model, the entrepreneur is not alone in his or her experiences, even though you don't share ownership of the business. How the entrepreneur feels about him or herself, and how the business is performing, will directly affect the quality of how he or she relates at home. Supportive spouses may advise, comfort, or encourage their entrepreneurial partners, but they often can't solve the problem. It can be heart-wrenching to be unable to alleviate your partner's troubles, to helplessly watch them struggle with business difficulties.

It is usually more difficult for a woman to detach from her male partner's mood swings, than vice versa. Men will generally try to help their wives solve the problem, and they may get angry at the source of their wife's trouble. Men usually find it easier to shield themselves from emotional codependency. Women find it more difficult to be in a relationship with an angry or despondent partner while maintaining their own sense of well-being.

The serenity prayer comes to mind:

God grant me the serenity to accept the things I cannot change, courage to change the things I can, and the wisdom to know the difference.

Supportive spouses need to find their own unique way of supporting their partners through myriad business ups and downs, without losing their own sense of well-being and integrity. They also need to identify the kind of support that is really effective for their partners. (Perhaps you would like a hug when you're feeling down, but your partner needs to have more personal space during those times.) Give what your partner needs, within your abilities, and then find ways to take care of yourself.

Male Supportive Spouse Role—A Unique Challenge

In my interviews with couples in the supportive spouse model, some male supportive spouses and female entrepreneurs experienced a difficult adjustment, summarized well by this man who now earns half the income his wife is earning as a successful business woman.

> When we got married, I took care of my wife and the kids and she was dependent on me for everything. Now her business has made her independent. She doesn't really need me anymore. If she needs someone to mow the lawn, she can hire a landscaper.
>
> *Male supportive spouse*

This challenge normally arises when the man is somewhat insecure or, if he is one who measures his self-worth by his ability to financially support his family. His wife's success, independence, or business contacts with other men may threaten his ego. She may feel stifled by his jealousy and resentful of his lack of support.

The assistance of a relationship expert/marriage counselor can be crucial to handling this challenge. Each partner needs to do his or her part. The man needs to work on developing his self-esteem and ability to support his partner's success without feeling threatened. The woman needs to find effective ways to reassure and include her husband in her success. When she can approach him with compassion for his vulnerability, rather than resentment for his lack of support, she will find this challenge easier to deal with.

Primary Rewards of the Supportive Spouse Model

Care for the Children: The Traditional Model

Millions of families still prefer a traditional model of marriage, (at least during their children's pre-school years), where the husband supports the family entirely, and the wife is a full-time mom and housewife. The couples I interviewed who thrived in this model had chosen their roles. For example:

> We both knew that we wanted a traditional marriage, with my wife home full-time with our children. We were each raised with our moms at home, and we wanted the same for our children. Our wedding song was Michael Bolton's "Soul Provider."
>
> *Franchisor*

Many of the male entrepreneurs I spoke with remarked they were better able to focus on their work because they knew that their wives were taking good care of their kids at home. Their wives felt great satisfaction in their role of running the home, while their husbands ran the business. They understood that their husband's ability to provide income for the family depends on not being distracted by home details. Husband and wife worked together as a team in a well-choreographed dance, with each role separate and defined and vital to the whole performance.

Care for the Children: Entrepreneurial Flexibility

The other supportive spouse model, where one individual is an entrepreneur and the other is working a regular job, also has its advantages for raising children. Entrepreneurs with flexibility in working hours may be more available for taking care of the children's needs during the day. Allison and Travis experienced this when Allison's stepson enrolled in his new school in Pennsylvania, after they moved from Denver. The school required several meetings. It was easier for Allison to work these appointments into her entrepreneurial schedule than it would have been for Travis in his corporate job. They often remarked that they didn't know how they would have managed moving into a new home and establishing themselves in a new community, if Allison hadn't been home to make the hundreds of phone calls required.

Enhanced Social Life for Supportive Spouse

> We frequently entertain foreign businessmen in our home. My husband's business contacts have expanded in many horizons and introduced him to many different cultures. By traveling to conventions and trade shows with him, I've been able to see the world.
>
> *Supportive spouse of international entrepreneur*

Entrepreneurs who travel or have a social component to their work often involve their spouses in the social end of the business, if the ages of their children allow for this arrangement. Their partners may develop longstanding friendships with the partners of other entrepreneurs in the same industry. The business may pick up the tab for a host of cultural events related to entertaining out-of-town business associates. Entrepreneurial wives and husbands often accompany their spouses to social business functions whenever possible or appropriate.

Greater Freedom and Personal Growth for the Supportive Spouse

> My husband travels for business most weekdays, returning to our home only on weekends. We have very happy reunions when he comes home, but I don't get upset when he leaves again Monday. We're happily married after forty-five years of marriage because we've spent so much time apart!
>
> *Supportive spouse of international manufacturing executive*

> Because my partner works so many hours, I've taken up gardening, improved my golf game, and joined the local men's club. I've created a satisfying life that doesn't depend on her.
>
> *Executive Chef*

Full partners in the same business credit spending more time together for creating intimacy in their relationship. In contrast, many couples in the supportive spouse model believe that spending less time together promotes individual growth and encourages greater sexual desire and appreciation for each other's company. They see their daily separation from each other as an advantage to their relationship.

Rewards for the Entrepreneur

In virtually every interview, entrepreneurs spoke with gratitude about how their spouses had made it possible for them to follow their dreams. These are just a few examples:

- My wife took care of the kids like a single parent while I worked over 90 hours a week for ten years. I think she had the harder job of the two of us!

- My partner was really there for me when my business was crumbling. I learned that she wasn't with me for my money or my prestige. She stuck it out with me because she loved me.

- My home was like an oasis for me. When I came home dog-tired from the office, my wife was waiting for me with dinner on the table—often at ten o'clock at night!

- My thriving business is only what it is because I had an incredible husband backing me every step of the way. If he hadn't been willing to support our family for the year my business wasn't making much money, I would have given up a long time ago.

The benefits for the entrepreneur of having a supportive spouse model of partnership can be numerous. Many entrepreneurs view it as the best of two worlds. They have someone who offers advice, encouragement, and assistance, without the legal hassles of sharing control with a formal business partner. They are better businessmen or women because of the contribution of their spouses, and all the profits of the business return to the family. They are truly "in it", this thing called life, together. Their spouse's support of their dreams enables them to do the work they love to do. Pulling together to conquer the challenges of entrepreneurship deepens their love and respect for their life partner.

CONCLUSION

Whichever entrepreneurial model you choose is ideally predicated upon what works best for your dreams, visions and goals for your business and your romantic relationship and/or family life. As entrepreneurial women, we know success is not dictated only by the bottom line but by happiness in our romantic and interpersonal relationships. This chapter should serve you well towards these goals.

If you would like to download copies of Discovery Exercise One go to:
www.relationshiptoolbox.com/partners.pdf

If you would like to download copies of Discovery Exercise Two go to:
www.relationshiptoolbox.com/dual.pdf

If you would like to download copies of Discovery Exercise Three go to:
www.relationshiptoolbox.com/spouses.pdf

III
HOPE FOR THE BEST, BUT PLAN FOR THE WORST!
Financial and Family Planning

> "When the business didn't earn what we projected, we invested $30,000 more than I had originally agreed to. After two years, we still weren't profitable. I gave my wife an ultimatum: turn a profit, or close the business down. I'm not willing to invest one more nickel in this business."
>
> *Elaine and Tyler, a couple in their mid-forties, who purchased a small business with severance pay Elaine received after a layoff. Poor financial planning devastated their bank account and their marriage.*

> "When I encouraged my wife to start her own business, I didn't realize that our house would fall apart. She stopped cooking, cleaning, and caring for the kids. Suddenly the only thing that was important to her was her business."
>
> *Disgruntled husband of business owner*

From the beginning of your marriage, you both had to decide whether to pool your money or keep it separate, how the bills would get paid, and who would reconcile the checking account. When one or both of you is self-employed, you may not need a new conversation about money management. For example, if you established your businesses before you married and you handle all the financial transactions of your business individually, or if you maintain separate bank accounts and don't merge your finances in any way, perhaps this entire topic of managing money isn't such a hot button in your marriage. But under most circumstances, when you are starting a business of your own, you will need to create new understandings with your spouse about money management.

I help couples with many different types of issues; however, consistent with research, the number one reason couples seek my help involve fights revolving around money, followed by sex and parenting styles. Contrary to what many people believe, money fights among couples cross all socio-economic barriers. Many individuals are unaware of what money represents for them and/or how these representations and values were conceived. When a person is in the dark regarding their own values, attitudes and beliefs about money, it makes it almost impossible for a couple to resolve their issues over money. You cannot understand your partner's position regarding money if your partner is unaware about what is running him or her when it comes to money decisions.

When you are single, you endure entrepreneurial hardships alone. When you are a married business owner, your spouse and children bear the personal and financial risk as well. If you haven't solidly prepared your family for the financial and personal sacrifices inherent in starting a new business, you put your marriage and the well being of your family on the line.

Guideline Exercises

The exercises contained in this chapter will help you and your partner build a strong foundation of mutual understanding. You may choose to do the exercises with your partner, separately from your partner (with discussion at a convenient time), or even entirely on your own, if your partner refuses or is unable to participate. You may choose to do all the exercises or only the ones that appear to be the most relevant and important for your present circumstances. I encourage you to complete all the exercises, even those you feel you don't need because you've got it all figured out already—you might be surprised what you will learn that will help you strengthen your marriage and your business.

At the end of every exercise you will have an opportunity to record any agreements you make with your spouse. Some couples find the process of formalizing their agreements reassuring and satisfying. If you lean toward the formal side, you may even want to consult your family attorney before or after constructing any financial agreements. Other couples prefer a looser approach—jotting down ideas on a piece of paper, or even talking into a digital recorder linked to a computer or iPad. Do what works for you and your spouse, provided that it helps you both clarify and express your expectations of and agreements on financial management and family goals. With only the few hours of preparation this chapter requires you invest, you will emerge with a strategic plan for merging your business, marriage and family goals.

GUIDELINE ONE:
ACKNOWLEDGE THE EXISTENCE OF RISK

> Our best friends warned us we were moving too fast when we decided to quit our jobs to go into business together. It was hard listening to their negativity, but it's a good thing we did. When we researched the new business more carefully, we realized that the financial risk was much greater than we were willing to take. I went back to my former job, and my husband worked the business alone for two years before I joined him.
>
> *Husband and wife business partners*

It takes enormous courage to become self-employed, and/or to start or buy a business, especially when family and business associates express great concern. Enthusiasm and optimism are essential for success in life and any entrepreneurial venture. To protect your family, you must balance optimism and positive psychology with thorough preparation and sound business advice. Acting on one's dreams, especially when your family is involved, can be quite risky. Some dreams are not meant to be actualized!

Dr. Victoria Felton-Collins, psychologist and certified financial planner, counsels, "There is a difference between prudent risk and wild gamble. Before you put one dime of partnership funds into any investment, know that difference." (Felton-Collins, *Couples and Money*)

Gary decided to leave his corporate job as an accountant to set up a consulting business, focusing on lowering clients' overhead expenses. Since Gary planned to sell his consulting services to company owners on a contingency basis, paid only through the savings he could find for them by reducing their operating costs, he expected clients to be knocking down his door for services. After all, he could potentially save them thousands of dollars a year, with no up-front consulting fee. He invested $12,000 to get himself the training and office equipment he needed. He thought he was taking a prudent financial risk, but he ran into serious cash flow problems from the beginning.

Gary's father and father-in-law, both experienced businessmen, saw potential difficulties in the sale of this service to business owners. They cautioned him about the risk of basing a consulting business on contingency sales. Gary could donate his time and expertise with no income to show for it. They predicted problems collecting accounts receivables, since Gary would have to wait until the company experienced savings before being paid for his services. The wait for full payment could be as long as a year. They warned him that company presidents may not be as open to change as he expected, even if it could save them some money.

Gary heard their warnings, but interpreted their advice as the caution of overly concerned family. He wanted this business option to work, so he listened instead to the enthusiasm of a few people successfully selling these services in other states. He figured if they could do it, so could he. Gary didn't test the market because he was so sold himself on the value of this business service. Unfortunately, the predictions of Gary's family advisors all ended up coming true and what he and his wife thought was a prudent risk evolved into a sizable gamble.

For a solo entrepreneur, financial risks related to one's business may be scary; for a married entrepreneur unacknowledged financial risks create enormous ramifications for not only the business but for the marriage and family as well. Enthusiasm and optimism are prerequisites for entrepreneurial success; however, it is imperative they do not blind you to the financial risks and potential pitfalls associated with any entrepreneurial effort. When performing due diligence, curb enthusiasm and optimism so you can objectively analyze your financial entrepreneurial risks with your eyes wide open. Just as young love may initially blind us to our partner's less than stellar attributes, unchecked enthusiasm and optimism may blind an entrepreneur to the obvious and not so obvious risks of an entrepreneurial business. The financial risk inherent for any entrepreneurial business cannot be underestimated.

Gary's experience is typical of many entrepreneurs who rush toward entrepreneurial dreams and away from confusion, distress, or miserable jobs. If you are in the early stages of exploration, examining the risks with your spouse is the best way to insure that your enthusiasm and mindset (key qualities for entrepreneurial success) are not interfering with the facts. Also, risky undertakings are more likely to gain the support of a spouse when they have been included in the evaluation process. Although they may or may not be an actual business partner, your spouse will reap the rewards or face the consequences of your business' success or failure. If you and your partner go white-water rafting, at least know the level of difficulty of the river before you leave the riverbank so that you can better prepare both of you for the journey that lies ahead.

GUIDELINE TWO:
IDENTIFY YOUR RISK PERSONALITY
AND THAT OF YOUR PARTNER

> When the needle on my gas tank is on empty, and the red light is flashing, I worry about getting more gas. My husband fills up his gas tank when it's still a quarter full.
>
> *Jenna*

If you are risk averse, marriage to an entrepreneur will be a formidable challenge for you. Your entrepreneurial spouse may drag you reluctantly from your comfort zone into your idea of a living nightmare. In contrast, if you are an entrepreneur who thrills in trading risk for reward, and you marry someone who doesn't feel the same way about risk, then your spouse's lack of support may drive you crazy, or even prevent you from achieving entrepreneurial success all together. Married entrepreneurs must be ever cognizant that the success and/or failure of their business impacts not only themselves but also, their marriage and family as well. Marriage is a partnership in every sense of the word.

Fighting about money is the number one reason for most couple fights. If you stretch too far outside your partner's financial comfort zone, you may need to accommodate your spouse's need to cap your financial risk. Even if your business is a wild success, your partner will still feel ignored and disrespected if you fail to consult with him or her about your entrepreneurial efforts.

Where are you and your spouse on the vast spectrum of risk tolerance?

> I quit my job without telling my wife in advance, risking everything, including our marriage, to start my company. Material security is meaningless to me, but it was hard on my wife. She doesn't feel the same way I do about money.
>
> *Alan, a forty-year-old CEO who put his family*
> *$1 million in debt to capitalize his startup business.*

> When I lost my job, we had three kids in college, paying out over $100,000 in tuition a year. When the perfect business opportunity came my way, I took the gamble. It nearly killed me when my daughter called home from college and said it would be OK if she had to take a semester off.
>
> *Yolanda, a high-tech executive, who started her own*
> *company after losing her job in a company downsizing.*

Chances are you and your spouse feel differently about the financial and personal risk that accompanies self-employment. To thrive in marriage, you must consider both sets of feelings when you are making major financial decisions. As with anything else in a marriage, planning and ultimate decision-making regarding an entrepreneurial venture should be made only after effective communication has taken place between you and your spouse. Brainstorming and strategizing together about the ramifications of your business' success and/or failure will help you create the appropriate contingency plans based upon the "what ifs." With few exceptions, risking joint assets should be a joint decision. As one spouse expressed, "It may be his business, but it's *our* money so it's *my* business too!"

The Origins of Your Risk Personality

Let's call your attitude toward risk your "risk personality." The following section explores four sources that influence the formation of your risk personality—family messages, adult experiences, friends and colleagues, and the media/pop culture.

Family Messages

How your parents raised you to think about money influences how you perceive financial risk in your adult life. Memories from your childhood have a tremendous influence on your adult money personality. Most of your money behavior as an adult probably reflects following in your parents' footsteps or rebelling against them. Couples bring an array of conscious and unconscious beliefs, attitudes, and feelings about money into their marriages, often having absolutely no idea how they were formed. Without this clarity and understanding, your marriage may become the Titanic unknowingly sailing into an unseen, yet just as deadly, iceberg without the protection of enough life jackets—and your relationship is sure to sink.

Conscious and unconscious attitudes about money are internalized by approximately age twelve, formed by the experiences of our childhood where money values were covertly and overtly communicated. The reason why many money fights between couples are left unresolved is because each partner's unconscious beliefs and attitudes about money are never brought into the open and discussed (since they are unconscious, partners are, by definition not aware of them). What remains unknown and undisclosed in one's unconscious remains unresolved in one's relationship.

Susan grew up in a home where debt was frowned upon and her widowed mom kept the first dollar she ever made. Her husband Mark grew up in a home where financial debt was a way of life and his parents were quite comfortable with it. Mark is a serial entrepreneur who has experienced considerable financial success and abysmal financial disasters throughout the past ten years. When Mark is on a financial roll, Susan cannot shake the terror that the day will arrive when the money won't be coming in anymore. Mark spends money as quickly as it comes in—and then some. No matter how much money Mark makes, he ends up in debt. Money in the bank represents security for Susan whereas for Mark, it represents a ticket to the good life.

Effective communication and the ability to compromise bridged the financial risk gap for this couple. They created a family plan that gave Susan responsibility to prepare the financial statements for the business, giving her full knowledge of the company's financial health. This provided Susan with the sense of control and financial security she yearned for. She and Mark also agreed upon a certain level of debt that she could learn to live with, above which, Mark needed to respect her insistence that old debt be paid before any new debt would be incurred. It took a few years before Mark learned how to give up his freewheeling approach to debt, but once he learned how to take care of his wife so that she wouldn't be living in daily financial fear, he adjusted, and his business grew even stronger—as did his marriage.

Childhood upbringing strongly influences your comfort with an entrepreneurial lifestyle, as this entrepreneur admits: "My dad was extremely security conscious. He worked for the telephone company for thirty years. When I lost my job and decided to start my own business, instead of looking for another job, his disapproval rang in my ears all day long." Another entrepreneur shares: "My parents taught me 'never touch the capital' and 'money in the bank equals security.' I panicked when I saw my inheritance begin to dwindle, as we invested it in our business."

If you had positive experiences as the child in an entrepreneurial family, you may naturally seek out an entrepreneurial life as an adult. If your early experiences with money were negative, you may be risk averse as an adult, vowing never to let your parents' experience happen to your family. Theresa's dad was a waiter dependent on tips for the lion's share of his earnings. Theresa craved an adult life with financial security, which for her meant a steady, predictable paycheck, paid sick days, vacation days and health benefits. Her husband Vinnie grew up in a home where his dad was a moderately successful entrepreneur. For Vinnie the thought of a 9-5 desk job was akin to a root canal without anesthesia. When this couple learned to respect each other's differing positions on financial risk, Vinnie could put together a business plan that satisfied Theresa's need for stability.

Adult Experiences

Have you experienced the consequences of financial risk as an adult? Once you begin taking risks as an adult, the outcome of your decisions, and your attitude toward success or failure, will influence your risk personality. Initially, I was quite hesitant to add an entrepreneurial business model to my traditional private practice model. The private practice model is referred to as an hours for dollars model. The entrepreneurial business model that I have transitioned to allows me to achieve my goal of helping more people be successful in business and life by leveraging my time with public speaking, conducting workshops and seminars, doing teleseminars and writing a weekly on-line newsletter, as well as this book. Initially, this new entrepreneurial business model was quite unsettling and raised my risk tolerance to uncomfortably high levels. But my determination to get my message across to a larger audience eventually quieted my fear. My husband's unwavering support and cheerleading went a long way to ward off any financial doubts I felt about expanding my relationship and communication work outside the comfort zone of my very successful private practice.

In contrast, Bella and her husband Fred have become more risk-averse the older they get, and the more obliged they are to come up with thousands of dollars in college tuition and second mortgage payments. Although they can dream about Fred quitting his job to start his own business, his steady salary and benefits are an anchor they rely upon, so in their marriage, only one of them is currently self-employed—Bella—and Fred has, for now, given up the entrepreneurial life—at least till the kids are out of college.

Friends, Colleagues, and Media/Pop Culture

A business owner who lost his shirt in a poor business decision or ran into some bad luck can dissuade you from taking a risk. If you are risk-averse by nature, you may interpret another business owner's difficult experiences as evidence to support your decision to avoid financial risk. On the other hand, successful friends, neighbors, or colleagues may inspire you to follow their lead.

Radio, newspapers, magazines and the Internet love to report the drama of business success and failure. We've all read about how WalMart put the mom-and-pop store out of business when it moved into town, or how the latest global earthquake destroyed hundreds of uninsured small businesses. We also love to read about how an ordinary guy or gal down the street achieved the American Dream and made it big with an idea they scribbled on a cocktail napkin at a party.

The stories you read, hear, and pay attention to influence your perception of risk. You will filter in or out the positive stories of risk and reward, or the tragic stories of loss, depending on your frame of mind regarding risk. Your mindset is a critical factor that dictates whether you focus more on the success stories or the failure stories of entrepreneurs, along with how you interpret these stories as an indicator for your own entrepreneurial efforts. Either way, the media and pop culture will have an invisible hand influencing your willingness to take a risk.

Many people are unaware of their risk personality until they find themselves locked in a never-ending battle about money with their spouse. This exercise will help you identify your risk personality (and that of your spouse), rather than waiting until you are in the midst of a financial catastrophe to figure it out. Don't start looking for your life vest when the ship is sinking.

Patty / Ann

DISCOVERY EXERCISE ONE:
FAMILY INFLUENCE ON RISK PERSONALITY

Completion time: 15 minutes

Research shows men and women hold different values and attitudes about money. These differences are operationalized in how a person wants to spend it (or save it) and what drives them absolutely crazy about their partner's view of money. Awareness and respect for these differences will be identified in the exercise below—creating a window of opportunity necessary for understanding each partner's differing views and attitudes about money.

Discuss the following questions with your partner to understand better the family influence on your risk personality. Note your similarities and differences. Also record any new insights you gained from thinking about these questions.

1. **What were the messages you received about risk from your family?** Was it, "Nothing ventured, nothing gained," or, "A bird in the hand is worth two in the bush"? What were the actual expressions about money and risk you heard in your house, at the dinner table, or in conversations between your parents? What kind of risk-taking in employment did your parents role model? Were your mom or dad entrepreneurs, corporate career types, or full-time homemakers?

2. **What was your actual experience with money as a child?** Did you worry about the family acquiring enough money? Did you get what you needed as a child? Were you given an allowance? Could your family afford family vacations or school clothes? Did you feel you had access to enough food to eat? What kind of condition was the house you lived in? How did you finance your education beyond high school? Where did you perceive your family fell on the food chain: wealthy, upper middle class, middle-class, lower class or poor?

3. **How did your parents manage their money (if you know)?** Did your parents invest in the stock market, real estate, mutual funds, or savings bonds? Did they ever lose a significant portion of their assets? What did they believe about savings accounts? What kind of assets do they own now, as a result of their financial decisions, or what did they leave as an inheritance? Did your parents ever argue about money?

4. **What messages about risk did your parents learn from your grandparents?** Were your grandparents immigrants who risked everything to come to this country? Did your grandparents work together in a family business, such as farming or shopkeeping? Is entrepreneurship in your family's blood?

Patty / Ann

DISCOVERY EXERCISE TWO: IDENTIFYING YOUR BASIC ORIENTATION TOWARD RISK, AND THAT OF YOUR SIGNIFICANT OTHER.

Completion time: 5 minutes

The following statement about couples often rings true: "There is his side, there is her side, and the truth is somewhere in the middle." To eliminate this pitfall of subjective truth, complete together the two discovery exercises below to better understand each other's basic orientation toward risk, thereby diminishing potential misunder-standings about money if your business falls on hard financial times.

First circle the number that most applies to you. Then circle the number you believe best applies to your spouse. Ask your spouse to do the same exercise. Do you find any differences in perception of each other? You might be surprised by what your spouse reveals!

HUSBAND

Risk Averse				Risk Tolerant				Risk Inclined	
1	2	3	4	5	6	7	8	9	10

WIFE

Risk Averse				Risk Tolerant				Risk Inclined	
1	2	3	4	5	6	7	8	9	10

DISCOVERY EXERCISE THREE:
RISK ASSESSMENT TOOL

Completion time: 30 minutes

The following risk assessment tool will help you identify what you and your spouse are willing to risk materially in order to reap the rewards of entrepreneurship. The assessment provides the basis for discussion about the allocation of cash if a business venture causes money to be scarce. It asks you to differentiate between events that would cause you discomfort and events that would cause you such distress that you need to avoid them under any circumstances.

For the assessment tool to be effective, you must be willing to suspend all predictions and assumptions about the projected risk of your business venture. Imagine for the purposes of this assessment that anything is possible.

Complete the following assessment by yourself and ask your spouse to do the same. Place the appropriate number in the space before each risk event.

Circle any questions with the answer 5, and you might want to do it with any 4's as well.

After completing the assessment, follow the instructions at the end of the assessment for sharing your responses with your spouse.

0 = not applicable

1 = no big deal, hardly uncomfortable

2 = somewhat disagreeable and uncomfortable

3 = very disagreeable, uncomfortable, and embarrassing

4 = extremely disagreeable, humiliating, way out of my comfort zone

5 = under no circumstances—would violate my sense of safety and stability

Rate your willingness to risk the following events.

SHELTER

- ☐ Take a second mortgage or home equity loan
- ☐ Postpone home repairs, like plumbing, maintenance, painting
- ☐ Postpone replacement of old appliances when needed
- ☐ Move to a smaller home or rent instead of own
- ☐ Rent a smaller home than you are renting now
- ☐ Lose your second home
- ☐ Shut off utilities (heat, light, telephone)
- ☐ Foreclosure and eviction from primary home
- ☐ Move in with in-laws, parents, or other family members
- ☐ Other: _____

Comments: _____

DEBT

Need to borrow money from:

- ☐ Parents
- ☐ In-laws
- ☐ Other family, friends
- ☐ Private investors
- ☐ Banks
- ☐ Venture capitalists
- ☐ Angel investors
- ☐ Bring in a partner to the business

Credit card debt:

- ☐ Up to $5,000
- ☐ Up to $10,000
- ☐ Up to $15,000
- ☐ More than $15,000

Other debt problems:

- ☐ Unable to make monthly payments on current debt
- ☐ Unable to make alimony and child support payments
- ☐ Unable to keep current on school loans or other personal loans
- ☐ Unable to make auto loan payments
- ☐ Creditors are calling the house
- ☐ Need to declare personal bankruptcy
- ☐ Other: _____

Comments: _____

FINANCIAL CUSHION

Savings account falls below

- ☐ $1,000
- ☐ $5,000
- ☐ $10,000
- ☐ $25,000
- ☐ $50,000
- ☐ Other: _____

- ☐ Loss of savings for retirement
- ☐ Loss of savings for college
- ☐ Loss of savings for life-cycle events (weddings, etc.)
- ☐ Loss of savings for new car
- ☐ Loss of savings for taxes
- ☐ Loss of savings for vacations
- ☐ Loss of savings for construction on home

Mutual funds and other short-term investments fall below:

☐ $1,000

☐ $5,000

☐ $10,000

☐ $25,000

☐ $50,000

What are your balances now? _____

Comments: _____

Long-term investments and IRA fall below:

☐ $1,000

☐ $5,000

☐ $10,000

☐ $25,000

☐ $50,000

☐ What are your balances now? _____

Other sources of financial cushion: _____

Comments: _____

FOOD

☐ Curtailing eating out at fine restaurants

☐ Curtailing eating out at family/casual restaurants

☐ Cut back on junk food

☐ Cut back by 25 percent on expense of meals at home

☐ Cut back by 50 percent on expense of meals at home

☐ Cut back by 75 percent or use food stamps

☐ Other: _____

Comments: _____

AUTOMOBILE

- ☐ Postpone car repair and maintenance
- ☐ Increase car insurance deductibles
- ☐ Lose car
- ☐ Reduce gasoline budget by 50 percent
- ☐ Trade in current car for used or less expensive car
- ☐ Postpone purchase of new car
- ☐ Lose use of second car
- ☐ Lose use of only vehicle
- ☐ Other: _____

Comments: _____

INSURANCE

- ☐ Lose health insurance
- ☐ Keep catastrophic medical insurance only
- ☐ Lose disability insurance
- ☐ Eliminate life insurance
- ☐ Reduce life insurance premiums by 25 percent
- ☐ Reduce life insurance premiums by 50 percent
- ☐ Lose dental insurance
- ☐ Other: _____

Comments: _____

CHILD EXPENSES

Unable to pay for:

- ☐ Hobbies
- ☐ Sporting activities
- ☐ Musical lessons
- ☐ Religious school education
- ☐ Summer camp
- ☐ New clothes
- ☐ Private school tuition
- ☐ School expenses—supplies, field trips
- ☐ Orthodonture or other uninsured medical expenses
- ☐ Other: _____

Comments: _____

ELDER-CARE EXPENSES

Unable to pay for:

- ☐ Travel to visit elderly parents
- ☐ Supportive services for elderly parents
- ☐ Renovation of home to allow elderly parent to live with you
- ☐ Other: _____

Comments: _____

CHARITABLE DONATIONS

- ☐ Donate less than 5 percent of earnings
- ☐ Donate less than 10 percent of earnings
- ☐ Donate to church or synagogue only, but no other
- ☐ Eliminate donations entirely
- ☐ Other: _____

Comments: _____

ENTERTAINMENT EXPENSE SIGNIFICANTLY REDUCED OR ELIMINATED

- ☐ Curtail or postpone vacations
- ☐ Reduce expenses for couple dates
- ☐ Reduce expenses for kids—ice-skating, sports events, after school programs
- ☐ Eliminate or reduce entertaining guests
- ☐ Eliminate or reduce cable TV and movies
- ☐ Eliminate or reduce personal computers, electronic games, gadgets
- ☐ Reduce the purchase of magazines and books
- ☐ Limit the purchase of alcohol and uninsured prescription drugs
- ☐ Other: _____

Comments: _____

GIFTS

- ☐ Unable to leave sizable inheritance for children/grandchildren
- ☐ Unable to give significant birthday or holiday presents
- ☐ Unable to support adult children who need financial support
- ☐ Unable to give gifts to friends and extended family
- ☐ Other: _____

Comments: _____

FAMILY PET

- ☐ Sell family pet(s)
- ☐ Go to veterinarian on emergency basis only
- ☐ Purchase cheaper food
- ☐ Reduce toys and treats
- ☐ Other: _____

Comments: _____

PERSONAL DEVELOPMENT

Eliminate or cut back for one or both of you:

☐ Therapy or counseling

☐ Personal growth workshops and seminars

☐ Books and magazines

☐ Fitness center membership, personal trainer

☐ Hobby expenses

☐ Chiropractic, acupuncture, massages

☐ Naturopathic Physician visits, vitamins and nutritional supplements

☐ Regular haircut

☐ Manicures; pedicures

☐ Other: _____

Comments: _____

If both of you are entrepreneurs or self-employed, complete the one applicable to your business.

PROFESSIONAL DEVELOPMENT FOR YOU

Eliminate or cut back:

☐ Office rental and utilities

☐ Travel

☐ National conventions

☐ Membership in professional organizations

☐ Educational classes, workshops, seminars, journals, books, newspapers

☐ Business supplies

☐ Public relations, advertising, business communications

☐ Professional clothes

- ☐ Business/client entertainment expense
- ☐ Professional services—accountant, lawyer
- ☐ Other: _____

Comments: _____

PROFESSIONAL DEVELOPMENT FOR YOUR SIGNIFICANT OTHER

Eliminate or cut back:

- ☐ Membership in professional organizations
- ☐ Educational classes, workshops, seminars, journals, books, newspapers
- ☐ Business supplies
- ☐ Public relations, advertising, business communications
- ☐ Professional clothes
- ☐ Entertainment expense
- ☐ Professional services—accountant, lawyer
- ☐ Other: _____

Comments: _____

Discussion of Risk Assessment Exercises with Your Spouse

The risk assessment tool provides an objective means for evaluating how far into debt you can go if you wish to keep your marriage secure while you are building your business. The conversations and ensuing discussions surrounding the findings of these risk assessment tools should be scheduled as an important business meeting with your spouse. The goal of this meeting will be to understand how an entrepreneurial undertaking will impact the financial aspect of your marriage. Come to it with an open mind and if possible, talk in a quiet environment free from all distractions. Shut off all electronic devices such as cell phones, computers, televisions and music to prevent distractions that might emotionally remove you from the conversation, even though you are physically present. Schedule this meeting when you and your spouse are emotionally and physically present. Honestly discuss the risk assessment findings and write down any agreements and/or deal breakers that materialize. Negotiate and compromise your agreement in good faith. Sleep on it for a day or two and then revisit the written agreement. Schedule a second meeting with your spouse in a few days to discuss anything that makes you feel ill at ease. Discuss a new and improved agreement plan and then write it down. Sign this agreement and put it in a safe place for future reference. Revisit this agreement as the business and your marriage evolves and grows; rewrite the agreement when necessary. Be creative, and remember, the shared goal is a prosperous business and intimately connected marriage.

Ground Rules for Using the Results of the Risk Assessment Tools Effectively

1. Don't judge your spouse for any of his or her number 4s and 5s. Each of you has your own truth, formed by your life experience and training. You are each entitled to your own boundaries and opinions without fear of criticism or denigration.

2. Be as flexible as possible, and look hard at whether you can renegotiate any of your own 4s or 5s, if necessary. Reserve 5 for those circumstances that you would find absolutely intolerable, not just uncomfortable. Could you move a 5 category to a number 4, if circumstances demanded it?

3. Remember: Boundaries related to risk and financial management are most effective if they are flexible. Ironically, if you give your partner permission to establish firm boundaries, he or she will often become more willing to turn those boundaries into gates and windows, rather than solid barricades. First he or she needs to feel accepted and safe.

GUIDELINE THREE:
FORM MUTUAL AGREEMENT ABOUT MATERIAL RISK

Use the insight the risk assessment tool provides you for completing guideline three, which follows.

Whether it's his business, yours, or you share the business as full partners, it's advisable to form a mutual agreement about how much material risk you can tolerate. After completing all of the risk assessment exercises we have provided you, you now have a much better understanding, and we hope, empathy, for how your spouse approaches financial risk. Hopefully you also learned about what triggers you, as well. Now, you and your partner can better negotiate a compromise to avoid triggering a catastrophic (5) loss for either of you. You each might be quite similar in your orientation toward risk, needing to negotiate only one particular issue. Or, you might be dramatically different from each other, requiring the negotiation of several financial decisions. Partnerships/marriages that work always honor the risk threshold of each partner. To not do so risks the foundation of trust in the marriage:

> "When my wife pledged the house to raise capital for her business, I didn't sleep for months. I would wake her in the middle of the night and scream at her, "What have you done? We're going to be out on the street!" She was angry with me for not believing in her, but my anger had nothing to do with her. Eventually her business became profitable and I calmed down, but it was six months of hell for both of us."
> *Panicked husband*

Let's take a look now at a few fundamental actions and mind-shifts you can make to solidify your marriage and to keep financial risk from sending it off track.

Appreciate your spouse's sacrifice: If you are the one who is asking your partner to step out of his or her comfort zone, convey your gratitude to your spouse on a regular basis. Just when your spouse needs your appreciation the most may be the time you find it hardest to provide support. The stress of your new business has you preoccupied. You may feel guilty, frustrated, embarrassed, or even humiliated because you are causing your spouse great discomfort. Instead of acknowledging your spouse's gift to you and expressing your gratitude, you could find yourself avoiding the subject altogether, but your spouse needs you to express your appreciation regularly.

Be as flexible as possible: Before Claire met her husband, Jeff, 29-years ago, she was single for many years and in total control of her own money. She was for the most part debt-free and preferred it that way. When they married, they merged their finances completely. Even though Jeff carried more debt than she did, and many new monthly expenses would now be hers, keeping their money separate was inconsistent with their view of marriage. Claire recalls, "Before I met Jeff, I said that I would never let my checking account fall below a certain level, I would never carry charge card balances, and I would never be willing to pay someone else's debt with my hard-earned money. I have done all of those things in our marriage, and guess what—it was difficult, but not as tragic as I had always imagined. I stretched beyond my self-imposed absolutes. Using the Risk Assessment Tool, my 5s became 2s and 3s. Some of the losses I once felt I could not endure under any circumstances became losses I learned to view as only disagreeable and uncomfortable. If I had been inflexible with Jeff about my risk threshold, I would have missed the opportunity to develop strength and courage and to redefine my relationship to money and security."

Writing this chapter also causes me to reflect on how my husband and I have handled financial risk in our marriage, and what our experience over a long-term marriage has taught me about myself. Since I was self-employed, I always thought that Mitch would work in a "secure" corporate job—with all the benefits that entails, including a steady paycheck, health insurance coverage, retirement monies, and more. (Much like the agreement that Bella and Fred, discussed earlier, worked out between themselves). But life didn't go according to my plan. After years of a successful career in corporate America, the entrepreneurial bug bit my husband and it became his passion. I'd like to tell you that I was a super supportive wife from the very beginning, but maybe not exactly... Initially I was distraught with the idea of losing the security a corporate job brought. Eventually, however, we began to enjoy the freedom and flexibility of a dual entrepreneurial relationship, and now I'm his biggest fan.

Be Willing to Compromise

What should you do when, with one item on the Risk Assessment Tool, you score a 2 and your spouse scores a 5? How do you "honor your partner's risk threshold?" Compromise about financial risk can take a wide variety of forms:

- Move faster on a business decision than what makes you comfortable, trusting the intuition or wisdom of your partner, or move more slowly on a business decision than you would like to, to accommodate your more risk-averse partner.

- Create financial safeguards to satisfy the security needs of your partner. For example, pay down the mortgage, or obtain life or disability insurance before making a bold business move.

- Keep your day job while you test out the new business idea part-time.

- Put aside a predetermined amount of money safeguarded from risk.

- Invest more money in the business for now than your preference, or accept less money invested in the business than you would like.

- Allow a business decision to be made without enough information to satisfy your need for data, or postpone a business decision until your partner can gather enough information to be satisfied.

All marriages must learn the art of compromise since two people will never agree on all issues, all the time. The ability to compromise becomes more imperative when dealing with a couple's financial situation. The most important aspect of compromise is being crystal clear on communicating exactly what the issue is that requires compromise. This sounds like common sense but some couples think they are compromising on the same issue, when they are actually trying to compromise on two different ones. Without effective communication, misunderstandings and conflict erupt, and compromise is totally unattainable.

Each partner can agree to compromise on an issue for a very specific time frame and then agree to re-visit this compromise at the designated future time. For example, a wife might agree to go into debt to support her husband's new entrepreneurial business for six months. After this six-month period, the couple would re-visit this compromise if the husband's business has not become profitable. This couple would then decide if they want to renegotiate the initial agreement and for what length of time. Or perhaps after the initial six-month period, the new agreement might be for the husband to terminate his entrepreneurial business and look for a traditional job. The key is to be clear about what will happen after this time frame passes if the financial goals of the business are not met. Are you willing to go further into debt or will your partner have to give up his entrepreneurial dream and seek a job? Ideally, these issues should be discussed at the beginning of the compromising process—not at the end. This avoids one partner feeling unsupported or betrayed by the other if the business needs to shut down.

Few compromises are completely equal. There is no such thing as a relationship that is a true 50/50 at any given period. At any one time, one of you may be compromising more than 50 percent. In a true equal partnership, it all "evens out in the wash." Sometimes it's your turn to do the bending, and then at some later time in your marriage, it will be your spouse's turn. Sometimes, you both bend toward the middle enough that each of you can stay within your comfort zones. Compromise is based on the principle of truly believing it is preferable to bend rather than to break (this is as true for business as well as personal relationships).

Patty Ann

DISCOVERY EXERCISE FOUR: OPTIONAL: FORM WRITTEN AGREEMENTS ABOUT RISK, DEBT AND SPOUSAL SUPPORT

Completion time: 30 minutes

If you choose to, you may wish to create written agreements with your spouse regarding the level of financial risk each of you is willing to experience. You can write a joint agreement or two individual agreements for each other. Consult your family lawyer if you are concerned about making these agreements legally binding, or if, in fact, you want to ensure that they would not be considered legally binding in the event of an unplanned and unfortunate divorce. These questions, and possible answers, will help you and your spouse formulate a written agreement that addresses several of the primary issues of concern.

RISK BOUNDARIES AND DEBT

What are your agreements about risk boundaries and debt? Here are some alternatives:

1. We should close down the business or find another alternative if continuing the business would require transgressing a number 5 risk boundary for either one of us.

2. I agree to do everything I can to avoid transgressing a number 4 or 5 risk boundary for either one of us. I will do so only with your permission.

3. No matter what, we won't, for the sake of the business, (Describe the number 5s for each of you.)

4. Let's revisit the Risk Assessment Tool on a quarterly basis or when faced with an unforeseen financial crisis.

Example: I agree to honor your risk boundaries, and I will not take any actions or make any decisions with my business that would require you to feel unsafe or unstable. To that end, I promise you that in no circumstances under my control will we lose the house, borrow money from your parents, or cancel our medical insurance. I will find another alternative before any of those things happens. I agree to negotiate with you about any business decisions that might result in taking you out of your comfort zone concerning the loss of our material possessions or financial stability. Let's revisit the Risk Assessment Tool once every three months.

PROFITABILITY OF THE BUSINESS

What are your expectations and agreements about the profitability of the business? Here are some alternatives:

1. We agree that if the business is not earning money by this date, we will cut our losses and look for another alternative.

2. As long as you can find a way to bring money into the household each month, it's your decision how long to keep the business operating.

3. When the business is earning money, on a part-time basis, then I will quit my full-time job.

4. When the business is earning \$_____, then you can quit your job and join me in the business full-time.

5. We understand that the purpose of this business is not to make a profit or a living wage for us. We'll keep the business operating as long as it does not require more than \$_____ (or_____% of our assets) over time.

6. We agree to reinvest \$_____ (or _____% of profits) back into the business for (period of time).

Example: We are starting this business expecting prosperity and success. We intend to earn a pretax profit of \$80,000 during the third year. We accept that it will likely take two years of development before we can expect profitability. We expect to invest \$50,000 in the first year, and \$40,000 in the second year to accomplish that. We agree that if the investment required in total exceeds \$100,000, or if the business is earning less than \$20,000 pretax after the first two years, we will reevaluate the feasibility of ongoing operations.

SPOUSAL SUPPORT

Sometimes the only way to start a new business is to depend on one spouse to provide income and benefits for the family. If that's the case for your family, which approach suits you best?

1. I have no problem being the primary breadwinner for this family. We can rely on my income and benefits. We do not need your income to survive financially.

2. I am willing to be the main breadwinner for the family for the time being, but these are my limits (not longer than a certain amount of time, not expecting more than a certain level of income, etc.).

3. I am willing to support the family while you are starting your business until (fill in date). At that point, it's my turn to have you support the family, because I want to (quit my job, go back to school, start a business, have a baby, etc.).

4. I am willing to support your business emotionally and to help in whatever way that I can part-time. I am not willing (or able) to support the family financially. I expect you to continue to fulfill that role, one way or the other, even if it means supplementing income from your new business with a second source.

Example: We can make it on Lisa's salary without any income from George for about a year if we cut way back on expenses and stick to our financial plan. Lisa is willing to support the family for a year while George grows his business. After a year, we hope to have a child. If Lisa is able to get pregnant, neither of us wants her to work full-time. We need the business to support the family within two years. If it doesn't look as if that will be possible, we will revisit our commitment to the business at the end of Year One.

GUIDELINE FOUR: KNOW YOUR MONEY MOTIVATION

We've spent a lot of time discussing the important concept of risk tolerance and aversion. Now we move on to another equally important topic that relates to the hot topic of money conversations and decisions in a marriage.

Money Motivation

Another factor that powerfully influences an individual's attitude toward money is what we will call "money motivation." It's not enough to work out all of your various feelings about taking risk and going into debt. That's important, but equally important is to recognize that individuals come from different approaches to lifestyle and debt, not only due to risk aversion and childhood experiences with money, but also, from their subconscious motivation to use money in particular ways.

The primary motivator for you, whether it be for freedom, security, power, or love, will drive your daily choices about what you spend money on, how you interact with your spouse about money, and your preferences for the type of business or work you choose. No motivation is more right or honorable than another, and what you think is motivating someone may not at all be the case. A person may spend a great deal of discretionary income on family members, but this generosity could be a clever disguise for a need to feel self-important or to manipulate relationships. The entrepreneur who appears motivated by ego may actually want to achieve power so that he can provide well for his family. The way in which money is handled, whether it is saved or spent, and on whom and what, may be a key indicator of what it represents for the person who holds the purse strings. The giving or withholding of money often represents power control and influence. When marriage is not a partnership, but rather, a one-up versus one-down power play, money is often a manipulator for power and control, which significantly compromises intimacy.

You've considered how your past and your personal money motivations impact your relationship with your spouse, and how you each feel toward business finances. Now it's time to examine how you operate around money in your daily life, so that you can better understand yourself, and your spouse, and avoid potential hot arguments on this contentious subject. Are your styles of spending money different? Is this a source of conflict for you as a couple? Let's create an understanding of how each of you typically handles money on a day-to-day basis.

DISCOVERY EXERCISE FIVE: IDENTIFYING YOUR DAILY MONEY BEHAVIOR

Completion time: 15 minutes

Take a few minutes, individually, and then collectively to discuss the questions raised in discovery Exercises Five and Six, to gain insight into this important question: "How do I relate to money in my daily life?"

1.   **What are your purchasing habits?** Do you buy the floor model to get a great deal, even if you risk quality? When you are shopping for a big-ticket item, like a new television, do you comparison shop in several different stores and on the Internet? Do you make decisions about big-ticket items on your own, or do you check with your spouse first?

2.   **What are your investment habits?** Do you prefer long-term conservative investments, choosing lower yield as a trade-off for safety? Do you enjoy playing the stock market? Are you a day trader? Do you prefer to have a balanced investment portfolio?

3.   **How long does it take you to make a financial decision?** Do you make decisions impulsively? Do you weigh all the data carefully before making a commitment? Do you reach decisions intuitively, or do you demand substantive, painstaking analysis and information to guide your decision?

4.   **Are you two peas in a pod, or is it amazing you can reach agreement on any financial decision for the home?** Do you balance each other well, or do you both tend to lean toward one direction? Do you never cease to amaze each other regarding how differently you view money? Are you comfortable with how you currently compromise to reach agreement?

Patty / Ann

DISCOVERY EXERCISE SIX: UNDERSTANDING YOUR MONEY AND RISK PHILOSOPHY

Completion time: 15-30 minutes

These questions help you identify what money means to you. You may or may not want to write your answers down, but these questions can spur meaningful conversation with your significant other. You might learn something about your spouse you did not know, even after years of marriage!

1. **Are you basically optimistic or pessimistic when it comes to your relationship with money? Do you have confidence in your ability to make money?** Do you trust in the benevolence of the universe? Do you worry incessantly about financial harm befalling you? Do you believe that money is a fluid resource that may come and go many times in your lifetime? Or, do you view money as an asset that isn't easily replenished once it is lost?

2. **Do you consider risk taking a necessary evil, like going to the dentist, or an exciting adventure, like mountain climbing?** Do you get a sick feeling in your stomach or a pleasant adrenaline rush when you are taking risks? Is the absence of risk boring to you or comforting? When you look back on your life, are the times you took your biggest risks your best memories or your worst?

3. **How does money represent freedom to you?** Do you dream of earning enough money so that you won't have to work anymore? So that you can hire housekeeping staff and a gardener? So that you will not be indebted to anyone? If you were able to achieve the wealth you long for, what privileges would be available to you that you don't have now? How would greater wealth influence the overall way you live your life?

4. **How does money represent security to you?** Does the provision of material needs give you peace of mind? Have you ever had enough money, and still felt poor, or afraid of losing it all? Is there ever enough money for you to feel secure? How much is enough? Do you feel that money is meant to be spent or do you prefer to save for a rainy day? Do you save twenty years away for retirement or only five years ahead, because anything can happen?

5. **How does money represent power to you?** Do you aspire to be managing a company with several employees working for you? Do you appreciate the status money provides? Is it important to you to influence people's actions with your money? How have you felt more powerful when you have had money, compared to when you haven't?

6. **How does money represent love to you?** Do you expect your partner to take care of you financially, as a demonstration of love for you? If you have discretionary money, do you prefer to spend it on loved ones? Do you ever attempt to buy love through giving? When you receive a gift from a loved one, what does it mean to you? If you don't receive a gift when you expect to, how much importance do you give the oversight? How much does it matter to you what a loved one spends on a gift?

7. **Who are your role models, the people you admire the most when it comes to financial success?** Do you wish you were the one who thought of Facebook or "Mrs. Fields Cookies," or would you just as soon enjoy the comfortable retirement of a corporate CEO? Who in your family, neighborhood, or circle of friends has achieved the kind of financial success you dream of acquiring?

GUIDELINE FIVE:
ESTABLISH GUIDELINES FOR MONEY MANAGEMENT AND DECISION-MAKING

Guideline five outlines some of the decisions you will need to make with your spouse that relate to money. With an overall conceptual conversation about risk and spending habits, you can now drill down to the basics, the cornerstones of daily spending and sharing money, to see how comfortable you both can be with certain practices. The devil is often in the details, especially when dealing with money differences. Here are some of the topics to discuss.

Joint or Separate Checking Accounts

Some happy couples swear the key to their successful relationship is keeping all of their money separate. These marriages are frequently second or third marriages, marriages with no children or grown children, and marriages in which the partners established businesses before they married. Sometimes couples in first-time marriages decided to keep money separate because they recognized significant differences in their spending patterns, or each individual wanted to maintain control over his or her own money.

The "traditional" view of a healthy marriage suggests a couple maintain a joint financial agreement, merging all savings, spending and investment accounts. This view was predicated upon each partner being equally committed to the marriage and each other. The marriage vow "for richer or poorer" is taken both figuratively and literally for these couples. Couples who merge their finances view this decision as a source of strength in their relationship. They view themselves as one financial unit and can't conceive of marriage with separate checking and/or savings accounts.

When partners elect to keep their finances separate, these marriages acknowledge both the pragmatic and financial complexity with which many individuals enter into marriage. For example, if one spouse attended graduate school in the fields of medicine or law they might

114

have easily accumulated $100,000 in student loans. Although you and your spouse may be powerfully committed to each other, the stark reality is that marriage is as much a legal and business arrangement as it is a romantic relationship. Couples who ignore the business aspect of their marriage do so at their own peril. Many couples feel totally committed and loyal to each other but, from their perspective, that has absolutely nothing to do with paying the debt off their partner incurred before marriage—so finances are kept separate.

Some couples cannot fathom separate finances as much as some couples cannot imagine keeping joint accounts. Neither strategy is wrong; the decision is up to each individual couple to decide which arrangement works best for them, taking into account their unique situation, their individual tolerance for risk, and their personal preferences. This decision, to merge finances or keep them separate, might also shift over time. A couple might start their marriage with separate finances and then merge them years later, perhaps when the woman has a child and they decide she will stop working full-time for a period of time.

Financial Decision Making for the Business

Whether your personal finances are held jointly or individually, business finances need to be kept separate from personal accounts for accurate accounting. Just as you made decisions about how to set up your personal accounts, you also must discuss who has access to business accounts and for what purposes.

When you introduce entrepreneurship into your marriage, you will also need to clarify the extent that joint money will fund one or both businesses. Is the business "my" business, "yours," or "ours?" If the business is yours, but funded in part by joint funds, then a certain level of joint decision-making comes with the privilege of using joint money for capital. If your business is self-sustaining or funded only by money you hold individually, decision making about business expenses might not be shared with your spouse. When you consult your spouse for advice, his or her lack of endorsement may, or may not, stop your actions, depending upon what agreements you've made ahead of time about how much control your spouse will expect over your day-to-day business decision-making. Make sure you discuss this in your financial agreements.

In some traditional marriages, wives are still expected to seek permission from their husbands to spend joint money, but their husbands make financial decisions without consulting their wives. Hard to believe this is still true in some marriages, but it is. Other couples make virtually every financial decision together. What are the decision-making ground rules you and your partner will operate with on a daily basis? For example, this is the agreement that Betty and Howard formed regarding financial decisions for her business:

Betty will consult with Howard about nonrecurring business expenses over $500. For any non-budgeted expense over $500, Howard must concur with Betty's request before she will spend the money. All major changes, like moving Betty's office, will be a joint decision. Howard expects Betty to consult him as if he were a full partner in her business, even though he won't be working with her in the business full-time, since a significant portion of Howard's income and savings is being used to capitalize her business. Both of them agree, if she finds sharing decisions with him unacceptable, she will find another way to fund her business.

Entrepreneurial couples that operate a business together may divide decision-making by function (e.g., he handles operations and she handles marketing), or agree to joint decisions when the expense exceeds a set dollar amount. Some insist on joint decision making for all decisions; other couples give each other wide latitude for unilateral decision-making. Again, there's no "wrong answer" here—the right answer is the one that works best for you as a couple.

Work together to establish decision-making ground rules optimal for you in your situation. Clarify which business decisions you will make jointly and unilaterally. For example, who will decide:

- How much to pay your employees and how much to spend on benefits (human resource issues).

- When to buy office supplies, and how much to spend (office management).

- When a customer should receive a refund and when to negotiate price with a customer (customer service policies).

- How much money to spend on advertising and promotion (marketing and sales).

- How much to charge for the merchandise, product, or service (product pricing).

Example: Sherry and Mike run a clothing consignment store together. Sherry is in charge of day-to-day operations. She will make all decisions related to operations expenditures. She will consult with Mike if she wishes to spend more than $300 non-budgeted expense. Mike is in charge of all marketing, sales, and promotion. He will make all decisions related to those expenditures. He will consult with Sherry if he wishes to spend more than $300 in non-budgeted expense. Mike and Sherry will meet weekly to keep each other informed of financial issues.

Resolving Disagreement

In a corporate hierarchy, "the buck stops here" reflects an understanding that, though democratic consensus may be ideal, a particular individual is ultimately responsible for any one problem needing resolution. Entrepreneurial life doesn't always provide a simple hierarchy to follow. Regardless of the type of business you and your spouse engage in, agree on a framework for negotiation and compromise when you disagree on a decision requiring joint approval. Establishing guidelines in advance will help you avoid trouble. When you reach stalemate, who or what will break the tie? Some couples agree that one of them will ultimately have authority over a certain functional area in business or in the home if they reach an impasse. Other couples use this simple rule of thumb: "The one with the stronger feelings gets his or her way." This rule operates in other areas of a healthy marriage, on both a small and large scale. One spouse might feel more strongly about going to a certain restaurant than the other. Or one spouse might really prefer a beach vacation over a ski vacation. Although both spouses have preferences, common sense suggests the spouse who feels most strongly about a specific preference is the one that is decided upon. Over the course of a long-term marriage, decisions over who gets their preference met evens out in the final analysis.

Adele rarely has a preference for where the family takes its annual vacation, however, her friend just returned from a trip to Alaska and she was in awe of her photos shared. Although her husband Bob was thinking the family trip would be to Utah this year, he acquiesced to his wife's preference for Alaska stating: "Adele never really cares where we go on our family vacations so if going to Alaska is that important to her this time, Utah can wait." This decision came out of a compromise conceived from empathy and love. Ultimatums and threats were never part of the conversation; rather, preferences and wishes were respectfully communicated. Bob recognized Adele's strong yearning to go to Alaska and he granted her this wish from a generous feeling of wanting to give to his wife. Now, since this is a chapter on money management, let's look at this same conversation from a money perspective. Bob might say to Adele, "it's okay with me if we go to Alaska this year, but you know that Alaska is going to cost us five grand more than if we went to Utah. Let's try to come up with some ideas on how we can fund the Alaska trip without going into debt."

Here's another discovery exercise that will help the two of you formulate these understandings.

Patty / Ann

DISCOVERY EXERCISE SEVEN: MONEY MANAGEMENT AND DECISION-MAKING

Completion time: 15 minutes

With your partner, articulate verbally or in writing your understandings of personal and business money management and responsibility for business decisions that impact your business or personal finances. Here are some alternatives:

1. All our money is joint. Therefore, we will equally share all money-related decisions.

2. Although we will fund the business with joint money, we agree that I must check with you only if the business goes over budget.

3. I agree to consult with you on any business or household decision requiring more than $_____ amount.

4. Since our money is separate, I will check with you only if my financial decisions will affect our lifestyle or joint personal possessions.

5. I agree to handle the bookkeeping for all of our household bills and for the business.

6. I will take care of paying my personal and business bills. I expect you to do the same.

7. Although we operate this business as full partners, I leave the daily financial management to you. However, I expect you to involve me in financial decisions requiring additional investment over $_____ as a one-time expense or $_____ monthly.

8. We agree that I will make financial decisions related to operations, and you will make financial decisions related to marketing and sales, as long as the decisions are consistent with our business plan, and not more than 5% over budget.

INVESTING MONEY IN THE BUSINESS

How much will the business be capitalized by personal money? Before you can answer this question, clarify exactly what defines personal money for you and your spouse. For example, is it everything outside of fixed expenses? Or does it include only your discretionary funds? Once you and your partner have determined what exactly constitutes personal money in the marriage, there are some alternatives to consider for how you and your spouse will view personal money invested in a business:

1. My business will never use joint money. It's my business completely, and I take full responsibility for supporting the needs of the business.

2. I won't use joint money beyond the initial investment. We agree now that you are willing to invest $_____ up front. I agree that my business must be self-sustaining before I would ask for more investment. (If that's not true, discuss whether and how often the business owner can come back to the spouse and ask for more investment).

3. Even though you quit your job, I expect you to continue to pay half of our living expenses.

4. Although we normally contribute equally to living expenses, I agree to pay _____% of them until you can contribute your fair share, as long as it doesn't go past these boundaries (amount of money I'm paying, and/or how long I'm doing it).

5. We will invest up to $_____ in the business over time. If the business requires more than that, we will close it down or seek outside investors.

6. I agree to invest our joint money into your business until I hit one of my number 3's on the Risk Assessment Tool.

Example from one couple's agreement: We will take $10,000 from our joint savings account to fund the start-up of our business. For the next year, while the business becomes profitable, we agree to fund the business with our joint savings and investments, as long as we do not exceed $40,000. If we need to cut back on expenses, we are willing to cut back on any of the 3s on the Risk Assessment Tool. Neither of us is willing to endure any 4s or 5s on the Risk Assessment Tool for the sake of the business.

Patty / Ann

GUIDELINE SIX:
ALLOW THE MONEY STYLE DIFFERENCES BETWEEN YOU AND YOUR PARTNER TO WORK TO YOUR ADVANTAGE

Money conflict is the most frequently cited reason for divorce and the hardest issue for couples to resolve effectively, but this guideline encourages you to view the differences in money style between you positively. For example, Jason (quoted below), appreciates his wife Joy's balancing influence:

> *"My wife, Joy, and I have the 'stop and go' approach to spending money. I'm the driver and Joy is the brakes. I'll call her from the field and tell her I want to buy something. She'll tell me I can't because money is too tight this month. She has a better handle than I do on how much money we have, so I've learned to listen to her."*

Jason has learned from experience to trust Joy's system for evaluating financial purchases. Frequently one partner is the big dreamer with ideas and chutzpah to act. If lucky, this person will team up with a partner who injects a regular dose of reality, a knack for details, and cautious money management—a complementary partnership.

Caution: the "stop and go" approach to financial spending, where one partner has steady control over stopping his or her partner's purchases can create friction. When the marriage is on solid ground this approach may work like a charm. When the marriage is experiencing emotional difficulties (as all marriages do), this approach might create resentment between partners when the partner who is told "no" begins to feel angry and controlled. At this point the 'stop and go' approach does not feel as if it is coming from a place of support and love, which was its original intent. When each individual approaches spending based on mutually agreed upon couple goals, both short and long-term, fighting over individual purchases will be less likely to occur.

Polarization

Polarization, a common block to couples working out money style differences, occurs when couples become argumentative and more opposed in reaction to each other. For example, the freewheeling spender's behavior becomes even more exaggerated in reaction to a tightwad saver; while the saver begins to hoard money as a response to the spender's spending. The qualities and characteristics, which initially attracted spouses to each other, are often the very same ones that become a point of contention in the future. This is especially true when it comes to the spending and/or saving of money.

Suppose Jason reacted to his wife Joy's insistence that he stop spending money by spending even more, just to prove to her that she can't control him. This may lead Joy to react to his overspending by trying to control him even more. Quickly they are in a vicious cycle. Polarization moves behavior to extremes. It replaces the sense of partnership in a marriage with a competitive framework. Polarization represents a serious danger to the bond and intimacy of the relationship because the couple is now competing against each other, instead of working as a team toward shared goals. The competitive aspect of the relationship, defined by a winner and a loser, begins to negatively shape and redefine the marriage.

If you feel you and your partner are in this struggle, here are some helpful tips to move out of polarization in your marriage and back into a true partnership:

1. Remember and acknowledge how you once liked the different attitudes and beliefs your partner brought into the relationship. Recall how you appreciated a different perspective from your own—especially regarding your partner's view about money. This allows you to view your partner's different attitude about money from a familiar and more comfortable place. If you are currently frustrated because your partner does not save as much money as you would like, remember how his or her ability to spend money in what now appears to be a carefree manner once liberated you making yourself save every cent you made. At an earlier time in your relationship your partner's spending allowed you to enjoy life's pleasures, which you withheld from yourself. This recognition and appreciation for your partner's

different approach does not imply you are comfortable with it; however, it allows you to view it from a positive perspective.

2. The technique of walking a mile in your partner's shoes, also known as "role reversal" goes a long way in understanding where your partner is coming from. (This technique is a great way to resolve other areas of conflict in your marriage and we will discuss this in detail in Chapter 6). The ability to understand your partner's money habits, even if you do not agree with them, creates a platform where you can begin to appreciate their financial perspective. This also creates a mindset shift from a negative to a positive place.

3. Try to remember, at least during the initial stages of polarization, that your partner is not trying to deliberately defy you. They merely feel differently about money than you do.

4. If needed, seek advice from an objective third party professional whose sole interest is the financial health of your relationship. It removes the negative cycle of criticizing and blaming each other for "bad" or "inappropriate" financial behavior. Consider hiring CPA's, tax attorneys, financial planners and a host of other financial professionals to navigate out of stormy financial seas.

One of the greatest challenges of your married life will be to celebrate the differences in your two individual money styles. I know a couple who, recognizing this challenge, included the following in their personal marriage vows: "I will strive for tolerance and acceptance of our differences, with the hope of coming to celebrate them." Make it your goal to move from annoyance, to tolerance and acceptance, to celebrating the differences that make you a stronger partnership. It would be very helpful to remember differences are not bad—they are just that, different. There is no one correct way to be married. Every relationship is unique and different. Celebrate your differences and view them as strengths in your relationship. Remember: you would not have married someone who is your twin, because if you did you would be bored to tears with them after a very short time. Let your differences complement and enhance your relationship, not devastate it. This is a clear conscious choice you can make.

DISCOVERY EXERCISE EIGHT:
APPRECIATING MONEY STYLE DIFFERENCES

Completion time: 15 minutes

To help guide your conversation about money style differences, and to appreciate these differences, do the following exercise together.

Complete the following exercise by yourself, and then share your responses with your partner.

1. When it comes to money management, my greatest strength is _____.

2. When it comes to money management, my spouse would say my greatest strength is _____ (Does #1 and #2 match? If not, discuss why not.)

3. When it comes to money management, my spouse's greatest strength is _____.

4. When it comes to money management, my spouse would say my greatest strength is_____. (Does #3 and #4 match? If not, discuss why not)

5. We recognize these money style differences between us: _____.

6. We're lucky those differences exist. We complement each other in the following ways, making us a stronger team: _____.

7. When we get polarized and rigid about our differences, this is what I do that contributes to the problem: _____.

8. When we get polarized and rigid about our differences, this is what you do that contributes to the problem: _____.

9. I want to come to celebrate the money style differences between us. To that end, I agree to _____.

10. We acknowledge the different values and behaviors we have about money is rooted in our family upbringing. (Now discuss these differences, not from a judgmental place, but from a factual place which will help lead to greater understanding and appreciation of each other.)

Dr.
Patty / Ann

GUIDELINE SEVEN:
DISCUSS MONEY ISSUES AT A TIME
AND PLACE THAT WILL BE PRODUCTIVE

Our worst money arguments are usually unplanned, triggered by some small event that takes the top off a volcano already poised to erupt. A reaction to your spouse's peculiar money habits puts you over the edge, or his or her failure to deliver on an agreed-upon task infuriates you. Whatever the event may be, it occurs at a lousy time when you aren't able to deal with it in a reasonable way. Tension mounts quickly, and before you know it, you and your spouse are discussing whether you should close down the business, get a job, or even get divorced. This happens when issues are left unresolved and resentment builds. Resentment acts as a roadblock to intimacy and effective communication; two essential "must haves" necessary for conflict resolution about any issue.

Here's an example: A check bounced from Karen's business account. Karen's husband, Roy, is her bookkeeper. Karen discovered the problem when she opened her mail and saw the notice from the bank. Roy is at his full-time job, but she is so furious she can't wait until he comes home to discuss it. She calls him at work.

Roy: *I'm right in the middle of an important meeting. Can it wait?*

Karen: *No, it can't! You told me you were taking care of balancing my checkbook. Obviously I should have hired someone to do it. You bounced a check to one of my most important vendors!*

Roy: *Well, if you weren't spending so much money on that business of yours, we wouldn't be bouncing checks. When are you going to start bringing in some money?*

Karen: *That's not the problem and you know it. The problem is you promised to keep my books up to date and balanced, and you haven't done it for the last two months. If you had kept your end of the bargain, we would have known we needed to transfer money and I wouldn't have bounced this check.*

Roy: *Where do you think we're going to get the money to transfer? I'm working sixty hours a week to support this family, and there still isn't enough money to take care of our bills. We're going to bounce the check for the mortgage this month!*

Karen: *Why didn't you tell me things were this bad? I wouldn't have printed my new brochure if you had warned me. What do you want me to do? Shut down after putting in all this effort? If you would help more with the kids, I'd have more time to work on my business.*

Roy: *Look, I told you this wasn't a good time to talk. We'll talk about it later. I have to go!*

Karen and Roy violated guideline eight in several ways. They talked about a serious money issue at the wrong time (interrupting Roy's meeting), in the wrong place (on the telephone), and in a very unproductive way (with seething hostility). They are speaking to each other with blame, defensiveness, and overreaction. Both Karen and Roy are unable to discuss the problem fruitfully with this approach.

The saddest thing about this scenario is that Karen and Roy are battling each other, rather than joining to problem-solve their current financial crisis as one team. Both Karen and Roy are responsible for this disastrous conversation. Karen insisted on talking about this issue even after she was told it was not a good time, while Roy proceeded to engage her in the conversation. This conversation was not urgent. The check had already bounced so the fallout of the financial situation had already occurred. The conversation was totally unproductive; it would have been best to have this discussion take place when cooler heads prevailed, at a time and place when both partners could hear and appreciate the others' concerns. As you can see, nothing productive resulted from it; conversely, negative feelings were increased with salt being added to the open wound.

Two truths are important in life and couples would do well to live by them. First, timing is everything. You wouldn't have had this discussion with your friend or client if they told you it was not a good time, so why would you do so with your spouse? Secondly, you can just about say anything to anybody—depending on how you say it. Conflict resolution skills, including managing the timing of your communication and the words you choose, are just as critical when enhancing communication with your spouse as they are when you speak with other people.

Ground Rules for Productive Discussions About Money Issues

Use the following ground rules to discuss a decision as significant as closing your business down, or a problem as major as being unable to make the mortgage payment.

Discuss Money Concerns Only in a Designated Meeting Scheduled at the Right Place and Time for Both Parties

If your money concerns could be an emotionally hot one, ask your spouse for a meeting at a mutually convenient time, preferably in a place that allows you to talk face to face and uninterrupted. Rule of thumb, the more emotionally charged the issue is, or potentially may become, the more imperative you follow this ground rule. For example, Karen could have waited until Roy came home from work and said, "I received a notice in the mail today that my check to the advertising agency bounced. I'm really angry about the possibility of losing an important business relationship. Can we talk about it before dinner?"

If possible, a meeting should take place within twenty-four hours of the request. If Roy didn't want to discuss the problem before dinner, he should suggest an alternative time before the end of the next day. With a family, it is often difficult to get uninterrupted time, but that is the ideal.

Agree that You Will Make No Significant Money Decisions as a Knee-Jerk Reaction

Avoid asking for any major changes to your current financial circumstances until the appropriate time for discussion with your spouse. This will prevent the further polarization of the relationship, which may have already begun. If you make a decision or demand based on an argument, cancel the agreement or request made in haste, and discuss it at a more appropriate time. In your conversation, approach the meeting with the tone of partnership rather than accusation or blame. Expressing concern over the family's financial situation will create goodwill, which will allow your spouse to actively listen to your genuine concerns.

For example, this is how Roy might have handled his outburst more effectively:

I'm sorry. I didn't mean to snap at you. I know you are working hard on your business. Our checking account balance has me really worried. I would like to set up a meeting to talk with you about how we can bring in some money quickly to help us get out of this jam. Can we talk about it this evening, after the kids are in bed?

Discuss Money Concerns Before They Become a Crisis

When you are in the midst of money difficulties, sometimes it is too painful or frightening to look at the reality of your situation. Procrastinating discussion until finances are at a crisis level is not an effective way to solve the problem. It is much more effective to deal with financial issues as soon as you feel its strain on your relationship. When the Titanic hits the iceberg is not the time to determine whether there are enough lifeboats onboard.

Roy gave Karen only a few weeks notice about their inability to make the mortgage payment. Yet signs of the problem were there for a few months. By the time he told Karen about it, there was little they could do to effectively respond. Another option would be for Karen to be equally involved in maintaining the checking account, so she knows the status of the account herself.

In every entrepreneurial venture, unpredictable money crises arise. Employees quit, accidents happen, natural disasters occur, customers fail to pay, or the cost of supplies increases. It may not be possible to prevent all problems ahead of time. Manage the crises you can control with proper planning, awareness, and discussion.

Use Conflict Resolution Techniques When Trying to Resolve Money Conflicts

When battling over an issue as sensitive as money, you will need your strongest communication skills to express your concerns and negotiate effectively. With practice, you will learn how to create a fruitful and calm discussion about your greatest money concerns. (Chapter 6 provides specific techniques you and your spouse can use to resolve your money conflicts effectively.) All couples fight. It is how they fight that determines their overall happiness and level of intimacy.

(If any couple tells you they do not have conflict, this means either the couple is in denial or one partner in the relationship has given up his or her sense of self—eclipsed by the other partner.) View conflict as an opportunity for growth in the relationship. It presents a situation where you can learn and grow from each other by adding a new dimension of understanding to the relationship.

These ground rules encourage the ideal environment for resolving your money conflicts. If you can't follow all of them all the time, that's okay. Start gradually, practicing with the money issues that aren't as charged for you. Work your way up to using these rules for all of your money discussions.

GUIDELINE EIGHT: DEFINE YOUR BOUNDARIES FOR PERSONAL SACRIFICE

So far, we have focused on the financial planning necessary to ease the pressures of entrepreneurship on your marriage and family. Now we move family planning to a deeper level than financial investment by exploring what you and your partner will sacrifice personally to be an entrepreneur and self-employed. Any experienced entrepreneur will tell you that business success comes with a personal and family price. Are you willing to pay that price? Is your spouse?

> We quit our jobs to buy our own business so that we could have control over our time. It hasn't worked out that way at all. Both of us have to be at the store six days a week, ten hours a day. Instead of giving us freedom, the business feels like a jail. It's gotten so difficult, we've put the business up for sale.
>
> *Husband and wife retail storeowners*

> Before I started my own law practice, I used to swim three times a week at the local club. Now I'm so busy, I feel guilty if I take the time out to swim. Since I stopped swimming, I am more irritable and I've gained twenty pounds. I know I should return to working out regularly, but it's hard to make the time.
>
> *Lawyer*

Many couples find out midstream that the personal or family cost of self-employment is greater than they predicted. The next exercise helps you examine the personal sacrifices you might be willing to make to create a business of your own. Take a few moments, alone or with your spouse, to consider the following questions. Keep a journal of your responses if you choose, and share your thoughts with your partner. If you are currently self-employed and feeling burned out, these questions may give you a clue to where your personal sacrifice has become too large.

DISCOVERY EXERCISE NINE: PERSONAL SACRIFICES TO BE SELF-EMPLOYED

Completion time: 30 minutes

Define the boundaries or fences you and your spouse will erect around private, relationship, and family time. Articulate your personal boundaries in writing. Commit to those activities essential to sustaining your marriage, your family, and your physical and emotional health. Here's one way to help you figure out what those boundaries should look like for you and your loved ones.

RELATIONSHIP WITH YOUR SPOUSE

1. What is the minimum amount of time you need to spend with your spouse to maintain an intimate and thriving marriage? Do you need "quality time" daily, weekly, or monthly? What constitutes "quality time" for you? Will your business allow for that? What happens to your relationship when you are unable to devote enough time for intimate connection? What are the warning signs that you need to spend more intimate time together? Do you know how your spouse would answer these same questions?

2. How much travel will your business require? Do you have any concerns about infidelity—yours or your partner's? How many days each month are you willing to be separated from your spouse? What happens if you go over that limit? How much does travel drain your energy and ability to be present for your partner? Will you consider limiting business growth in order to curtail travel?

3. Is your relationship strong enough to weather financial crisis, exhaustion, the demands of business ownership, or working together? Where is the evidence from your history together that you will be able to manage? Are you both on board and committed to the same goals and dream? Are you willing to

close the business down, or seek outside help, if business starts jeopardizing your relationship?

4. Does your business leave you with enough energy to be emotionally and sexually available to your partner? Does the pressure of your work distract you from being able to focus on your partner's needs? How are you able to balance personal and work commitments? What happens to you, and your relationship, when you get out of balance?

RELATIONSHIP WITH YOUR CHILDREN

5. What is the minimum amount of time you need daily or weekly to develop and maintain a rewarding relationship with your children? How will your business allow you to have that? Does this time change as the ages of your children change? What are the consequences of absence from your children? Are you willing to miss key developmental milestones and moments in order to achieve business success? To what extent?

6. Will you be able to be present and available for your children in the ways that are important to you? (For example: attending little league games, school performances, teachers conferences, car pooling.) Will your business require your absence in new ways that you and your children aren't used to? If so, how have you prepared yourself and your children? Do you have the support systems necessary to take care of your children's' needs without your physical presence? What are you willing to do if you think you feel one way about these questions, only to find out later you feel differently? What, if anything at that point, changes?

7. Do any of your children have special needs that require your attention? (For example: help with homework, learning disabilities, chronic medical conditions, preparation for Bar Mitzvah, athletic coaching, emotional difficulties, trouble with drugs or alcohol, physical disability.) Will your business allow you to be available for your children's needs? If not, do you have resources to help you?

YOUR HEALTH

8. What are the daily and weekly routines you need to maintain in order to stay healthy? (Consider food, exercise, sleep, hygiene, and personal growth. For example: eating home-cooked healthy meals, running twice a week, working out at the gym, playing tennis, sleeping six hours a night, attending AA meetings.) How much time alone do you need to recharge, unwind, and keep mentally fit? How will your business allow you to take care of yourself the way that you need?

SPIRITUAL LIFE

9. How will your business enable you to pursue the spiritual exploration that is vital to your centeredness and well-being? Will you be able to attend church or synagogue services, if that is important to you? Will your schedule allow for regular daily prayer and meditation? Will travel and eating out interfere with any religious commitments? Are you able to devote time to community service, if that is an important dimension of your spiritual life? How is your business consistent, or inconsistent, with your spiritual values?

FRIENDS AND FAMILY

10. Will you be able to keep up with your current individual and couple friendships? Contact with close family members? How much time, energy, and creativity will that require? How will your business allow or encourage developing new friends or business colleagues? How important is that to you? Does your commitment to entrepreneurship change any of your current friendships or make it more difficult to remain in your current social group or neighborhood? Will your business allow you to get together with family and friends at important holidays or occasions? How will business travel impact your relationships with your spouse, children, friends and community?

HOBBIES

11. Will any of your hobbies require more time and money than you may have once your business is under way? Are any of them essential to your mental and physical well-being? What

else might you do instead? How could your business support and involve your personal interests? Are you committed to spending time with other people involved in your hobby? Will any of these commitments have to change as a result of your business demands?

SELF-ESTEEM

12. How will you handle rejection and failure if you have to? How have you handled it in the past? How will you respond to naysayers who predict you won't succeed? How will you cope with being judged poorly by your spouse, parents, and in-laws, or business colleagues, if the business fails to thrive? How will you confront and overcome your personal weaknesses and fears? Are you willing to face your worst demons? How would a decrease in your social status, as a result of making a career change, make you feel? How will you handle your spouse's greater success or contributions to family support while you launch your business?

OTHER

13. What other personal sacrifices do you expect to make as a result of being self-employed? Will you have the time necessary to be a vital member of your community or children's school, if that is important to you? Will you be able to stay current in local, national and/or global politics if that is your passion? Will you be able to deal with the uncertainty entrepreneurship will bring to your life in total: i.e., financial, scheduling, etc.? Will you be flexible enough to adapt to change when called for to reconcile your work/life responsibilities?

Patty / Ann

GUIDELINE NINE:
PLAN FOR THE DETAILS OF
ENTREPRENEURIAL FAMILY LIFE

A married entrepreneur who works an average of one hundred hours a week offers this advice to new entrepreneurs: "Make sure you plan out the details of what each day is going to look like, not just the big stuff that goes into the business plan."

> When Jenny and I started our new business, neither of us had any time for keeping up the house. Before we knew it, we were too embarrassed to invite even our best friends over for dinner because the house was such a disaster. One day I wrote HELP in the dust on our living room coffee table.
>
> *Co-owner social service agency*

> When I told my wife Ellen I wanted her to join me in my business, she was enthusiastic. Ellen had always been home with our boys full-time, and she was ready for a change. Unfortunately, it took three months to find reliable day care that we both felt good about.
>
> *Retail store owner*

Business responsibilities place a strain on family life. Interviews with experienced entrepreneurial couples reveal that even those who prepare complex business plans often overlook the day-to-day details of caring for a family while running a business. You may have the big picture all figured out, but it's the small stuff that can sometimes cause your business or family to collapse. No detail is too small to prepare for.

Satisfying family life depends on establishing dependable routines. Discuss often with your spouse and children, in advance if possible, and throughout your entrepreneurial journey, how your daily family life will look, feel, and accommodate to the demands of your business and the ever-evolving needs of your family. These regular conversations bring forth your family's fears and fantasies, which help you better prepare and manage.

Your children will often wonder about the smallest of details, rather than the bigger concerns. (Can I still play with Jennifer after school? Who will give me my lunch money in the morning? Who will put me on the school bus? Can I still play on my basketball team?) Your spouse may be supportive of the idea of your being self-employed, but need reassurance that you'll still get the grass mowed. You may be gung ho about starting your own business, but need to resolve how your elderly mother will continue to get the biweekly visits you have been providing her. Don't underestimate the importance of asking and answering these kinds of questions. Caution is the word of the day. Do not assume these details will work themselves out, or try to wing them; rather, plan for an open and honest discussion about them from the beginning.

Simple "old school" tools for managing daily communication are a wall calendar and a dry erase board. On the family board go instructions for the kids, reminders to put the garbage out, grocery shopping lists, important phone numbers, phone messages, and sometimes, just a note of greeting. Everyone in the family checks the board when they enter the house.

When the kids were growing up, we used a dry erase board for everyone's weekly activities. With a large family (four kids, two adults and a dog, who hadn't as of yet been trained to write with a dry erase marker, but you never know what's possible in the future) this method allowed everyone to know where everyone else was, or should have been, during any given day and time. If changes were made to someone's schedule, it was the responsibility of the person whose schedule had changed to amend the board, if this was age-appropriate. The board was consistently updated every Sunday, with new activities added and old ones erased. This kept all the parts moving smoothly and immediately showed scheduling conflicts—giving everyone the opportunity to brainstorm a solution to the conflict on Sunday—before it occurred. Weekly reviews minimized the advent of crisis mode—which sometimes occurred anyway, but was prevented from becoming the modus operandi for the Tublin family, which would create undue stress and complications to any jam-packed week.

Depending on the complexity of your family life, you may wish to create a weekly schedule to be posted on the wall—or depending upon the ages of your children, utilize computer technology such as Google or Outlook for scheduling, reminding each of you of your daily responsibilities and commitments. You can get quite creative and involve your entire family in the creation of the family calendar. Check out an office supply store with a selection of tools for keeping employees informed and prepared. Many of these tools can be used for your family as well. You might also consider using the same calendar for your business and family commitments, as I do. This way I can immediately see where conflicts between my professional and personal schedule arise—allowing me the opportunity to make changes based upon my personal needs as a mother, wife and professional at any given moment. This eliminates the element of surprise—and guilt—with which many working mothers are all too often plagued.

DISCOVERY EXERCISE TEN: PLANNING THE DETAILS OF FAMILY LIFE

Completion time: 30 minutes

All aspects of family life must be considered when venturing into business ownership. The exercises below will assist you in anticipating the needs of your family and provide an opportunity to devise a plan that gets these needs met.

Listed below are activities of family life to consider. Jot down as many daily concerns for each category as you can think of, and a way to care for these details.

INTIMATE RELATIONSHIP

Example: We like to walk together every day to stay connected.

Plan: Walking together three times a week, in the early morning, is all that is likely, given our new schedule. We'll get up extra early on those days to fit it in. Plan an alternative activity if the weather prohibits these walks.

CHILDREN

Example: Molly needs to be transported to Girl Scouts two afternoons a week.

Plan: We'll take the evening shift in the car pool if someone can bring her in the afternoons.

EXTENDED FAMILY

Example: Someone needs to look after Mom during the day.

Plan: We'll arrange for a home health aide to visit her daily. Or, we will call an extended family meeting to get the input of other family members to resolve this issue.

PETS

Example: Someone needs to walk the dog in the late afternoon, before we get home from the shop.

Plan: We'll hire one of the neighborhood kids to walk her. Or, we will contact the local schools and/or religious communities to see if their members need to complete hours of community volunteering.

HOBBIES, PERSONAL GROWTH, AND EDUCATIONAL PURSUIT

Example: Russell plays golf every Sunday, and Cheryl plays tennis twice a week.

Plan: One of us will babysit our daughter, while the other is at the club.

SPIRITUAL EXPLORATION

Example: Maude has a Bible study class every Tuesday night.

Plan: We'll cover the store with Suzanne on Tuesday nights, so Maude can attend.

HOUSEHOLD

Example: Someone needs to make dinner every night.

Plan: Larry and I will alternate cooking meals for the family. We'll eat out every Saturday night. Or we will buy healthy prepared food at the local Costco or BJ's to make it financially feasible.

HOPE FOR THE BEST, BUT PLAN FOR THE WORST

Heading into a new venture, you can only estimate financial and personal risk. Most business owners will tell you, "If I had known how much risk I was taking, I might not have been willing to start." Visionary entrepreneurs may enter a state of semi-denial to summon the courage to move forward. It's a bit like having children. We focus on the positive rewards of raising children when we are planning to have a family, because if we focused on the (un)predictable hardships, we might never be willing to give it a try!

Financial advisers and seasoned business owners will tell you the dangers of wishful thinking, rather than careful planning. They will say something like, "Create a business plan, and then double the expenses you are planning for," or, "Keep six months of liquid assets available not pledged to the business." Take an honest look at your business plan. Is it a wishful fantasy or a solid realistic guide? Did you base your calculations on input from others in your industry?

Talk with your partner about how you will handle potential difficulties. Describe your worst-case scenario, and imagine how you will handle it if it should happen. What are the warning signs that will let you know you are headed in that direction? Don't base your financial planning on the assumption that you will be wildly successful or that your partner will be faithful to your dream no matter what the cost. Hoping for the best, but planning for the worst isn't negative thinking—it's smart business and goal-oriented family planning. Some small businesses won't survive in the long run, and every supportive spouse has limits. As you work on achieving your dream business it is important you keep both your feet on the ground and your finances planted firmly in reality.

Patty / Ann

CONCLUSION

In this chapter, you have learned about setting boundaries, assessing financial risk, defining your needs, communicating proactively with your spouse, and planning for hundreds of family details. If you have completed the exercises in this chapter, you now collected all the information you need to prepare a thorough, considerate and adaptable family plan. These guidelines won't prevent all hardship or distress, but they will support you and minimize family difficulties. The secret to marital harmony lies in being thoroughly prepared for the predictable stressors on financial and family life of entrepreneurship, bending like a palm tree rooted firmly in the ground.

Wondering how your relationship measures up when it comes to money issues? Take this money fight quiz by going to:

www.relationshiptoolbox.com/moneyfightsquiz.pdf

IV

HONEY, SINCE YOU'RE HOME, CAN YOU PICK UP MY DRY CLEANING FOR ME?

Working From Home, The Good, The Bad, And The Ugly

> When I took early retirement, I switched from VP of a $45 million budget, to becoming my husband's assistant in his business. We argued about how to set up my home office to allow me to join him. He wanted me to use his workspace which was really a man cave!
>
> *Partner in my husband's consulting business*

Perhaps you've heard the famous saying, "I married him for breakfast and dinner, but not for lunch." Years ago that expression referred to a housewife coping with her husband's sudden presence at home upon retirement. Now millions of self-employed individuals work from home full-time; others work remotely from home for corporations, large and small. Couples across America are adjusting to a shift from the tradition of the husband working outside the house, and the wife home full-time. Husbands now work from home and their wives leave for the office in the morning. Business partners manage their businesses together from a shared home office. Spouses with separate offices at home meet each other for lunch in the kitchen.

Dozens of home office experts have responded to the burgeoning home office market, offering practical guides on how to set up and manage a productive and organized home office. If you need advice on practical business matters, such as what kind of office equipment to purchase, how to maximize the tax advantages of working from home, or how to market your services, you'll find thousands of resources available to help you.

This chapter focuses exclusively on how working from home affects your marriage, family, you, and your business. No fixed rules exist. The home office environment that delights one couple could be troublesome to another. This chapter will help you answer these six questions:

1. How will a home office suit your marriage and family?
2. How will working at home affect your relationship?
3. What are the challenges and rewards of sharing a home office with your spouse?
4. What house rules will protect both your home and your business?
5. How do you work at home as a parent?
6. When should you move the business elsewhere?

ASSESSING HOW A HOME OFFICE WILL SUIT YOUR MARRIAGE AND FAMILY

If you're not sure how well-suited working in a home office would be for your relationship and your business, then complete this assessment. If both you and your spouse will work at home, then take the test separately and compare your results. If you are already working from home, taking this assessment will also give you additional insight into what aspects of working from home suit your personality—or do not.

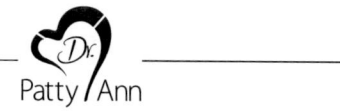

CLARIFICATION EXERCISE ONE: ASSESSING HOW A HOME OFFICE SUITS YOUR MARRIAGE AND FAMILY

Completion time: 15 minutes

Score each question from 1 to 5, 1 indicating "strongly agree" and 5 indicating "strongly disagree." Then total your points.

☐ My significant other is enthusiastic about my working from home.

☐ Our home has private office space where I can work uninterrupted.

☐ My children understand how they must behave in the house when I work at home. They are cooperative and responsive to house rules.
or
No children live with me at home.

☐ I don't have children or elderly parents I am caring for in my home.
or
If I do, someone else will care for them during my workday and I am confident I will not be checking on them constantly.

☐ If I plan to care for my children or elders while working at home, I have realistic expectations about how much work I will accomplish and how much business I can handle.

☐ My spouse and I have talked a great deal about how our routines and household rules will change when one or both of us start working from home.

☐ I can ignore nonessential household repairs and clean-up when I have work to do. My spouse has reasonable expectations about how much household work I will accomplish while working from home.

☐ I can easily set boundaries in my business so that I spend adequate time with my spouse and children. I don't tend toward workaholism.

☐ Working at home doesn't exacerbate any personal addictions (for example: overeating, sleeping, watching TV, drinking alcohol).

☐ I already have the essential equipment needed to operate a productive business at home, or we have enough capital to buy or lease the essential equipment.

☐ I am self-disciplined, well-organized, and a self-starter. The isolation of working from home doesn't scare me—I even look forward to it! Working from home suits my personality.

☐ I don't mind family interruptions and distractions when I work, as long as I can get uninterrupted time when I absolutely need it.

☐ My spouse and I handle transitions well. We are generally flexible and cooperative, and we work effectively as a team to overcome obstacles.

☐ We have no choice other than a home office at this time.

☐ Both my spouse and I have active support systems outside our marriage that we turn to if we need assistance.

☐ I'm not reluctant to pay for outside help if I need it, either in my home or in my business.

☐ The well-being of my marriage and family is my highest priority, above the success of my business. If working at home seriously troubles my family or my spouse, then I will consider other options, even if it increases my operating expenses.

SCORE

16-36: Green Light! You and your spouse appear to have a marriage conducive to making a home office work. You'll still experience some challenges, but if your business and lifestyle choice is to work at home, go for it!

37-58: Proceed with Caution. You have some challenges ahead, but with increased preparation, dialogue with your spouse, and a lot of hard work, you can pull it off. Make sure that you *and* your spouse read this chapter in its entirety before you commit to basing your business primarily at home. Be aware that a home-based business might present challenges for your family and discuss issues as soon as they arise with your partner and your children so resentments do not build.

59-80: Trouble Ahead. You either haven't thought through the implications of your home office on your marriage and family, or the early signs are that this could be a difficult and risky transition for you. You may want to consider other options. If that isn't feasible at this time, make sure that you and your spouse read this chapter in its entirety. Start talking about how you could make it work. Hire outside help right from the onset. Commit to regular meetings with your spouse to discuss how well the arrangement is working.

DISCOVERING HOW WORKING FROM HOME CAN CHANGE YOUR RELATIONSHIP

Working from home will affect your relationship with your spouse in unforeseen and significant ways. Many couples who have sought my help have stated they were totally unprepared for the unique challenges and stressors working from home would place on their marriage and family. Following are five common challenges entrepreneurial couples experience with home-based businesses, followed by ground rules for coping with these kinds of challenges.

How Working from Home Can Challenge Your Intimate Relationship (and What to Do About It)

When You and Your Spouse Change Roles

When a woman changes her identity from corporate employee, housewife and/or mother to a work-at-home entrepreneur, the change can be difficult for her husband. Though he may initially express his enthusiasm and support for her endeavors, his expectations and discomfort may eventually undermine her home office efforts in subtle or not-so-subtle ways. He may come to resent his wife's spending more time in the office and less time being a caretaker. One man, on the brink of divorce, expressed his indignation:

> My wife tried to make a profit with her little business for three years. I was working an average of one hundred hours a week to get us through financially. Since my wife was working in the house I expected her to pick up the house at least and make the meals. I'd come home exhausted and she had done nothing. She said she was too busy working on her business. I said, until she starts earning some money, the least she could do is keep the house clean.
>
> *Disgruntled spouse*

For this couple, the home office became an arena for fighting over marital roles. He was angry about being the sole breadwinner and felt unsupported by his wife. He was angry that she had ceased to take care of the house, and of him, the way that he expected of a wife. She resented her husband's expectations and felt unappreciated. His lack of support for her business hurt her feelings, and she wondered if she might not be better off living alone.

Another equally difficult transition can be when a husband who normally worked away from the home suddenly comes home to work. He may have lost his job and decided not to return to corporate life, or quit his job to pursue his entrepreneurial dreams. Even if his wife supports the idea of his self-sufficiency, his working at home is unfamiliar to her. If she is also at home most of the time, she worries that her husband will interfere with the rhythm and routine of her day, or demand more of her. She fears unsolicited advice about how she should care for the kids, keep the house, or run her own business. If she works outside the home, she is unaccustomed to coming home to her spouse's presence – and like the husband discussed earlier, may have unrealistic expectations of what he should have accomplished for their home during the day.

Marilyn worked part-time as an adjunct college professor and her husband Jack was a computer engineer. When Jack was laid off from his Wall Street firm he decided to become self-employed and work from home. Marilyn was accustomed to having her home and the care of their two school-aged children to herself—with little, if any involvement from her husband. Having worked on Wall Street since before the kids were born, Jack regularly worked 14-hour days. Now Jack was home all the time—or at least that is how it felt to Marilyn. Tension between this couple escalated because Jack could not understand why his wife would become angry when he offered his well-meaning unsolicited advice on how to make the kids breakfast, how to help with homework, what to cook for dinner, etc. Marilyn was at her wit's end when she contacted me for relationship expertise. She loved her husband but his butting in about every little detail of how she ran the home and took care of the kids was driving her crazy!

> Before my girlfriend moved in, I had been working at home in silence. Suddenly I had to learn how to live with another human being who wanted to listen to the radio, watch TV, talk on the phone, or just talk to me. We lived in a small apartment and I couldn't get away from the distractions.
> *Creative consultant*

The best way to resolve these work-from-home issues is to effectively communicate and strategically plan how working from home will play out in advance. It is imperative that clear boundaries are established so spouses' and children understand that the person working from home is not available for house maintenance and other responsibilities just because they are, in fact, at home. The best way for couples to think about this is to create similar expectations for the spouse working from home as if she (or he) were working outside the home. Use common sense here. If the plumber needs to come, of course it is reasonable for the person who is at home to let them in. It is not reasonable, however, to expect the person at home to clean the house, do the wash, cook dinner, etc., unless those agreements are negotiated in advance, taking the needs of the business into account.

Coping with a Judgmental Spouse

The tendency to judge how the home office entrepreneur works is a difficult passage for some couples. When your husband works from the house, he may spend some of his day planting a beautiful garden; you might want him to focus more on planting money in the bank account. Your husband quit his job so that he would no longer have to report to a boss. Then, you became his new boss. When you come home from work and say, "How was your day, Honey?," he hears, "Did you spend your day the way I think you should have?" He will become quite defensive. Your husband wants you to trust him and leave him alone. Working at home puts his behavior under a microscope for you to see, and it may be impossible for you to withhold judgment. (The same is true of course if you are the work from home entrepreneur with the worried and judgmental spouse).

If you have the tendency to be a controlling spouse, you may intrude on your spouses' home-based business in an unwelcome way. Couples will also struggle with this aspect of home office life when trust is tenuous, criticism is prominent, and money is tight.

If the spouse of an entrepreneur has trust issues, it is critical to discuss these concerns at the first hint of trouble so they do not spill over and affect the business. For those married to a controlling or jealous spouse, working from home may invite concerns about infidelity of an emotional or sexual nature—especially if a lot of work is conducted on the internet. Unfortunately, technology has been an instrument of relationship destruction, due to sexting, porn addiction, sites created to foster extra-marital affairs, and spouses reconnecting with old lovers and new "friends" on social media sites.

Although it is tempting, it would be a fatal mistake for a spouse to micro-manage his or her work-at-home spouse's every moment of every day. Some people think they are the most creative when engaging in physical activity like gardening or walking. I spend much of my daily exercise thinking about my work. Although I appear to be exercising, more often than not I am also thinking about work while working out. Be careful about judging or rushing to conclusions on how productive your spouse is being when working from home. Work does not always look like work in the traditional sense of the word.

Setting Boundaries Around Personal Space

A home office infringes on the privacy of both partners. When a spouse starts a business in the house, personal space is lost. It's hard to achieve the perfect balance for both partners.

> I see clients from noon until 10:00 P.M., four days a week. Before my life partner, Marie, moved into my small house I used my mornings to meditate, walk, eat, and center myself, to prepare myself for the demands of the day. Now Marie is always around. I can't even get dressed in private. I didn't realize how much I needed privacy to run my business until Marie moved in.
>
> *Psychologist*

> My girlfriend is a different woman in the office than she is in the kitchen. If I kiss her in the kitchen, she loves it, but if I try to kiss her in the office, she takes my head off. When she steps into her office she becomes a whole different person. She's no longer my lover. She's made it very clear: she's off limits when she's at work—even if she's working at home.
>
> *Boyfriend and business partner*

Gender differences are not necessarily the driver of these conflicts. Consider a gay couple, Adrienne and Sheila, who had great difficulties with setting boundaries around personal space. Adrienne complained about Sheila being a control freak; she was always coming into her office to rearrange files and paperwork, ostensibly to get Adrienne "organized". Sheila even had a "correct" way to unroll the toilet paper! Adrienne experienced Sheila as controlling and overbearing in both her personal and professional life. Sheila was one of those people who believed "its my way or the highway." Sheila's controlling behavior was the result of being parented by a mother who constantly criticized and micro-managed all aspects of Sheila's life. In fact, Sheila's mom was so controlling that once Sheila and her siblings left home, her father left her mother. Sheila's father said he could no longer bear to be the sole target of her mother's controlling ways. Because Sheila carried this baggage from her childhood into her work life, she confused control with caring and Adrienne grew to resent Sheila's intrusion on her office space.

To overcome this problem, Adrienne can write down all her issues with Sheila's controlling ways and verbally communicate them to her during a pre-arranged meeting. Since Sheila truly believed she was acting as a concerned partner rather than controlling, Adrienne should present her issues to Sheila in a respectful, non-accusatory manner. For example, Adrienne might say to Sheila, "Sheila, I know you are trying to help, but I put my papers on my desk in a way that works for me. I understand my desk is not as organized as you would keep your own, but it's my desk and it is organized enough for me. I appreciate your efforts to help but I do not need you to organize my desk. I realize you are trying to be helpful, but I am starting to find your behavior intrusive and constraining. Please stop touching the stuff on my desk and in my office."

Oil Spill Phenomenon

A home office can take over an entire household, leaving no room sacred. The computer and fax are in the bedroom, materials are spread over the dining room table, clients walk through the kitchen and peek at dinner, and the business cell phone rings or vibrates morning, noon and night. Employees share your living space, know your family affairs, and use your bathroom.

Oil spills are notoriously difficult to contain, once they have spread. They kill what's around them, as the oil oozes into a wider and deeper area. With no physical boundaries around the business in your home, your home-based business becomes toxic to intimacy and destroys a comfortable living environment for your family.

To clean up the oil spill, consider keeping business paraphernalia out of the bedroom, or at least out of the bed. If you can, avoid using your bedroom as an office at all. A bedroom should be a safe haven from the stressors of work and life—and a place to reconnect with your spouse in an intimate way.

Remember, your home includes the space that contains your office; do not allow your office to become a place where you happen to live. Unplug yourself from technology at the end of your workday. Do not feel obligated to immediately answer every email, text, social media post, etc., that you receive, especially late in the evening if this is when you prefer to spend time with your husband and family. If clients come to your home, be strict about designated business hours. Talk with your family about ways to contain your work physically (to one or two rooms), within time limits (i.e., no calls taken after 6:00 p.m.), and emotionally (to allow for daily activities with family and your spouse that have nothing to do with your business). If business associates, employees, or clients visit your home regularly, devote one bathroom in the house to them. Set the boundaries that both you and your spouse need, agree upon and then enforce them. If your home stops being a private and pleasant place to live and work, then you jeopardize your business success and your marriage.

It does not help your business to have every area of your home littered with work material. This prevents your brain from resting. Your brain needs to be cleared and decluttered on a regular basis as much as your office space needs to be organized. Without this rest, your brain cannot perform at its optimal level. Many professional breakthroughs occur when you are thinking about something other than work. In that light, establish a specific space for your office within your home. This will help set physical boundaries between your role as worker, spouse and parent. For example, I once had a client make a big red STOP sign and put it on her home office door when she wanted to make clear she was not to be interrupted. It had been previously communicated to her family the importance of this STOP sign. A very clear sign, in a very distinct space, with a very clear message helped this mom work from home without a steady stream of interruptions, and unrealistic expectations from her husband and kids. Similarly, both her kids and husband knew that when she was not in her office, she was fully available to focus on them and would not allow her work to intrude, or take precedence over their family life.

Tendency to Overwork

It is easy to fall prey to overworking when you work from home. We have all heard ourselves say: "Let me check just one more email." The next thing you know, you have proceeded to work for two more hours. If your business is always in your face, you will need self-discipline to contain work to a reasonable number of hours. Consider your family by reducing the number of hours you work, permitting interruptions only at certain times of the day, sharing child-care duties, or even just showing up for dinner. Engage your spouse to help you set limits.

> The business obsessed me and became my life. Even though I was working at home, I never spent any time with my boyfriend or kids. When my boyfriend threatened to walk out on me, I was angry with him for not being supportive. Now I realize I needed my boyfriend to set limits for me because I couldn't do it myself. To my surprise, our relationship and my business both improved after I cut back on my work schedule.
>
> *Personal trainer*

All work and no play makes a business owner unproductive and boring as hell. Research consistently shows after a certain number of hours at work, people cease being productive. With technology and the capability of 24/7 communication in our global world, entrepreneurs are easily seduced into believing they *must* send out one more email at the end of their designated work day—which turns into 10 more emails and significantly cuts into the time they could be spending with their husbands and children.

People find true happiness not in the balance sheet but in the balance of life. Many women become entrepreneurs because they want a more balanced life—one that includes a healthy marriage, time to effectively parent, to be an active member of the community, and more. They rejected the corporate model of working crazy hours that left little, if any time for the creation of a fulfilling life. It would be unfortunate if they lose the very balance they sought when choosing to become self-employed because of the availability of modern technology. Use technology to grow your business and enhance your life; not consume or control it.

> When we began our business a few years ago, we made ourselves available around the clock to our clients. I burned out after a year of always keeping the house clean, and answering phone calls until midnight. When I came down with pneumonia, we started setting limits with our clients. I don't think we lost any business because of it, and I got my health back.
>
> *Female partner in a business referral service*

You don't want to create for yourself a health scare in order to slow yourself down. Too many entrepreneurs wait until they hit a wall and come close to a nervous breakdown—or a divorce—before setting limits on themselves. You can put safeguards in place to improve your odds of success. The first step is acknowledging your vulnerability and addressing potential issues before it erupts into life-altering trouble.

You have now learned about five common challenges home-based entrepreneurial couples confront:

- When you and your spouse change roles.

- Coping with a judgmental spouse.

- Setting boundaries around personal space.

- The oil spill phenomenon.

- Tendency to overwork.

Some or all of these challenges may apply to you. Undoubtedly, you may have experienced challenges not presented in this section. Refer to the following ground rules for meeting whatever challenges come your way.

Ground Rules for Coping with Home Office-Related Tension in Your Relationship

Besides the advice I recommend that is specific to each unique home office source of tension, here are some general guidelines for protecting your relationship from potential harm when you run a business from home:

Keep Emotionally Current with Your Spouse

When you withhold feelings of any kind because you fear hurting or angering your spouse, remember that:

- Your spouse can usually sense your anxiety, even if you don't express it clearly or directly, and

- You may emotionally erupt for a completely unrelated reason, doing far more damage—a concept referred to as displaced anger. This refers to expressing unwarranted anger towards a situation or person who is not responsible for your angry feelings.

Rather than withholding your feelings, be straightforward and discuss problems openly and in a timely fashion (which does not always mean as they immediately unfold). If you can't work out your complaints effectively and come to a constructive compromise, do not despair. I have counseled hundreds of couples who arrive at my doorstep a hair's breath away from divorce. Many times it seems as if they will never figure out how to speak to each other in a loving, calm way; but believe me, even the couples who express great difficulty with this process do eventually learn how to communicate effectively. If this is a hot spot for you, be sure to also read Chapter 6 in this book about conflict resolution or seek professional counsel. You might also consider going to this link: www.relationshiptoolbox.com/lmf to obtain my product: "Love, Money. Freedom" which provides proven strategies for women business owners who are struggling to solve the unique challenges of working from home.

Look for Simple, Immediate, and Beneficial Changes

One small adjustment to the way you manage working at home—a "do-not-disturb" sign on the door, an extra computer, a self-imposed schedule for when you will read and respond to electronic messages, a designated time when you shut off all forms of electronic communication— can make the difference between an unworkable and a satisfactory arrangement. Send out an email or other electronic message letting clients know you are going "offline" every day at a certain time. This way you begin to train the people you interact with not to expect instant responses from you during these designated time frames. People sometimes resist this advice because they are afraid they will lose business or clients if they are not available 24/7. Yet, when business owners have taken this step, more often than not their business actually *increases* because they have more peace of mind and their clients have greater respect for the business owner's time. I make it very clear I am not immediately available at every client's beckoning call, text, email, or instant message. Clients and colleagues will respect your boundaries only if you respect them yourself, so once you implement this policy, do not make exceptions (unless of course your work involves life-threatening emergencies).

Get Outside Support or Read Books, Newsletters, Blogs and Magazines for Home Office Workers and Entrepreneurs

Reach out to build your networks, join a home office association, a networking group or any of the working women professional organizations. Attend conventions and seminars or join a mastermind group with people who share your unique challenges as a business owner working from home. Provide yourself with as many varied venues as possible to vent your feelings of frustration and concern to others who will be able to relate and empathize with your feelings. This will help you avoid criticizing your spouse in a manner that is unproductive—leaving him feeling disenfranchised with your work situation. You are not alone. You don't need to suffer with this problem alone. Refer to the resources available that are listed in the back of this book, or go to this link: www.relationshiptoolbox.com/products for a list of invaluable products.

Take Responsibility for Your Part of the Problem

Creating tension takes two people; there is no such thing as a one-handed clap. I have worked with couples who "waste" countless hours explaining what their spouse is doing that has caused problems in their relationship, what their spouse should be doing differently and how all the problems are their spouse's fault. Rather than pointing the finger at each other, I counsel them to take a long hard look in the mirror and ask themselves, "What am *I* doing that contributes to the problems in my marriage? What can *I* do differently to improve my relationship and my attitude? Am I effectively communicating and listening to what my partner is telling me? How can I be more cooperative, flexible, forgiving, or patient?"

You can provide creative solutions to relationship difficulties by shifting maladaptive patterns of response, even if you're not close to divorce. Address issues in your relationship as soon as they appear. I also recommend going to www.relationshiptoolbox.com/toolbox to view my revolutionary product called *Relationship Toolbox™: How to ReKindle Romance and Happiness in Your Relationship*. This comprehensive product is designed to stop the fighting and increase romance and happiness in your relationship.

Review Your Priorities

Did you start your own business so that you would have a better quality of life, more time with your family, or a better relationship with your kids? If your life is out of balance, then remind yourself of why you are working so hard in the first place. The family plan I guided you to put together in the beginning of this book will help you structure that conversation. If you are feeling out of sync at any time, it would then be a perfect time to revisit this family plan.

How Working From Home
Can Enhance Your Marriage

Although we have been focusing on the challenges, the home office lifestyle can also positively affect your relationship. What are the potential rewards for your marriage of working from home? This section brings you the stories of several thriving home-based couples to demonstrate.

Greater Involvement in Each Other's Lives

Earlier in their marriage, Elaine and Gary worked together in separate businesses, in the same shared office for months. They conversed throughout the day about business developments and turned to each other for practical assistance, emotional support, and companionship.

Recently Gary took a job outside of the house, so he now tells Elaine about his day in summary fashion. Elaine doesn't know his work or his colleagues, and a certain kind of distance has developed between them when it comes to discussing work. Connecting deeply to your partner's professional life is easier if you are able to witness or experience it with them. Mitch and I are both entrepreneurs with offices within and outside the home. However, we share neither space at the same time. Although our professional lives seem enmeshed at times, we can go for days and never discuss work issues. Our lives are so full of family and friends we seek balance in our life and enjoy each other's company as partners, parents and friends. When business matters need to be discussed, we schedule business meetings to discuss work topics and business planning issues.

More Flexibility for Household Maintenance Leads to Greater Intimacy

Fatigue is the greatest killer of a satisfying romantic and sexual relationship. If you work outside the house ten or more hours a day, then you are usually exhausted by the time you return home from your job and take care of the demands of the household. A home office may afford you the flexibility to do household chores and errands throughout the day, releasing more time and energy for intimacy.

> Before I started working from home, I devoted all my free time outside work to child care and cleaning the house. I was too burned out to be interested in any kind of intimacy with my husband. Now that I'm working inside my home, I take time out during the day to take care of some of the household demands. I'm much more relaxed and easier to live with now. Working from home has improved our marriage considerably. My husband even comes home every once in awhile for a "lunch date!"
>
> *A business owner with a renewed interest in sex & intimacy*

A home business can encourage a more relaxed breakfast time together or a therapeutic neck and shoulder massage in the middle of the day. If you are both self-employed, you can be more spontaneous, leading to creative romantic encounters. Family life often works better when at least one partner has professional flexibility. When family life is running smoother, romance and sex are more likely. Happily married people tend to be more successful and make more money than people who are in unhappy marriages or relationships. Think about this from a simplistic perspective—there is strength and power in numbers. The whole is greater than the sum of its parts.

Additionally, when you feel supported by your partner you are obviously not dealing with the distractions of an unsupportive spouse (more on this later). If you are both home-based, there are additional benefits. Mitch and I enjoy the flexibility of a dual entrepreneurial marriage. We take comfort in knowing we can immediately access each other if we are really excited or upset about something—whether it is a personal or professional issue—and not have to wait until the evening to do so. We relish the ability to take vacations without needing "permission" from a boss. And of course, we love the ability to engage in spontaneous romantic interludes at any time when we are in the mood!

Dual Home-Based Entrepreneurs Keep Each Other Honest

> My wife, Harriet, and I both work out of the home in separate offices. If I was totally on my own, I would probably sleep late and watch TV. Harriet keeps me honest. When I see her working all day, I feel too embarrassed to let her see me goofing off.
> *CPA*

We See Each Other More Often

The average working couple spends less than an hour a day together, and even that isn't always private. I believe the concept of "quality time" for marriages (and parenting) is a myth. You can't have "quality time" without sufficient "quantity time" and one hour a day alone for a couple really slims down the chances of creating "quality time" in any sense of the word—including time for intimacy. You can enhance intimacy merely by increasing the time you see each other; one spouse working from home increases your chances for creating intimacy exponentially.

> My husband's corporate career took him away from home so often we hardly knew each other after fifteen years of marriage. We decided to change our life radically. We both quit our jobs, we sold our home and we bought a small working farm in another state.
> *Farmer*

I counsel my clients about the importance of scheduling time together to protect the intimacy in their marriage and keep the flame alive. Many couples have sought my help with the stated problem that they just seem to have drifted apart, not really knowing why or how that happened. Unfortunately, many couples put the intimacy and romance of their marriage on the back burner, thinking they will rekindle it once the kids are grown, or their careers are on track, etc. By doing this, they later find there is not sufficient intimacy left to be able to rekindle and in some circumstances, no relationship to get back to at all.

Working from home provides you with the envious opportunity for flexibility of scheduling both date times and sex with your partner. Some couples resist the suggestion of scheduling sex because they say if they have to schedule it, it wont be sexy. If you don't schedule sex, chances are you aren't going to have any! How sexy can that be?

Let's be really honest here. Running a business, being a spouse and raising a family can consume all our time, leaving us physically and emotionally exhausted. Just like anything else that is important to us, we must prioritize intimacy and romance by literally putting it on our calendars. Once the time is scheduled, honor the commitment you made to spend that time in a loving way with your partner. There are couples who will schedule time to spend together, and put this time on there calendars. However, this schedule time is not prioritized and becomes "bumped" off their calendar if a client call or important business meeting appears. This is a grave mistake. Not only have they failed to honor their commitment to their partner, but their partner will feel rejected as well. Scheduled time with a spouse should be treated with even higher priority than an important client meeting!

SHARING A HOME OFFICE WITH YOUR SPOUSE

The next section of this chapter relates to the unique challenges and rewards of sharing a home office with your spouse.

The Challenges of Sharing a Home Office with Your Spouse

The key elements to sharing an office successfully with your spouse are (1) the nature of the relationship and the business, and (2) whether the office space allows each partner to carve out distinct space within it. People are creatures of habit. They work best when they can organize and use their physical space however they please, to be productive. Here's a self-assessment you and your spouse can take to identify whether or not sharing an office is a feasible solution for your partnership. Sharing an office is not as easy as it looks! Conscious decisions need to be made that will support you in sharing space. Even mundane matters, such as whether either spouse is left-handed are important to consider because they might influence where you place office equipment. Annoying little habits like loud gum chewing, frequent throat clearing, or sneezing can also become major obstacles to sharing the same office with your spouse.

Sharing an office when you are both home can be as distracting as working in a large corporate office space divided into cubicles. Your partner speaking on the phone next to you breaks your concentration. It's difficult to have a private conversation without feeling eavesdropped upon. Productivity decreases because of frequent interruptions. Couples who make this arrangement work often schedule private time in the office to respect each other's needs for uninterrupted work time. They make sure that they have space enough and access to their own office equipment when needed.

Patty / Ann

CLARIFICATION EXERCISE TWO: CAN YOU SHARE AN OFFICE SUCCESSFULLY?

Completion time: 15 minutes

If you are considering sharing a home office with your spouse or are sharing one now, then this quiz is for you. Complete separately and compare your responses.

Score each question from 1 to 5, 1 indicating strongly agree and 5 indicating strongly disagree. Then total your points.

☐ My spouse and I have the same need for tidiness, organization, space, and clutter in our work area.

☐ I can easily share a computer or desk space with my spouse, or we have separate workstations for each of us.

☐ My spouse and I enjoy being together a great deal. We can work together in close quarters without friction.

☐ I don't need private uninterrupted space to do productive work.

☐ I work better when I am working nearby my spouse than when I am working alone.

☐ My spouse and I are able to negotiate and problem-solve well. We easily resolve conflicts that arise.

☐ I really appreciate having my spouse available for advice, encouragement, and constructive comments throughout the day.

☐ My spouse and I can share office equipment efficiently and still meet our individual business needs.

☐ The only space available is shared office space, so we will make it work one way or the other
or
We have other space available, but it's our strong preference to share a home office if possible.

☐ Even within our shared space, I am able to carve out my own separate work area.

☐ My partner may have work habits that annoy me but even if I feel judgmental, I've learned how not to express it, unless it gets in the way of my work. When I do need to express it, I have learned how to do so in ways that don't offend my partner.

☐ Both my spouse and I have a sense of humor. We laugh and have a good time together throughout the day.

☐ My spouse and I find private personal and working time away from each other and our shared home office when needed.

☐ My spouse and I have learned to keep our business and personal conflicts separate. We don't fight dirty, carry fights over from work to home, or vice versa. When we do fight, we don't stay angry with each other for very long.

☐ My spouse and I both work best at different times of the day, so we are able to coordinate private time in our shared office.

☐ Sharing a home office is our first choice right now. If doing so begins to jeopardize our relationship, we will look for other alternatives.

SCORE

16-36: Looks Promising! You have the potential to share a home office with your spouse quite successfully. You may produce better work and enjoy a more satisfying relationship as a result of sharing space. There will be some issues to negotiate, but you'll likely work them out over time.

37-58: You Have Your Work Cut Out for You. With positive intention, hard work, and regular open dialogue, you and your spouse may meet the challenges ahead. But don't underestimate the potential difficulties. Prepare to compromise—you can't always have your own way.

59-80: Danger! Sharing an office could spell trouble for your marriage and your business. If you have no other options, prepare for a significant growth opportunity! Your relationship could become stronger, as sharing a home office forces you to learn how to accept each other's differences, to give and take, and to resolve conflict. This will only work, however, if both partners are committed to making it work.

> My husband and I own eight computers. We each have our own computers at the store, our own computers in our shared home office, individual laptop computers, and even separate computers in our weekend house. We like to be able to work wherever we are and neither of us can stand sharing a computer. Eight computers may seem excessive, but $25,000 is a minimal investment when you're running a $10 million a year company.
>
> *Retail executive*

Sharing Space and Equipment

The most challenging arrangement is sharing equipment, a computer, workstation, printer and filing cabinet, etc., with your spouse. One female entrepreneur we interviewed commented, "My husband Sammy and I always got along beautifully—until we started sharing a computer and a desk. I decided that buying a new computer for a few hundred dollars would be cheaper than getting a divorce!"

Separating Personal and Work Conflict

For most couples, the greatest challenge of sharing a home office is learning how to separate personal and work conflicts. If you fight in the morning about one of the kids and then walk downstairs to begin your business day together, you may struggle to leave the conflict behind. Likewise, an unresolved business conflict can easily spill over to the dinner table. Blurring of boundaries invariably results. Entrepreneurial couples who hope to work together at home for any time must learn how to move through conflict quickly and to separate their work and personal conflicts. Many couples struggle with this process before they find a system that works for them.

One couple I interviewed fought passionately in their marriage before he lost his job and joined his wife's business as her partner. When they began working together in her basement office, the fights increased and carried into the evening hours. In desperation, the wife devised this strategy to manage the fighting:

> I knew we'd never stop fighting completely, but I came up
> with a new rule: Business fights had to take place in the
> basement office, and personal fights had to take place
> upstairs. One day we got into an ugly personal fight in the
> office. I excused myself, went upstairs, called my husband
> from the upstairs phone, and yelled all the insults and
> obscenities that I wanted to say to him in the office. Another
> day, when we started fighting about work at the dinner table,
> I grabbed my husband and dragged him down to the
> basement so that we could finish the fight down there.
>
> *Grace, small business owner*

All couples fight—even loving, healthy couples fight! The difference is that happy couples fight fair. What does fighting fair in a marriage mean?

Fighting fair means you stay on the topic at hand. Many couples begin fighting about one issue, then eventually bring all other kinds of disagreements, some of which may have occurred years ago, into the argument.

Fighting fair means dealing only with the issue at hand and not expanding the focus of the argument in an effort to "win" the argument.

Fighting fair means maintaining respect and courtesy toward your partner throughout. This means no yelling, cursing or name calling. As soon as one spouse raises his or her voice, the other spouse usually stops listening.

Fighting fair also involves practicing the art of active listening. Active listening is the ability to listen without a hidden agenda, to listen with an open heart, an open mind and an open soul. These listening skills allow couples to better understand the basis for their differences. Understanding your differences is at the heart of all conflict resolution. It is the key ingredient necessary for compromise and negotiation.

Happy couples know how to respectfully agree to disagree. All couples have at least one or two issues they will never resolve or agree upon. Happy couples learn to ignore these differences, or refuse to let them irritate them. These couples realize it is more important to be together, in peace and harmony, than to always be in agreement—and that some differences are just not worth fighting about. This requires an element of maturity for each partner.

Ground Rules for Resolving Conflict in a Shared Home Office

Following are tried and true solutions that work, shared with me by entrepreneurial couples who have, as they say, "been there, done that." No matter what the individual circumstances of your partnership, chances are, these ground rules will serve you well.

Create a Symbolic Separation Between Business and Personal Conflict

Designate places in your home, like your bedroom, as sacred from business conversation. Identify where business discussion is most appropriate. Refrain from continuing a business argument over the dinner table or a personal fight in your office. The more often you reinforce these boundaries with each other, the easier it will become.

Schedule Business Meetings Regularly to Resolve Business Issues

If you can't tackle something in one session, then plan another session, rather than continuing to debate or argue throughout the evening. You may need daily, weekly, or biweekly meetings to stay current on business issues. Follow this same process for relationship issues. It is a huge misconception that all marriage conflicts should be resolved before you go to bed—or that you should never go to bed angry. I advise couples to take a "time out" when an argument appears to be escalating to the point of no return. Once hurtful things are said they cannot be taken back. Current neuroscience research shows the old adage "Sticks and stones may break my bones but names will never harm me" is false. Words can inflict as much pain as real physical blows based upon the current findings of functional MRIs. As conflict escalates, the best way to avoid hurtful words that cannot be taken back is to take at least a 24-hour break from discussing the conflict. After that time, revisit the discussion when cooler heads prevail. Anytime I've failed to take my own advice on this topic, I have deeply regretted it.

In today's modern age of technology, calling a hiatus on an argument is more difficult to do since couples can (and do), fight using email, texting, instant messaging, and more. Electronic battles can prove extremely damaging to your relationship because they create a permanent paper trail of hurtful words that can create irreparable damage. When you allow your arguments to take place, or continue ad infinitum through electronic communication, it is very easy for your message to be misinterpreted, because non-verbal forms of communication, especially body language, is eliminated from the discussion. What you write as a simple question designed to gather information ("Why haven't you called our client yet?"), may sound accusatory to your spouse—creating conflict where you intended none.

Don't Take Advantage of Your Partner's Hot Buttons and Vulnerabilities

Belittling your spouse in anger will never lead to a positive outcome. For example, to bolster her argument for spending more money on a laser printer for the office, Kim accused her partner of being a tightwad and unreasonably cheap because of his upbringing. Kim sidetracked from a straightforward business analysis of purchasing a specific laser printer to a personal attack on her husband's spending habits. She hurt her relationship and failed to convince her husband to buy because he was defending himself.

If you use secret emotional weapons to win an argument, you create a toxic environment where your spouse feels angry, exposed, and defensive. Speak to your spouse with the same respect given an outside business partner, to the best of your ability. Better yet, speak with your partner using the same negotiation skills you would use with a potential client to close the deal.

Take Time away from Each Other When Necessary

If tension is building, or you are recovering from a personal fight the night before, then structure the day so that you can regroup. Get out of the house. Lunch with a friend or exercise at your health spa. Reschedule meetings where you might need to discuss difficult business planning issues. Create a "no-business" date if business arguments intrude upon personal time.

Keep Your Sense of Humor and Lighten Up When You Can

Marvel at your ability to work together most of the time. The majority of couples would never attempt it! Go insane by working for a day with clown noses on. Play hooky together and shut off all technology while you crawl into bed to watch a video in the middle of the work day. Take the kids on an outing. Working together at home in your own business gives you an enormous amount of flexibility. Use it occasionally to lighten the mood. Above all, keep your sense of humor and maintain your ability to laugh at yourself.

There Are Cycles and Seasons to Everything

Every relationship has it peaks and valleys, some of which may last for days, weeks or even months. Accept that your relationship sometimes bores, angers, frustrates, or annoys you. Some days you will be just plain grumpy. That's life, at home or in a corporation. Working together in a home office is more uncomfortable when you aren't getting along well, but you'll tend to work through fights faster if your marriage is strong and you keep the perspective "This too, shall pass."

Change the Setup If Sharing a Home Office Isn't Working

If you've really tried, sought outside help in person or by researching information, and your relationship and/or your business still deteriorates, then look for other alternatives. Many couples discover their need for more private space or time away from each other to keep their relationship healthy and enjoyable. Our needs change throughout our lives and our marriages will reflect these changes. What we are comfortable with in our 20's might not provide comfort for us in our 30's—or after the kids are born. We are constantly evolving and growing as individuals and as a couple. In the final analysis remember this: "To thine own self be true." Find creative ways to be together and to be separate at the same time. This is not an oxymoron but rather, a prescription for strengthening your marriage.

The Rewards of Sharing a Home Office
with Your Spouse

Sharing a business and a home-office certainly has its advantages and is a pleasing arrangement for many couples. Don't be surprised though if it's more challenging than you expected. Although it looks easy to do when a couple is doing it well, it's actually quite difficult to pull off.

On a practical level, sharing office space conserves resources. Couples share copy and fax machines, laser printers, expensive business investments on a lean start-up budget. For some couples, sharing an office significantly adds to the quality of their life together as well. Couples who enjoy sharing a home office cherish each other's company, the ongoing exchange, advice, brainstorming, and companionship. They have a low need for privacy or quiet to work productively and can't even relate to couples separated for days at a time. A female entrepreneur who loves sharing an office with her husband might say, "Because I work with my husband at home all day long, I feel really connected to him, and our business and marriage are thriving."

This entrepreneur started out working on her own at home, but then her husband joined her, and she's much happier now:

> Working at home was lonely at times. Except for the occasional conversation with a client, I could talk to no one for hours at a time. I gained twenty pounds working at home because I kept going to the refrigerator when I was restless. When my husband decided to work out of the same office, my productivity and creativity increased. Now when I'm bored or lonely I ask my husband for a hug instead of hitting the refrigerator.
> *Home-based web designer*

I often have to reassure couples who seek my help that just because they don't work well together in a home-based business doesn't mean that they shouldn't be married! Some individuals would feel totally suffocated sharing an office with their spouse; this is not a referendum on how they feel about each other emotionally—it is merely a personal workspace preference. The most important thing is for each individual in the relationship to know what their preference is for sharing or not sharing office space with their spouse, and then respecting that preference. Do not try to make an arrangement work that you know, in your heart, will not work for you or your spouse. If your spouse is insulted because you need a separate work environment, let him know this is your professional work preference and does not in any way reflect upon your personal feelings for him. Once you make this distinction clear, there is a good chance your partner will no longer feel insulted or rejected by your choice for independent work space.

Patty / Ann

DEVELOPING HOUSE RULES TO PROTECT YOUR HOME AND YOUR BUSINESS

House Rules

So you've decided together that one or both of you will work from home. How will you organize household routines and responsibilities to work synergistically with your home office? What do we mean by house rules? Who is going to do what when, and who is not going to do what, when? For example, the kids will never pick up your business cell phone, the entrepreneur at home will make dinner four nights a week, etc. Your family operates by implicit social rules all the time, based on your expectations of one another. Do you openly communicate the rules and renegotiate when they no longer apply? This successful entrepreneur who is now running a million-dollar business learned the hard way that the absence of explicit rules can backfire on the work-at-home entrepreneur and small business owner:

> When my kids entered high school I decided to start my own business. My business took off and I was working almost every night and weekend. Since I was working out of the house during the day, my family still expected me to cook every meal, clean the house, chauffeur the kids after school, and do everyone's laundry. I killed myself for six months, playing superwoman. Then one day I lost it on my husband. He told me he had no clothes and he needed his laundry done before he went to work the next day. He's fifty-five years old and he can't even wash his own damn underwear? I dumped the laundry basket out on the floor and told my husband that from now on he could do his own damn laundry. You should have seen the look on his face!
>
> *Successful entrepreneur*

Since this woman failed to communicate her new needs and expectations to her family, they naturally expected that nothing in the household routine would change. If she were single and living alone, she could change her routine without affecting anyone. If the dishes piled up in the sink, the food in the refrigerator turned green, or the laundry didn't get done for a week, who else would care? As a wife and mother she is an integral part of a system that depends on every individual to play his or her role in an established way. When one member of the system changes the routine, then all must adjust. Your partner and your family do not have a crystal ball—they cannot read your mind. Similarly, you will not always be able to predict changes in your life when you begin a business. This is why an entire chapter (Chapter 1) was devoted to making a family plan—and then revisiting this plan as your business and family needs evolve with time. Communication is key; assuming your husband or kids will pick up the slack is a dangerous, and often futile position that creates negativity and angry feelings, damaging to your relationships and becoming a distraction, in time and energy, from your business.

Most households establish house rules to prevent a negative situation from occurring. One of Ginny's most memorable step-parenting moments prompted her, many years ago, to invent an immediate house rule that she has never forgotten.

One September brought an unseasonably sweltering Indian summer. Ginny was eight months pregnant and working part-time out of the house. Her home lacked central air-conditioning and in desperation, she removed all her clothes and worked naked at their kitchen table by an open window to stay cool. The kitchen was about ten feet from the front door. She had all of five seconds notice when one of her then teenage stepsons came flying in the door from school, two hours earlier than expected. She screamed like a lunatic at him to get out of the house until she dressed. When she allowed her stepson back in, she spontaneously implemented a new house rule: no working unclothed at home, no matter how hot it gets! And, the children have to be sure to let Mom know in advance when they are coming home earlier than expected from school!

This section explores four categories of house rules to articulate if you have a family and will work at home:

1. Assigning household responsibilities.
2. Conducting business in the home without intruding on the needs and privacy of household members.
3. Protecting the business from interference by household members.
4. Caring for and supervising the children.

CLARIFICATION EXERCISE THREE: DEFINING HOUSE RULES

Completion time: 60 minutes

The following exercise should help as you embark on a home office or if you have a home office already established but haven't yet defined systems to keep your home and business operating smoothly together.

This exercise stimulates discussion about important family issues. Read the questions together with your spouse. Establish a mutual understanding of how you will handle and negotiate each if necessary. If your children are old enough, then involve them democratically in the rule-making process, or, if you prefer, hold an autocratic family meeting to share your decisions with them. Writing down the agreed-upon rules is particularly important with children. Agree to review the rules monthly, quarterly, or even weekly at the beginning if necessary.

HOUSEHOLD RESPONSIBILITIES

Cleaning. Who is going to keep the house in order, clean, polish, dust, vacuum, empty the garbage, clean the bathrooms, keep the office clean and straightened? How often will someone complete these tasks? Are children responsible for keeping their rooms straightened? Who does extra work when a client comes to the house, like maintaining any bathroom a client uses? Who decides what the cleanliness standards are? Will you hire a housekeeper?

Meals. Who prepares breakfast, lunch and dinner—how often, what time? Who sets the table, cleans the kitchen afterward, empties the dishwasher? Who grocery shops? Will you designate mealtime as family time, with everyone expected to attend? What exceptions are there? If the kids have changing schedules due to seasonal after-school activities, how is this accounted for? If your husband travels with little notice, how is this accounted for? What are your emergency plans if a child gets sick or if your child care or car pool help does?

Laundry. Who does laundry for whom, and how often? Who washes, folds, and puts away the clothes? Are children responsible for their own laundry at a certain age?

Maintenance. Who does household and auto repairs and maintenance? How often? When will you hire outside help instead of doing it yourself? If outside help becomes necessary and it has not been budgeted for, where will the money come from? What maintenance will you do around the house to prevent breakdowns and repair them? If money is tight, what repairs will be left undone?

Errands. Who goes to the Post Office, dry cleaners, office supply store, etc.?

Clutter. Who's the clutter cop? Who straightens, sorts the mail, keeps the business and household paperwork organized and filed? Who recycles old newspapers and magazines, puts away children's debris, keeps miscellaneous household clutter manageable? Who puts away business materials at the end of a workday? Is there a need to hire a professional organizer in the event clutter from both personal and professional items become unmanageable and distracting?

Pets. Who walks the dog, feeds the cat, cleans the guinea pig cage, buys the bird food, and takes the pet to the vet?

HOW WILL YOUR BUSINESS RESPECT YOUR FAMILY'S NEED FOR PRIVACY, RELAXATION, AND ATTENTION?

Public space. If you locate your work area in the family room or kitchen, where does everyone go to hang out while you are working? Is your business area off-limits to the family at certain hours?

Dress code. Do the members of your family have to dress a certain way when clients are in the house? (For example, can your 16-year-old daughter parade through the house in her string bikini?)

Client visiting. Can clients drop by unannounced or call at anytime? Is business ever off limits, so you can devote focused, uninterrupted time to your family?

Children's activities. Does your home office restrict your children's time on the computer, watching television, playing music, or inviting friends over to the house?

Accessibility. How will you respond to your children's requests for attention? What kinds of requests must the children postpone until your work is done? How will your children know when it is OK to interrupt your work? Define what constitutes an emergency.

HOW WILL YOU PROTECT YOUR BUSINESS FROM INTERFERENCE BY HOUSEHOLD MEMBERS?

Telephone/PC Computer. Are children prohibited from using the business line or your business cell phone to make telephone calls? Are children prohibited from using the PC or laptop you use for your work?

Privacy. How will you maintain privacy in your work area and keep your office secure, especially if your workspace is not a separate room with a door? How will you prevent your children from turning your home office into a play area?

Client visitors. How will you ensure a positive impression for your clients or customers when they visit your home? Will they have a reserved parking space? Do you expect anyone in the family to answer the door? Will you introduce business visitors to your family? How should your family behave toward clients if they do interact? How will you control unruly or excitable pets, a barking or jumping dog, unattractive smells, sounds, or sights? How and when will you notify your family that visitors are expected? All of these variables, although not directly related to the actual work of your business, will impact whether a meeting with your client in your home office is considered to be a success. Just as you "dress for success," first impressions are also made by how your office and its surrounding area looks; if this were not true business firms would not have fancy furniture and expensive art work on its walls.

HOW WILL YOU CARE FOR AND SUPERVISE THE CHILDREN?

1. Who wakes the children up in the morning to start their day?
2. Who gets the children off to school or day care in the morning?
3. Who picks them up from the bus stop or connects with them when they return in the afternoon?
4. Who chauffeurs the children to after-school activities? Does the car pool need to change?

5. How will you supervise, feed, entertain, diaper, or calm infants and very young children if they are home during the workday? Or will you hire someone?

6. Who will supervise, guide, and keep teenage children out of trouble?

7. Any extra household chores you expect of the children?

8. Any new restrictions you would place on the children?

9. Who will help the children with their homework?

10. Will the children help in the business? Will you pay them?

11. Any rules for the kids regarding off-limits business space and materials?

12. How will you minimize interruptions when you are on the phone or visiting with a client? When is it urgent enough for the children to interrupt you?

13. Have you discussed these rules with your children and received agreement?

14. Who gives the kids their bath, reads them bedtime stories and puts them down to sleep?

15. Who will take time off from work to take care of sick children when necessary?

16. Will you still be able to volunteer in the kid's classroom activities: i.e., class mom, supervise field trips, etc.?

17. Will you still be able to be involved in community activities you enjoy or those your children enjoy?

18. Write here any other house rules you can think of that need clarification or discussion: _____

WORKING AT HOME WHEN YOU ARE A PARENT

No matter what combination of work and parenting you choose, your family will experience frustration, guilt, anger, sadness, fatigue, and resentment. These experiences are natural and healthy, provided that you acknowledge them. There is no perfect setup that will eliminate all stress and difficulty. Raising a family and working is stressful, whether you work out of or in the home. You and your spouse must choose which set of challenges you wish to take on. Don't let anyone guilt or coerce you into their recommended option—like staying at home to raise your children or returning to the executive career you have worked hard to achieve. Find the right scenario for you, your spouse, and your children at this time. Be willing to change it, as needed, throughout your family life.

Working at Home with Young Children (under school age)

An author I know had a plan: During her three-month maternity leave from her full-time job, she would write the book proposal required for publishing her first book. Babies mostly sleep in their first three months, right?

Six months later, she finished the proposal, after returning to work, even though she was back at the computer within a few days of her daughter's birth. Her daughter slept for an hour or two at a time and then was hungry again—day and night, day after day. By the time my friend diapered, nursed, and cuddled her baby, she had only a few hours left to write. She has since published several books, but she learned that watching over a newborn or toddler brings with it certain limitations, and unless you are going to hire someone to watch your child so you can work, there is a limit to multi-tasking while caring for a young child.

I also managed a home business while caring for a busy brood, and I learned the importance of setting realistic expectations of myself as well. I clearly remember taking an emergency phone call from a client while home with three young children. Needing to find a quiet room, I went into the bathroom, sat on the floor with my feet on the door to block the kids from entering, and spoke to my client who was in such distress, she did not hear my kids banging on the door asking to get into the bathroom. When you are a self-employed mom who works at home, you will be surprised at how creative you can be when it comes to handling awkward work situations that develop. I don't recommend sitting on the bathroom floor to conduct business; however, nobody knows better than working moms that necessity is the mother of invention.

The bottom line here is to have things set up as much as possible so you are not working and parenting simultaneously; this is the biggest mistake many female business owners make, leaving them feeling inadequate at both roles.

Give up any fantasy of working full-time from home and caring for an infant or small children, unless you have child care help coming into your home, or you can work at night when your children sleep. You'll set yourself up to feel like a lousy parent, or an ineffective entrepreneur, and you'll wear yourself down to exhaustion quickly

On the other hand, if your expectations of yourself as a parent and businessperson are realistic, working at home while raising your babies can go well, allowing both quality time at home with your children and a business of your own. Following an extremely complicated pregnancy, I gave birth to premature twin boys. The infants were in the Neo-Natal Intensive Care Unit for weeks; upon discharge, they required many months of follow-up care with a variety of developmental pediatric specialists. I had planned to go back to work soon after the twins were born but their health and my physical and emotional exhaustion prevented this from happening. As John Steinbeck wrote, "The best laid plans of mice and men often go astray."

Patty / Ann

CLARIFICATION EXERCISE FOUR:
CAN YOU WORK AT HOME SUCCESSFULLY WHILE CARING FOR AN INFANT OR SMALL CHILDREN?

Completion time: 10 minutes

Here is a quick assessment to help you determine in advance if you are the kind of personality that can work well at home while caring for an infant or small child. One caveat: We are speaking about a physically, mentally, and emotionally well child. All bets are off if you bring home a colicky, special needs, premature, or otherwise more-demanding-than-normal infant from the hospital. Really, you may be amazing, but you are NOT superwoman. Of course, you will prioritize caring for your child, and there are only so many hours in the day!

Answer yes or no to the following questions.

1. Can you complete your business effectively in part-time hours, in short spurts of time, with distractions and interruptions from the children?

2. Can you work fatigued and feeling pulled in two different directions?

3. Will your spouse, parent, or older children share child care responsibilities with you?

4. Do you plan to hire child care and/or housekeeping help to come into your home?

5. Are you able to take a sabbatical from your business for a time, without destroying the business?

6. Do you have the financial means to earn less than a full-time income?

7. Do you have the flexibility to set your own pace in your business, so that if your baby gets sick, has a cranky day, is teething, etc., you can let the work slide a bit without jeopardizing a deadline?

8. Does your spouse have a realistic assessment of what you can accomplish while staying home with a young child?

9. Are your children reasonably healthy and even-tempered, not demanding more care than the average child of their ages? (For example, not colicky or emotionally or physically challenged).

10. Have you spaced out your children in age so that you aren't caring for more than one infant or toddler at a time?

11. Is raising your children at home your highest priority? Will you sacrifice business success, if necessary, to accomplish that goal?

If you can answer yes to all or most of these questions, you may be ideally suited for a home business, even though you have small children. If you answered no to several questions, reevaluate your alternatives rather than feel like a failure because you tried to achieve the impossible. Be true to yourself and the life you and your spouse have agreed upon.

Working at Home with Children Between Ages Five and Eleven

With your children in school at least part-time, you can usually plan uninterrupted work for at least four to six hours a day. Thousands of parents choose entrepreneurial options that allow them to work "mother's hours" when the children are either at school or asleep. Some parents abruptly stop their work upon their children's arrival from school. Others work through the distractions and interruptions that children may bring.

What has been referred to above as "mommy hours" is similar to the "mommy track" in Corporate America. Although this concept has received mixed reviews from men and women alike, the fact of the matter is most women with children make different career choices than men with children or women without children.

What works for you depends on your business, your children and your family goals. Children ages five to eleven are normally still too young to leave for a long time without adult supervision. They become bored and want to be entertained, interrupting your work, or getting themselves in trouble. You can plant children in front of the computer to play video games or use a television set to act as a baby-sitter for only so long and certainly not habitually. The computer and television do not substitute for adult interaction or supervision. If you have multiple children, remember that bickering between siblings is natural and frequent; it won't disappear just because it's inconvenient for you. If your children are bored or miss you, they will fight just to get your attention. They may also become physically hurt if let unattended for long stretches of time since many kids have a way of finding trouble. Business or no business, kids will be kids.

Paul and Sarah Edwards discuss what you can expect with children at home in their book, *Working from Home*.

> *Whatever their ages, kids will be kids. Don't expect your children to act like grown-ups just because you are working at home. Don't expect them, for example, to be quiet. Remember, by nature children are not quiet, and to be so for more than short periods of time is unhealthy for their development. Constantly trying to hush them will be a losing battle for you in the short run and not good for them in the long run. A good rule of thumb, applying to children of all ages, is to "child-proof" your home office rather than trying to "office-proof" your children. In other words, let your kids be kids. Set up your office and your schedule so that having "normal" children around will not disrupt your work.*
>
> *Young children may resent your work and act out even more if you force them to constrain their natural behavior and to act like adults when they are too young for those expectations. Even worse, they may act like adults and sacrifice their childhoods to your small business. This is a high price for them to pay. On the other hand, if they receive adequate attention, then they can come to love the fact that you are there when they return from school and available when they need you the most.*

Most young children don't know what their parents do for work. When one or both of you works at home, even very young children can start to understand what your business is for and about—if you take the time to speak with them about it in an age-appropriate manner. Over time, they will appreciate your effort to make money for what they want. All young children have a fantasy that money just appears when they need it. ATM cash machines and credit cards increase the illusion. Working at home can help to dispel that myth. One clever woman responded to her daughter's plea for a pair of designer jeans by telling her how many extra hours the family would have to work to buy the item. The child put down the jeans.

> My kids grew up helping in the family business from the time they were five years old. Some of our best family times were spent sitting around our large worktable, working together to get a mailing out. Our kids have always known that Mommy and Daddy had to work very hard to pay for groceries and movie money, and they appreciated us more as a result.
>
> *Partner in a retail-order business*

> When she was ten, my daughter took a bad fall on her bicycle, requiring several stitches. Since I was working at home, I was only minutes away to comfort her and take her to the hospital.
>
> *Bed and breakfast innkeeper*

> When we built our new custom home office, I had a special extra-wide desk designed that allowed my kids to do their homework at my desk in the afternoon. They get a kick out of working at the desk like "a big person," and it's easier for me to stay connected with them.
>
> *Midwest psychologist and consultant*

You may elect to bring day care or babysitting help into your home to cover the time during the day that the children aren't in school. Stay flexible and open to alternatives, and be creative. Start a babysitting co-op in your neighborhood for other work-at-home parents. Join with other parents to hire a babysitter to watch all the children in one place. Either you or your spouse may elect to work afternoon or evenings to have one parent always available to the children. Bring a live-in nanny into your home if you have the financial means and the space.

Working at Home with Teenagers

I have been working from home at least part of the time all through the growing up years of our children, from infancy through teenage years. The good news is, as they age you no longer have midnight feedings and dirty diapers, but anyone who has raised teenagers will tell you they bring their own unique challenges! I came to appreciate that I could make client appointments without worrying about whether or not there would be coverage for the children at home, but I also found it challenging to be available for the myriad of school and after-school activities our children engaged in. I also found teenagers to be most communicative immediately upon arriving home from school or after-school activities. There appears to be a "magical" half hour window when they talk about their day non-stop—and then all of a sudden the flood gates close, so I often scheduled my work to be available during this precious time, as much as possible.

The other time teenagers appear to speak freely is when they are in a car. I believe the non-communicative teenager will talk during a car ride because there is a definitive beginning and end to the time they are alone with you and this frees them up to speak—and then they are "outta there." Teenagers act like they really don't care if you are interested in their life or show up at their activities—until they think you aren't going to be involved or show up at an event. My teenage daughter once said she didn't care if I attended her softball game, and then when she misunderstood a conversation I was having with my husband said to me, "What do you mean you're not coming to the game tomorrow?"

Children over the age of twelve can entertain themselves and follow and respect house rules, even if they don't like them. Now you may have to contend with normal teenage behavior, like having the TV on too loud, video chatting loudly on the computer, walking through the house in ragged clothes with a punk hairstyle when your best client is there, expecting or demanding to be chauffeured, cooking up a storm in the kitchen and leaving it a mess, or not doing homework unless supervised. The same children who enjoyed having you at home may wish you'd leave, so they can have more freedom.

Depending on your relationship, working at home with teenagers can be a very positive experience. Your children may become even more active in your business as essential assistants. As a trade-off, you may be more available for transporting them to and from after-school activities. You can get to know their friends better, and have a better handle on any worrisome teenage behaviors, such as drug or alcohol use, trouble in school, depression and the omnipresent issue of the times: bullying and cyberbullying.

> I noticed that my son Charlie always came home directly after school and went straight to his room for the afternoon. He never had any friends over and appeared quite depressed. We got him into counseling and discovered that he was considering suicide. I felt much better keeping an eye on him during this fragile time. I would have worried sick about him if I was away front home all day.
>
> *Multi-level Marketing consultant*

The best way to work well with teenage children at home is to keep dialogue open, continue to hold realistic expectations, and be prepared for good days and bad ones, remembering that many of their mood swings are predicated upon hormonal changes out of their control. Teenagers themselves often do not know why they feel the way they do half the time—anymore than you do. It is a casualty of the age. As much as we don't like to admit it or remember, we were moody teenagers once also. If you have forgotten this fact, ask your parents or older siblings; I am sure they will be happy to remind you.

DECIDING WHEN IT IS TIME TO MOVE THE OFFICE OUT OF THE HOME

Some entrepreneurs set up a home office when they start their business, and their business never leaves home. If the business prospers, the quality of their home office will improve—even to the extent of moving to a new home so they can build a more spacious home office. For these entrepreneurs, the notion of eliminating a home office is out of the question. If relocating to a new house becomes necessary, a place for a suitable home office is a key criterion to the choice of a new house. They have discovered that their business, their personality, and their family needs are entirely conducive to a home office. Some business owners, however, find that working from home eventually becomes counter-productive and they decide to close or move out of their home office. We found there are typically four reasons this happens:

1. Zoning difficulties.
2. Business expansion.
3. Working at home doesn't work for either the entrepreneur or his or her family.
4. The business closes down.

Let's explore each of these scenarios.

Zoning

The town or city you live in determines whether it is legal for you to operate a business in your home, through zoning laws. Nine out of ten localities restrict using residences for offices or businesses in some way. You might run into restrictions like the following:

- Restrictions limiting increases in vehicular traffic
- Restrictions on use or size of outdoor signs
- Restrictions on on-street parking
- Limitations on employees
- Limitations on floor space used
- Restrictions on retail selling times on the premises
- Prohibitions on outside storage of materials
- Restrictions on inside storage of materials

Your building or neighborhood subdivision or community may also have rules that make it difficult for you to run all or part of your business from home. For example, some communities restrict the parking of commercial vehicles in your driveway; others prohibit customers from coming to your home.

Zoning ordinances, created on the local level, differ widely from town to town. Depending on your business of choice, they can severely restrict your ability to operate a legal home-based business. If you are conservative, law-abiding, and risk-averse, you will check with your local city hall to find out what the restrictions are for your neighborhood before you set up the home office. This will be particularly essential if you are considering a business that will bring traffic, noise, commercial vehicles or disturbance to your neighborhood. Complaining neighbors uncover most zoning violations.

If you take the route of selective denial or choose to "take your chances" by operating a home office that is not in total compliance with local zoning ordinances, you could get caught with an expensive battle to keep your business operating. Fighting a zoning ordinance can destroy your business and your relationship with your neighbors, so knowingly operating a home office in violation of zoning restrictions is risky. On the other hand, some home-based entrepreneurs have successfully defended their right to operate a business at home and have changed zoning laws as a result. You may be able to band together in the fight with other similar home-based businesses in your neighborhood.

Business Expansion

For some entrepreneurs, the home office is a necessary first step to growing a business. The dream has always been to expand to a large facility with dozens of employees. For them, the move out of the house is cause for celebration, or at least a big leap of faith that their business is now ready to absorb the increased overhead. That doesn't mean that moving out is easy.

> My husband and teenage daughter forced me to move my business out of the house when our home started feeling as if we were living in my office. My business had taken over the dining room, the living room, half of our bedroom, and even the hallways. It finally got to be too much for my family to take. I realize now that as our business expanded, our house was simply too small to accommodate employees and so much traffic.
>
> *Audio/video consultant*

This entrepreneur experienced the pull between striving for a successful, prosperous business, and wanting to work at home in a space too small to accommodate her growing business and a family. Some entrepreneurs intentionally limit their growth by turning down business or charging higher fees to reduce demand, in order to continue working at home. The critical decision for some is whether to expand beyond a one- or two-person business, to a larger business requiring employees. Others use the profits from their business to improve their living space, build an addition, or finish the basement. Some entrepreneurs move to a larger home, rather than relocating their business.

You may feel claustrophobic after attempting to coexist in too small a space with a spouse, employees, clients, and children. Stepping all over each other in cramped quarters gets old. Without the opportunity for at least some privacy during the day or evening, work is less productive and conflict usually increases among family members.

Couples are imaginative with available space when the need dictates. One couple with two children turned a small, two-bedroom New York apartment into an office for their thriving service business. Every day they shared their one-thousand-square-foot apartment with three employees, two children, and a baby-sitter. Another couple created and delivered personal growth seminars in their home, turning their home over to a dozen people or more for a week each month when they gave the seminar. Both couples eventually profited enough to move their businesses out of their original home offices, the first couple building a larger home in the suburbs to accommodate a more substantial office, and the second, a separate facility for delivering their courses.

If you are struggling with this dilemma, you may consider renting an outside office or professional suite on a part-time basis for selected work activities such as visiting with clients. Many major hotels have office space and conference rooms available you can rent by the hour and many professional business organizations provide free office space, on a limited basis to their members. Rent outside storage space instead of crowding your home with boxes and filing cabinets. House your staff in an outside office, but remain in your home office for most of your workday. Work in an outside office part of the day, but still work at home when it is preferable for you or your family.

> I rent a professional suite that I share with three other women. Since none of us needs an office outside the house full-time, it's the perfect arrangement for us. I can still be home in the afternoon for my children.
> *Translator*

It's Not Working to Work at Home

Working at home may not be conducive to business success and/or harmony in your marriage or family. Maybe you figured it out after just a few months, or after a year or two of valiant effort.

Some work at home entrepreneurial couples decide to move his office outside the home after six months, even though the additional overhead strained their budget. The entrepreneur wasn't productive at home, and their relationship, as well as bank account, was suffering. Mitch and I, who both maintain offices within and outside our home, find there are times where we just need space from each other so separate offices within and outside the home works like a charm for us.

Sometimes the increased cost of overhead is necessary to improve business performance or to diminish tension in your relationship or family. Rather than seeing the move out of the home as failure, consider it feedback. You tried the home office approach, and it wasn't for you. Fine, try something else. There is no "right" way to run a business. Do what works best for you, your marriage and your family.

The Business Closes

A home-based business can be a lifetime career choice or a brief adventure. Your business may last a year or two or a decade or more. You may switch to a new business venture that requires working outside of the home. Many retired, down-sized, or fired executives try their hand at self-employment and working from home after leaving behind their corporate routine. Contrast these two experiences:

> When I stopped working as a controller I missed talking with people and having an assistant to type my letters and file my paperwork. I was lonely working as a self-employed accountant. After a year, I gave it up and secured a job as a controller again.
> *Controller*

No more stiletto heels and expensive suits, and sitting inside a building with no windows for ten hours a day. I would never go back to corporate jail, for any kind of money. I will be working for myself, regardless of what it takes, for the rest of my working life! I have discovered how much I love the entrepreneurial life, and I'm well on my way now to a successful business that will support my family without ever putting on a pair of heels again!

Artist

You and your spouse may experience many variations on the home office lifestyle during your lifetime together, as your family and business needs change. You may shut the business down all together, or the business may prosper, but not in your home. Sometimes, in fact, the only way the business will prosper is if you move it out of your home! Here's a quick assessment to help you determine if now is the time to do so.

CLARIFICATION EXERCISE FIVE: IS IT TIME TO MOVE THE OFFICE OUT OF THE HOUSE?

Completion time: 10 minutes

The following quiz for the home-based entrepreneur will give you a sense of whether it's time to consider moving the office out of the home, for the sake of your business, your marriage, or your children.

Answer yes or no to the following questions.

1. Are you finding it difficult to focus on your work productively because household demands and repairs distract you?

2. Are your children complaining a great deal about the restrictions placed on them because of your home office? Are they rebelling frequently against your requests? Has it turned out to be impossible to create a productive work atmosphere because of your children's or spouse's presence in the home?

3. Are you and your spouse fighting more because of tension created by the home office? Do you argue over lack of space in the house, the blurring of personal and business conflict, boundaries around work and family time, or how you should manage the home office?

4. Is your home atmosphere interfering with the professional image you wish to project to your clients? Is it preventing or limiting new business development? Do you tend to network less often than you need to because your business is located at home?

5. Do you frequently feel torn between caring for your children and your spouse and caring for your business? Have you been unable to do either one to your liking? Would it be easier for you to compartmentalize and separate those aspects of your life?

6. Have you been unhappy, lonely, anxious, or bored more often because of your dissatisfaction with working at home? Are bad

habits, like overeating or sleeping too much taking over and jeopardizing your business and your health?

7. Is your presence at home unnecessary (for child care, elder care, or caring for a disabled spouse), so that you could consider other options that might work better for all concerned?

8. Does your gut sense and intuition tell you that it's time to move out?

If you answered yes to three to five of these questions, put some serious energy into researching out-of-the-home office alternatives, at least part-time. If you answered yes to six or more of these questions, start packing! Expect to go through an adjustment period when the office moves out of the home. Your spouse may be happy to reclaim his or her house, sad to see you go, or a little of both. He or she may feel more disconnected from you and your business once it's out of the house. The routines of the family will change again. Prepare children for the move and expect some adjustment difficulties. Revisit the family plan and re-negotiate, as needed, all of the household management activities discussed in the exercises earlier in this chapter. Remember, any change in the family system will disrupt the routines you and they are accustomed to. Anticipating change and discussing revised expectations will help you make the transition smoother for everyone involved.

CONCLUSION

Memories of boxes on dining room tables, computers in the kitchen, and baby's rooms converted to work stations bring a smile and a feeling of disbelief—"how did we ever do it?" Most couples are proud of what they have been able to pull off working at home with limited resources. Most also acknowledge how much of a struggle it was to keep their sanity and their relationship healthy during this start-up period. And then, there are many couples who feel the only reason why their family life works so well is because one of the spouses is working from home, on a flexible schedule, able to put the needs of the family first when called for, and they won't have it any other way until they are fully retired! My husband and I both love our work and never plan on retiring. Our future plans include working more closely together creating dynamic interactive workshops. They would incorporate Mitch's expertise of developing leadership skills and business strategies and my expertise on relationship and communication skills.

Openly communicate your evolving needs to your partner and your family if you work from home. Remember to be flexible and creative when it comes to problem solving home office issues.

Working from home—some will never stop, some will never do it again, and many will incorporate it into their lives some of their working career. Which one are you?

—m—

If you would like to download copies of Clarification Exercise One, "Assessing How A Home Office Suits Your Marriage and Family Needs" go to:

www.relationshiptoolbox.com/homeoffice.pdf

—m—

PART 2

SUSTAINING A THRIVING MARRIAGE

Not Tonight Dear, I've Got a Business to Run!

V
COMMUNICATION SKILLS

Assume Nothing, Discuss Everything

> I used to look forward to coming home to my husband. Now, I find myself making excuses to work late at the office because we've drifted so far apart, we have little in common anymore.
>
> *Retail sales owner*

> My wife and I share a home office. Lately, she's been driving me nuts. She talks to me all day long, even when I'm busy working. When I tell her to leave me alone, she does—she doesn't talk to me for the rest of the day. How can I get her to understand that I need privacy so that I can concentrate on my work? I wish she wouldn't take it so personally.
>
> *Environmental consultant*

Are any of the following statements true for you?

- I can enjoy a productive day at work, but when my husband comes home, he'll say something sarcastic to me that ruins my whole mood.

- Sometimes I'm convinced that my wife and I are from different planets. We both experience the same event, but see it entirely differently.

- I love my girlfriend, but I don't know how to make her feel better when she's upset. I wish I knew how to be a better friend to her.

- When I tell my husband a complaint, I get a hostile, defensive reaction. How can I make a simple request without causing a fight?

- Whenever I share a problem with my husband he always tell me how he thinks I should solve it. I don't want him telling me how to fix it—I just want him to listen with a sympathetic ear.

- If there are two ways to do things, my husband and I always pick the opposite one. I'm beginning to think we don't belong together anymore.

- When my live-in girlfriend and I began dating a few years ago we could finish each other's sentences. Now we can't even agree on how to drive home from the train station.

George Bernard Shaw once joked, "The single biggest problem with communication is the illusion that it has taken place." Couples often falsely think they are communicating merely because they are saying words to each other. In reality, they are just talking "at" each other instead of "with" each other. You cannot solve a problem if you haven't learned how to communicate effectively. Effective communication requires the ability to say what you mean and mean what you say. Repeating the same ineffective communication patterns, rather than making real breakthroughs in understanding, leads to greater conflict and escalates the problems which need to be resolved.

Loving, empathetic, and helpful communication will energize and support you as a couple. Unproductive negative communication will leave you lonely, angry, overwhelmed and in some circumstances, feeling emotionally distant and isolated from each other. You may wonder about your sanity and the intimacy of your relationship after failing miserably to connect with your spouse. Lacking effective communication skills will make the entrepreneurial journey much more difficult than it needs to be.

Julia has repeatedly asked her husband, Wesley, to stop walking through the house with his dirty shoes on. He agrees when she asks, but later doesn't follow through. The more often she requests, the more he ignores her, until she nags him almost daily. He complains of being henpecked and she of being ignored. Julia and Wesley wonder how they can negotiate more serious life issues together, if they can't even resolve a small disagreement like dirty shoes. Of course, this argument is not really "about the shoes."

This couple is communicating in a manner which escalates the problem rather than resolving it. Wesley verbalizes the response he knows his wife wants to hear—to get her off his back. Later, he does what he wants to do anyway. He doesn't really mean what he says. Julia is not really saying what she means either; what she desires is a clean house, but that is not what she says. This couple is in a power struggle for control and trouble is brewing.

When we communicate with our partners the way that we want to, but not necessarily the way that they feel comfortable communicating, we often feel frustrated and confused. Julia believes that asking her husband more often will get the desired response, because he will better understand how important a clean home is to her. Constant repetition like this is as futile as speaking more slowly and loudly to a person who speaks a foreign language, hoping they will better understand you. In this example, it is easy to see the absurdity of this thinking; you are speaking a different language and it doesn't matter how slowly or loudly you speak—you will not be understood. Julia doesn't see that what Wesley is hearing touches on his fear of losing his independence. The more repetitive she becomes, the more his fear is exacerbated. Wes needs to avoid taking orders from her, a need stronger than his desire to meet her standards for cleanliness. The more often she asks, the harder he resists. Her repetition reinforces his need for independence.

Let's look at research related to gender-related differences, to help all entrepreneurial couples, like Wesley and Julia, experience more satisfaction in their communication with one another.[1] Every couple wants to be able to:

- Comfort each other in times of distress.

- Make requests that get lasting results.

- Offer constructive criticism that avoids being painfully received and gets heard from a place of love and respect.

- Connect more intimately, in ways that are meaningful.

GENDER-RELATED DIFFERENCES

Comforting Each Other in Times of Distress

One of the benefits of marriage or serious commitment to a significant other is living with a best friend—your sounding board, safe haven, and battery recharge. However, if your partner doesn't understand how you need to solve problems, complain, and be comforted, then your relationship can stress you more than relieve your pain. Too often we give our partners what *we* need in difficult times, rather than what *they* need. Though we mean well, our partners find no comfort in the results.

Life offers a daily series of problems to solve, from the mundane, such as what to wear to work, to the significant, such as how to increase sales. Although we dream of a life without problems, we get some daily satisfaction from solving our problems. (Problem-solving provides us the opportunity to use our intelligence and creativity which enhances our self-esteem.) When you live with a partner and children, your problems are not just your own. Your worries, complaints, and frustrations affect those dearest to you, directly and indirectly.

---

[1] If you are in a gay or lesbian partnership, or if classic gender-related research doesn't seem to apply to your partnership, substitute "right-brain" or "left-brain" for male and female.

Georgia and Kurt are not responding effectively to each other's distress. When Georgia drags herself home after a horrendous day at work, she experiences the following frustrating conversation with her husband:

Georgia:	"Somebody should shoot the idiot I work for. He treats me like a slave, and I can't take it anymore. The commute to work is driving me crazy. There are so many trucks on the Interstate. God, I'm so exhausted, I don't know how I'm going to make dinner tonight. Damn it! Andrew left his coat on the floor again. I'm sick and tired of cleaning up after everyone. No one ever helps me around here!"
Georgia means:	"I want empathy, support, a listening ear, and appreciation. I need to hear something like, 'Gee honey, it sounds as if you've had an awful day. You work so hard, you must be exhausted. Is there anything I can do to help?'"
Kurt hears:	"She wants me to solve the problem for her."
Kurt responds:	"Don't you think you take things too personally at work? If it's so hard for you, why don't you just quit?"
Kurt means:	"I hate to see you this upset. It's OK with me if you quit your job, even if it would be hard on the family. I don't want you to fall apart."
Georgia hears:	"If you didn't take things so personally, there wouldn't be a problem. This is all your fault."
Georgia responds:	"You know I can't quit. We need the money. Don't accuse me of overreacting. I hate when you do that. If you could see the kind of abuse I put up with at work, you'd understand."
Georgia means:	"I need validation and reassurance. I expect you to support me and say something like, "You're right—no one should have to put up with that kind of crap. I'm sorry you feel you can't quit your job right now. It's really hard on you supporting the family while I get my business going. Let me give you a hug!"

Kurt hears:	"This is all your fault. If it wasn't for that stupid company of yours, I could quit my job and every thing would be fine."
Kurt responds:	"I've also dealt with horrible bosses. Sometimes you just have to toughen up and not let them get to you."
Kurt means:	"I'm sorry that you can't quit your job and it's because my company isn't doing well enough yet. I know you are strong enough to handle a lousy boss. If you do what I've done in the past, when I've been in the same situation, maybe you'd feel better."
Georgia hears:	"I've had a lousy boss too, and I had no problem dealing with him. You're just too much of a wimp."

What went wrong? Georgia wants to vent her misery and receive emotional support. Exasperated, she lets her husband know about four problems in the first thirty seconds. She doesn't really expect him to solve any of them. Complaining makes her feel better, even if some of the problems have no immediate solution. She exaggerates with expressions like, "I can't take it anymore," because she is feeling overwhelmed and exhausted. She needs reassurance of her strength and to be assisted with something practical like cooking dinner that evening.

Kurt responds by giving her what he thinks she needs the most—a solution to her worst problem and reassurance that her problems aren't so bad. That's what he would want. He thinks her cry, "I can't take it anymore," signals an impending nervous breakdown, so he offers her permission to quit her job. He's trying to be helpful.

Georgia and Kurt can each improve their communication by making some small changes.

Georgia needs to:

- Reassure Kurt that she's really OK, even though it was an awful day.
- Tell Kurt clearly that she's looking for a listening ear, not a solution to her problems.
- Ask for help in the kitchen when she needs it.
- Complain to Kurt about a few things at a time.

Kurt needs to:

- Recognize Georgia's unspoken request for comfort and reassurance.

- Listen empathically and show concern.

- Remember that Georgia has always pulled out of it when she's hit a wall in the past.

- Remind himself that he is not responsible for fixing Georgia's problems.

A slight shift in Kurt's response will dramatically improve his ability to comfort Georgia when she is distressed. Because of the differences in the way the genders communicate, figuring out how to best support your spouse when they are complaining is an excellent tool for avoiding major blowouts. The following scene between Georgia and Kurt illustrates how a slight shift in Georgia's response to Kurt can also improve her ability to comfort him in distress.

Neck-deep in employee problems at his manufacturing plant, Kurt fired his vice president of operations for sexual harassment when several of the women in the plant threatened to sue. On a particularly harsh day, he gets home at 8:00 P.M. and just wants to surf the web, drink a shot of whiskey, and go to bed.

Georgia: "How was your day?"

Georgia means: "You are looking really upset and I'm worried about you. What happened today?"

Kurt hears: "She's in one of those moods to talk, and I don't feel like it."

Kurt responds: "Rough."

Kurt means: "Please leave me alone to solve my problems by myself. I don't want to talk about it right now."

Georgia hears: "It was so bad I will need some prodding to be able to open up to you."

Georgia responds: "I can tell you're upset. If you tell me about it, maybe I can help. Burying yourself in the newspaper won't solve anything. Besides, just because you had a rotten day, you don't have to take it out on me."

Georgia means: "I hate to see you suffering and I want to make you feel better. It scares me and makes me angry when you pull away from me."

Kurt hears: "You have no right to be alone. Take care of making me feel better, along with whatever else is bothering you." He would rather hear something like, "I know you're having a rough time at the plant. If you want to talk about it, I'm here." Or, "I know you like to have your space when you're upset about work. Would you like to have dinner in an hour or so?"

Kurt responds: "Can't a guy get any peace and quiet?"

What went wrong? While women usually feel better talking about what's bothering them, men often pull away to mull over the problem in silence. John Gray refers to the place they go as their "cave." Georgia is trying to help Kurt the way she would like him to respond to her, but her approach is not what he needs.

Men can often become distant and preoccupied when troubled, and therefore emotionally unavailable to their mates or family until they solve the problem. This behavior triggers fear and resentment in their female partners, who try to pull their husbands out of their caves, to make themselves feel better. Their efforts backfire, as the man retreats farther back into his cave and resents her intrusion.

Georgia needs to:

- Support Kurt's need for privacy.

- Let Kurt know she is available if he wants company, and then get on with her life so he doesn't have to worry about making her happy, along with all of his other problems.

- Refrain from punishing him or making a scene because he pulled away.

- Trust Kurt's ability to solve his own problems.

Kurt needs to:

- Reassure Georgia that he wants to be alone temporarily, but he'll be back.

- Appreciate her intrusiveness as a well-intended gesture to help.

- Reassure Georgia that his upset has nothing to do with her.

- Ask for the space that he needs, and thank her for giving it to him.

Both Georgia and Kurt hold enormous power to help each other solve daily problems, if they can learn how to listen and communicate in ways that resonate and support their partner's natural problem-solving process.

Saying What You Mean To Get What You Want

When we are single, we do everything for ourselves. No one really needs or demands anything of us, a huge difference from living with a spouse and family. Though we may fantasize about having no demands on our time other than what we choose to dedicate ourselves to, accommodating reasonable requests for assistance from our husband, children, and stepchildren is part of what it means to be a wife and mother. One of the benefits of marriage is that we also have people to ask for assistance. The key is to ask for help in ways that are not received as a demand.

Here are some simple techniques for getting the assistance you want or need, when making the myriad of requests we make of each other to handle household and business details. For example:

- Would you mind picking up the kids from soccer practice tonight? I'm pushing a deadline here.

- Would you put the baby down for her nap?

- Would you mind paying the bills this month? I am swamped with paperwork for the next few weeks.

- Will you cook dinner tonight?

- Can you take the dog to the vet for her shots on Saturday?

- Can you call the electrician? The light switch in the kids' bathroom isn't working.

Men genuinely want to meet their spouses' needs; however, they don't want to be ordered around or nagged to death. They also need to feel as if they have some sense of control over how they spend their time. If we want him to change, we need to ask for that change so our request is clearly heard and not misinterpreted as a demand.

In a healthy committed marriage, we come to accept the differences between ourselves and our partner, in how we act, think and behave in everyday situations. We come to appreciate them for who they are—not who we want them to be. This appreciation helps us understand how and why our spouse's position differs from our own, thereby creating more tolerance for their position and decreasing our need for them to change. We come to realize that they are not deliberately doing something to or against us.

Current neuroscience research shows men and women do indeed communicate differently. Verbal and non-verbal cues activate different regions of the brain for men and women. Although one must be cautious not to stereotype, we can understand how people labeled "right-side" thinkers (generally women) communicate differently than "left-side" thinkers (generally men). Exciting new research is on the horizon for gaining a better understanding of male/female communication patterns based on neuroscience.

The exercises that follow will help you and your spouse gain an understanding of how your problem-solving styles differ. Some of these differences are related to gender, and some are not. As mentioned above, we must be careful not to stereotype, because gender does not explain all communication style differences, and each individual brings to the relationship a myriad of approaches to communication, some influenced by gender, some by family background, some by preferred ways of speaking and listening, and much more. I recommend you benefit from understanding communication and problem-solving from many different perspectives. Then you can engage in an informative conversation about your similarities and differences.

CLARIFICATION EXERCISE ONE:
HOW I SOLVE PROBLEMS BEST AND HOW
MY SPOUSE CAN HELP FACILITATE THAT

Completion time: 5 minutes

How can your intimate partner best facilitate, and not frustrate, your problem-solving process? Complete the following questions, in the presence of your partner, and see for yourselves. Choose either *a* or *b* for the following statements:

1.

    a. When I have a problem on my mind, I tend to want to be left alone. If I want to talk about it I will bring it up for discussion.

    b. When I have a problem on my mind, I generally want to talk about it.

2.

    a. I don't even mention most problems to my spouse, unless my spouse really presses me about it.

    b. I tell my spouse all the problems I have encountered during the day, if he or she is willing to listen.

3.

    a. I don't like to talk about a problem with my spouse unless I am asking for help to solve the problem directly.

    b. I use my spouse as a sounding board when I want to think something out. I don't necessarily want my partner to solve the problem for me.

4.

    a. I tend to focus on one problem at a time, so I can concentrate and don't get overwhelmed.

    b. I usually think about several problems at the same time.

5.

    a. I approach problem solving systematically, breaking them down and analyzing them, and then looking for a rational solution.

    b. I approach problem solving holistically, relying often on my intuition, as well as objective data, to reach a solution.

6.

    a. I would speak more to my spouse about my work problems except she/he has enough to worry about without me adding to her/his already full plate.

    b. When I share my work problems with my spouse, he/she usually tells me I shouldn't worry so much. He/She is trying to be encouraging but sometimes I feel that my concerns are being minimized.

Discuss your differences and similarities and how they affect your daily communication with each other. Although we might surprise our partner from time to time, we tend to rely on consistent, predictable patterns of communication and problem-solving styles. Knowing our spouse's style makes it easier to be heard when we need to discuss a problem or request a change of behavior. Playing to their strength allows us to avoid their third rail, if you will.

WHAT MEN OFTEN WANT IN COMMUNICATIONS

We all know what scientific evidence confirms: men and women communicate differently. You do not need to be a neuroscientist to know women tend to be more verbal than men. Watch pre-schoolers or school-aged children at play. Three girls will sit and play "make-believe," their play dominated by verbal interaction, talking with each other. Three boys will play in a manner I describe as "boys-in-motion," their play dominated by physical activity. This is not to suggest girls cannot be physical when interacting and boys cannot be verbal when at play, but for the majority of the time girls–and women—socialize with words, while boys—and men—socialize with physical activity.

Differing communication styles between men and women must be addressed in your marriage and your business (if you have a male partner, male employees or male clients) for effective communication.

In my research, I have learned that typically, men prefer for women to avoid certain behaviors and ways of communicating that either anger or frustrate them. Understanding a man's "don't do this please" list will help you stay on his good side and communicate more clearly. Just as you have your wishes, often that he will communicate more often in a style you enjoy, he also has his favored approach to communication with you. When you "get him," you'll probably get more respect and love, too.

WHAT MEN WISH YOU UNDERSTOOD
ABOUT WHAT THEY NEED

Don't make a request that is really a demand, taking away his freedom to say "no" without being a "bad guy."	**Try this instead:** Ask him to do something when he's not in the middle of doing something else, like when he finally sits down at 8:00 P.M. to watch the ballgame.
Don't ask him to do something by a certain time without respecting his time frame for accomplishing the task.	**Try this instead:** List household chores and prioritize tasks in order of importance to you. Discuss the list with him and ask him if the time frame you have in mind is realistic.
Don't *repeatedly* ask whether he's going to do a task you've requested (nag).	**Try this instead:** Let him decide when to do something and leave him alone, unless you need something done by a specific time. If you do, clearly communicate your time frame when you request he complete the task. Don't blindside him at the time you need something to be completed.
Don't bombard him with more requests as soon as he completes one task.	**Try this instead:** Express more sincere appreciation for what he has done, and complain less about what he hasn't. Positive reinforcement works for men and women (and children).

Don't interrupt him when he's concentrating, relaxing, and clearly doesn't want to be disturbed.	**Try this instead:** When he appears receptive, start by asking, "Is now a good time to ask you a question or two?" or "It would be great if…," or "I'd love it if you would…," or " I know you have a lot to do, but do you think you might be able to find time to…?"
Don't bombard him with demands as soon as he comes in the door from work.	**Try this instead:** Give him a chance to change out of his work clothes, check the mail, say hi to the kids, or whatever it is he likes to do when he first gets home. Once he has completed these tasks, then ask him if he is open to a request from you. Do not take any requests denied as a personal injury. Accept his refusal of requests graciously, without a scene. Cut him some slack if he doesn't follow through exactly as promised.
Don't act entitled to his positive response to your request, as if he owes it to you, and pester him to do something he doesn't view as important or worth his time.	**Try this instead:** Ask, "Will you…" rather than, "Can you…," since using the phrase, "Can you" may suggest that you question his competence, rather than his willingness. Or ask him, "I know you planned on doing some other things with your time this weekend but I was wondering if you could find the time to…"

WHAT WOMEN WISH MEN UNDERSTOOD ABOUT WHAT THEY NEED

Just like their male counterparts, women also need to feel appreciated and to receive emotional and practical support at times. Generally, the more you give a woman, the more she will give back. Women want their male partners to know they really get upset when their husbands/boyfriends do the following:

Don't express appreciation and instead, take them for granted.	**Try this instead:** Women love to feel cherished and appreciated. Express loving sentiments and provide consistent acts of kindness to her often, and she will be much more eager to fulfill your requests.
Don't assume that certain household and child care jobs are "women's work,' and act as if it's a big deal that you do one thing (like going to work every day), when she's doing twenty things a day.	**Try this instead:** Verbally recognize the many accomplishments of her day, singling out one or two to show that you recognize and appreciate her effort(s).
Don't overload a woman with requests until she burns out. She may have trouble saying no until she has reached the point of exhaustion or resentment, at which point she may explode.	**Try this instead:** Volunteer to help her with something without being asked.
Don't make a scene and act annoyed when she makes a simple request.	**Try this instead:** Say, "Sure, honey," instead of grumbling or mumbling under your breath.
Don't ask for, or demand sex without fulfilling her need to feel important and connected to you.	**Try this instead:** Give her plenty of physical affection. Do little romantic things for her like you used to when you were dating. Foreplay starts first thing in the morning by being nice!

Before going further on this topic, it is important to ask the following questions. Are there changes you and your partner can readily make that would make your life together easier, changes that do not touch on your emotional vulnerabilities? Are you willing to make changes in yourself that require similar sacrifices and compromises that you are asking of your spouse? Look in the mirror and be a positive catalyst for the change you seek in your marriage. When your spouse sees your willingness to accept him or her, and that you are willing to compromise and make concessions about what you would like, you significantly increase the chances of your spouse accepting you for who you are and make the changes you request.

Ask yourself: Are you willing to change for the sake of your relationship?

Answer these questions to help you gain more understanding of how to effectively communicate with your partner and gain a positive response.

Patty / Ann

CLARIFICATION EXERCISE TWO: ELICITING POSITIVE RESPONSE TO REQUESTS

Completion time: 5 minutes

Complete the following sentences, and ask your partner to do the same.

1. I feel the most cooperative and respond the best to your requests when you (positive actions). For example: give me a hug, thank me, enjoy sex with me.

2. I feel the most cooperative and respond the best to your requests when you refrain from (actions). For example: nagging me, interrupting me when I am busy, lecturing, belittling.

Criticizing Your Partner and Asking For Change

We enter an intimate relationship hoping for unconditional love and acceptance. In our early romance, we focus on the positive aspects of our partner's character and ignore or are charmed by the idiosyncrasies that later become a source of irritation. After a few years of marriage many couples report feeling annoyed or upset with the very same personality traits they initially found attractive and admirable in their partner.

Know your partner's hot buttons and avoid them at all costs, especially when requesting their help. An easy way to do this is to choose your words carefully. Different words evoke different feelings. For example, using the word "liar" to describe a false statement elicits a very different response from someone than using the word "untruth" instead.

Research shows that more than half of all communication takes place non-verbally. The issue for many couples is the discrepancy created between their verbal and non-verbal messages. This discrepancy creates ambiguity and distrust between partner. If you and your spouse are not actively listening to each other, your message will fall on deaf ears.

Active listening requires the ability to listen without a hidden agenda; that is, to have a truly open heart, open mind and open soul. Couples who listen hoping to find an error in their spouse's facts—or those just waiting to have their turn to speak—are not actively listening to each other at all.

Delivering and receiving criticism in an intimate relationship can be our most painful communication challenge. Sometimes you will speak critically to your partner directly (verbal communication) and there will be no mistaking your message: *I'm sick and tired of you being late for dinner and I want you to come home earlier.* Other times your critical message may be more indirect. Nonverbal messages often convey a deeper message and are more powerful than the verbal words themselves. For example:

Request for change: Would you change the shirt you are wearing?

Underlying message: That shirt looks hideous on you and it would embarrass me to be seen in public with you.

If the person delivering the request conveys a non-verbal message with a disgusted or demanding tone, then the communication shifts from being about the shirt to being about love and approval.

Here's another example of a critical question. Take the three letter word, *Why?* This innocuous word causes difficulty when it's used to convey indirect criticism. Most people react defensively when asked "Why?"

Question: Why did you mail this bill out late?

The underlying message: I don't approve of this bill going out late. I wouldn't have done that. You better have a good explanation.

Alternatives to asking "why," such as, "could you explain to me," or "how come," or "what do you think about…," help soften the non-verbal message of interrogation and disapproval or what Deborah Tannen refers to as the metamessage. It's also helpful to explain why you are asking the question. For example, "I am keeping track of our cash flow this month. I notice that you mailed the electric bill out late. Could you explain to me why, so that I can keep better control over our cash flow?"

One of men's greatest complaints about women is their tendency to become what John Gray refers to as a "Home Improvement

Committee." To help their partners achieve their full potential, women often nurture their partners with a constant barrage of well-meaning suggestions and unsolicited advice. "Why don't you…," or "If you did this instead…," or "Don't forget to…." The overriding message to a man of constant requests for improvement is that she does not accept or love him as he is. By questioning his competence, his self-esteem takes a hit and he begins to feel he is not capable of taking care of himself or his partner.

Helpful Hints for Managing Critical Communication

Little acts of appreciation, like a simple thank you for taking out the garbage, or a compliment on how nice your partner looks in a new shirt, goes an extremely long way in creating good will within your relationship. This good will comes in handy later on when offering critical communication and constructive criticism, to our partner. If the only time we communicate with our partner is to criticize him or her, after awhile they will totally ignore us or tune us out.

Weigh the pros and cons of criticism. Will the criticism help your partner? Is it a behavior that he or she is able to or likely to change? Do the possible benefits of speaking up outweigh the potential negative response from your partner? Keep quiet if a negative outcome is predictable, unless it is absolutely necessary.

Timing is everything. If possible, plan the time and place of your requests for change. Don't speak your mind whenever the impulse grabs you, if the moment is the worst time for your partner to hear your comments. Keep your primary goal in mind: to influence a change, not just vent a frustration.

Communicate critical feedback with "I" messages, and direct suggestions for a solution. Which complaint will likely result in positive change? Reframe your message from the negative to the positive, which is always easier to hear.

a. "All you ever do is work. I don't even know why you bother coming home. Why don't you pay some attention to your family for a change?"

b. "When you work late into the evening, I feel lonely and ignored by you. I really miss spending time together. Can we schedule some time together this evening?"

Sentence *a* will likely generate a defensive reaction and it doesn't tell the receiver how to solve the problem. Sentence *b* is more likely to create a loving and open response in the receiver by assuring him or her that a few hours of scheduled time that evening would be enough to satisfy the complaint.

Avoid late-night problem solving if possible. Women often complain of difficulty sleeping with an unresolved complaint between them and their partners, but men hate talking late at night when they are tired. They fear the discussion will go on endlessly and insufficient sleep will lead to an unproductive workday the next day. Postpone discussions of a critical nature until the time is right for both of you. If you feel you must speak your peace before going to bed, get your partner's agreement for a time-limited, simple, and direct conversation. It is a myth to think all problems in a marriage can—and should—be solved before going to bed.

Wait for your partner to ask for help. Your partner may ask for advice regarding how to change problematic behavior when you accept who he or she is right now. Create a feeling of safety for your partner, and he or she may come around. Your partner will change problematic behavior if self-motivated, not just in reaction to a complaint. Be patient.

Learn to let some things pass. Your relationship and the quality of your life together will disintegrate if you process every issue and confront every conflict. Talking about every complaint won't resolve every difference. Keep silent sometimes and bite your tongue. Pick your battles carefully since you do not want to win the battle only to lose the war. In other words, learn to just let some things go.

Encourage and notice positive change. When children learn how to walk, we celebrate every clumsy attempt to move on wobbly legs. They soon practice the skill more often to get the applause. Adults need the same positive reinforcement of progress, no matter how small. If you demand a change of your partner and fail to acknowledge any improvement, then your partner will quickly develop a "why bother" attitude when you register your next complaint. He or she will interpret your silence as either not noticing or not caring about the change.

Connecting in Ways that Are Meaningful to Your Partner

The last time you went to the zoo you may have bought a two dollar bag of corn kernels to feed the giraffes. Would you get excited about a bag of corn kernels? Of course not; it's not your food of choice. Yet, to the giraffe, there's nothing better! Imagine that your partner is an animal from another kingdom. He or she may be nurtured, sustained, and excited by very different experiences than you are. The secret to meaningful connection is to know what to put in the paper bag that will get your partner salivating!

Expressing and Feeling Love

If you don't know what makes your partner feel loved, you will automatically demonstrate love in the ways you want to receive love. Because your needs differ, neither of you will get what you are looking for. "If he really loved me, he would tell me more often." "If she really loved me, we would have sex more often." A sentence that begins with, "If my partner really loved me," expresses your need to be loved in a certain way.

You may have resented your partner because he didn't properly appreciate significant efforts of yours to express your love, only to discover that something else you did that took you no time at all was received with great enthusiasm. It is especially painful when efforts to be loving are actually interpreted as unloving behavior. For example:

I couldn't wait to see my husband at the end of a workday. As soon as he pulled in the driveway, I had dinner waiting, and I was eager to talk to him about the day. My husband hurt my feelings when he told me he felt smothered. He preferred for me to delay dinner for an hour so he could check his fantasy team scores and watch ESPN when he got home. How could he love me if he doesn't even look forward to seeing me?

My wife is a great cook. Every night I come home to a gourmet meal. I should be grateful, but I've been trying to lose a few pounds, and it's impossible when she's feeding me all the time. I've tried to tell her that I would prefer simpler meals, but she doesn't really get it. She thinks she is loving me by serving me meals fit for a king—and his entire army!

My husband is Mr. Fix-it. He spends all weekend working around the house. I appreciate being married to such a handyman, but I wish he would spend a little more time with me and less time with his tools and gadgets. If I got as much attention as his hammer, I'd be a lot happier!

Here are four powerful means to express love to your partner in the most effective way:

1. Pay attention to what really works and what doesn't work and give your partner more of what works for him or her.

2. Don't resent or judge your partner for being turned on and off by different experiences than you. No method of receiving nurturance is superior to another.

3. Express love as a daily habit. Don't wait for a good time or pour it on once a month or when you want something. Find a simple way, every day, to let your partner know he or she is loved, appreciated, and cherished.

4. Timing is everything. Sometimes it's not what you do, but when you do it that counts. Connect with your mate on his or her schedule and you'll get better results.

You may be surprised when you discover how your spouse prefers to be loved. Perhaps you feel most loved when your husband makes an effort to connect with you, and your husband feels most loved when you give him space and independence. If you catch yourself thinking, "If my partner really loved me, he or she would know what I need," STOP and do the exercise that follows instead. You will feel more satisfied by telling your partner exactly what you want than by demanding that your partner figure it out alone. Discuss the questions that follow as an opportunity to get to know each other better.

Patty / Ann

CLARIFICATION EXERCISE THREE:
HOW I LIKE TO BE LOVED

Completion time: 10 minutes

Number each of the following expressions of love according to the following scale. Then compare your responses with those of your partner.

1 = That behavior does nothing for me. In fact, it can turn me off.

2 = That behavior is neutral for me—it doesn't hurt, but it doesn't help.

3 = That behavior makes me feel somewhat loved and appreciated.

4 = Most of the time that behavior makes me feel really loved.

5 = That behavior always makes me feel sensational and much closer to you.

- ☐ Written expressions of affection—notes, poems, cards.
- ☐ Receiving a personalized gift, just because you were thinking of me.
- ☐ Receiving a gift for my birthday or our anniversary.
- ☐ Spending private intimate time with me.
- ☐ Giving me a massage or a neck rub.
- ☐ Sex.
- ☐ Creating a special meal.
- ☐ Calling me at work just to say "Hi" or to share something exciting.
- ☐ Telling me that you love me.
- ☐ Being affectionate in public.
- ☐ Confiding in me your deepest feelings and secrets.
- ☐ Telling me all the details of your day, after we've been apart.

☐ Giving me space and privacy when I need it.

☐ Listening to me attentively when I need to talk.

☐ Keeping the household in working order.

☐ Accepting me for who I am and letting me know.

☐ Admiring me and telling me why you love and respect me.

☐ Admiring me and telling others why you love and respect me.

☐ Encouraging me when I am down.

☐ Hugging, cuddling, and other physical expressions of affection.

☐ Surprising me with a secret date or romantic rendezvous.

☐ Offering to help me with household chores or the kids.

☐ Keeping the house clean.

☐ Complimenting me on my appearance.

☐ Forgiving me when I've made a mistake.

☐ Apologizing to me when you've hurt me.

☐ Checking with me before you make plans that will affect me.

☐ Talking about our future together, sharing your dreams.

☐ Other: _____

WORKING WITH AN OPPOSITE

The second section of this chapter, "Working with an Opposite," focuses on the challenge to working partners whose communication styles substantially differ from one another. Though focused on working couples, anyone who lives or works with an "opposite," even within a corporate setting, can benefit from learning how to:

- Communicate effectively when one of you is right-brained and the other is left-brained.

- Keep each other informed and make joint decisions.

- Share work space when your work styles radically differ.

Working Together as Partners

Couples who work together usually have extraordinary communication challenges. They must learn how to manage different communication styles and take advantage of complementary skills, or they can find themselves in divorce or bankruptcy court or both.

If you are a predominantly right-brained individual partnered in business with a primarily left-brained mate, your business team is stronger and more complete, but you'll often need a translator or mediator to communicate.

As you read the following composite of a typical team profile, switch the *he* to *she* or the *she* to *he* to best describe your situation.

He is right-brained. He's the creative one, the visionary, the idea man, the dreamer. He's always in the middle of several projects at once, constantly multi-tasking, and he likes it that way. When you are both at work, he wants to talk, talk, talk. He doesn't pay attention to details. He makes decisions intuitively, not always considering the facts. His highs are high, and his lows are low. He prefers to be spontaneous. Too much planning in his day will drive him nuts. He'll start a project, but if it goes on too long, he'll get bored or discouraged and he is easily distracted.

She is left-brained. She is the analytical one, the anchor that holds down the ship. She keeps the checkbook balanced and makes sure that business decisions are based on the facts. She keeps the office in order and designs routines and systems to organize the day. She loves to plan and often keeps a "to do" list. She brings logical, analytical thought to problem solving. She works best when able to focus on one project at a time and is detail-oriented. She makes sure that a long-term project gets finished. She encourages her husband over the long haul when he gets discouraged and she has the ability to keep a laser focus on the task at hand without being distracted.

The Challenges of Working with an Opposite and How They Can Become Advantages

Making Decisions

The challenge: Right-brainers (RB's) are creative individuals who decide intuitively and are frustrated by left-brainers (LB's) who are analytic in thinking and focused on facts. LB's who decide rationally are often frustrated by their RB partners who make spontaneous, illogical decisions because of a "gut feeling."

The key to successfully working together is clear and consistent communication. This helps couples understand each other's perspective of where the business currently is and where they see it going. Since RB and LB individuals bring such a different orientation and set of skills to the work at hand, failure to consistently check in with each other may, over time, may create a gulf too wide to bridge. Steady communication allow these couples to run the day-to-day operations of their business while simultaneously growing it in a manner which stays true to their long-term vision. This becomes a win-win for the couple and their business since they simultaneously combine the best attributes of both sides of the brain.

The advantage: RB's learn to appreciate the "devil's advocate" position of their LB spouse. LB's come to admire their RB partner's creative ability to promote business growth.

Who Does What

The challenge: Working partners must share decision-making and job responsibilities.

The advantage: Rather than arguing about "who does what better," RB and LB couples usually have very clear and distinct job descriptions, capitalizing on their individual strengths. You have the creative artist and the logistical thinker in the same company—providing countless advantages to ingenuity, vision and strategic planning.

Sharing Work Space

The challenge: RB's and LB's usually disagree about what constitutes the perfect work environment. LB's want privacy, an organized office, and systems to rely on. RB's like someone to talk to, organized chaos, and clutter.

The advantage: If RB's and LB's can work in separate offices and meet throughout the day to converse, each can learn to respect the other's work space and style. Certain aspects of business development and operations lend themselves better to a LB or RB ideal setting. Ideally, you won't share an office. The disorganized desk of the right-brain spouse will drive the left-brain spouse crazy, since they prefer a highly organized, clutter-free, and systematized space.

Meetings

The challenge: RB's would prefer to keep meetings spontaneous, informal, and frequent. LB's like having at least one scheduled meeting a day, or week, with a planned agenda to keep on track.

The advantage: Sound business communication requires both forms of communication. If two RB's pair together, they may neglect planning details. If two LB's pair together, they could lose spontaneous inspiration.

The Seesaw

The challenge: The emotional experience of their partner frustrates or puzzles RB's and LB's. Why is LB making a mountain out of a molehill? Why is RB talking about closing the business down, just because it's been a slow month?

The advantage: RB's and LB's are rarely discouraged at the same time. What triggers one into despair or negativity bounces off of the other, and vice versa. When RB's and LB's move from judgment to compassion, they can lift each other up like partners on a seesaw.

Planning a Work Project Together

The challenge: RB's are impatient and resistant to LB's slower analytical thinking style. They want to plan several projects at once and are often looking five years ahead. LB's prefer to carefully plan one project at a time. LB's may share a dream for five years ahead, but spend meetings talking about the practical details of how to make here and now work.

The advantage: An RB/LB team can handle long-range planning and current details, simultaneously. RB's don't sacrifice visioning and planning for the future for managing day-to-day operations. They encourage progress. LB's keep the company solvent and successful, building a foundation for future growth.

CONCLUSION

Effective communication influences the overall quality of our lives; it impacts our success in business, in our marriage and in all our relationships. The greatest business concept and plan will fail miserably if it is not effectively communicated to clients, employees etc. After all, what is the purpose of a marketing department other than to get the company's message/product effectively communicated? Many companies struggle because they do not know how to effectively communicate their message to their clients. And many marriages fail because the couple has lost the ability to say what they mean and mean what they say—and they fail to be heard. At the deepest level, most daily communication with our intimate partner amounts to, "Do you love me enough?," "Do you accept me completely the way that I am?," and, "Do you trust me?"

Wondering about your communication skills in your relationship?
Take this Communication Quiz by going to
www.relationshiptoolbox.com/communicationquiz.pdf

Patty / Ann

VI
STAYING OUT OF DIVORCE COURT: WHAT'S LOVE GOT TO DO WITH IT?

How You Can Both Win
When Resolving Conflict

> In the beginning of our marriage, my wife and I couldn't decide how many pencils to order without questioning whether we should be married to each other. When I wanted to order office supplies in a smaller quantity than she, she accused me of being cheap. When she bought fresh flowers for the office staff, I complained she was being extravagant. We didn't trust each other and every business decision became a forum for debating whether we should be married, instead of running a business.
>
> *Manufacturing business partners*

> I quit my job in my husband's store for four months, because I was sick of being unappreciated and taken for granted. Once when my husband was mad at me, he told me that no one would ever hire me. So I went and got another job in a week, just to prove him wrong. He apologized when he learned how difficult it was to manage the store without me. Now he's more conscious about expressing appreciation.
>
> *Wife of retail store owner*

Webster's dictionary narrowly defines conflict as "a fight or battle." The word *conflict* may lead you to think of a nasty fight with your spouse, or a mild disagreement over where to eat dinner. I've created this working definition of conflict: *An unresolved, or potentially unresolvable, disagreement between two people or parties that requires some resolution to ease tension, maintain goodwill, and strengthen the relationship.*

Why is there conflict between people, and what leads to it? Dr. Robert Schwebel, clinical psychologist and author, sees marital conflict rooted in a power struggle:

> *Most couples have no idea how to stay close when the going gets rough, and no awareness that it is possible to remain a team and to solve problems together. They lack a vision of cooperatively sharing power. We are thoroughly programmed to compete and to feel comfortable in power-based relationships—one person on top and the other on bottom. We tend to approach conflict as adversaries pitted against one another. We see the world as either I win and you lose, or you win and I lose. Or we hope to sidestep a power struggle by trying to avoid all conflict. In the long run, this eventually leads to even more trouble.*

All couples have conflict and fights; the difference between happy couples, unhappy couples and those that divorce lies in how they fight. Studies of thousands of couples reveal it is not how similar or different you are, it's how you handle differences when they arise that counts. The way in which couples handle disagreement predicts with startling accuracy whether the couple will remain married. In a healthy marriage, a couple views their relationship as a partnership—they are on the same team. In the pursuit of victory, what is good for one team member is good for the entire team. When conflict transforms your relationship from being on the same team and turns it into a competition, the relationship becomes adversarial and perhaps even toxic. You know you are in a toxic marriage if either partner *has* to win an argument at all cost, taking priority over the integrity and intimacy of the relationship. Conflict within a competitive relationship creates a winner and a loser. In a marriage, or a business, if the relationship turns into a competition, a hollow victory is claimed because for one spouse to win, the other spouse has to lose—and therefore, the relationship loses.

Ignored or avoided conflict can also be devastating to a marriage; it acts like carbon monoxide—it is odorless, colorless and silent, yet deadly to your relationship. Mastering conflict resolution skills can protect your marriage as well as your business.

Conflict is an opportunity to develop a deeper more meaningful relationship with your spouse based on the ability to *understand and respect your differences.* If couples were in constant agreement with each other, their relationship would stagnate due to a lack of excitement that stems from a healthy challenge. Conflict handled in a productive, respectful, positive manner provides an opportunity for growth, which eventually strengthens the bond between partners. That doesn't mean you should fight or manufacture conflict to grow closer, but if handled appropriately, conflict potentially allows your relationship to grow through adversity.

This chapter will teach you some simple techniques for preventing and managing conflict, so that you reach win/win resolutions more often than not. These simple techniques are by no means exhaustive of the many conflict resolution techniques and skills couples may employ to keep their relationship a partnership, allowing couples to avoid or settle disputes in a way that allows both of them to feel satisfied. Learning successful conflict resolution skills allows you to face disagreements and differences with respect and confidence so your personal and professional relationships stay strong and healthy. As each conflict is resolved, the relationship matures with the knowledge it can survive, and even thrive, in the face of adversity.

Four Different Kinds of Conflict

Marital and business conflicts fall into four general categories:

1. *Taking responsibility:* Discord that you can mitigate alone by changing your own attitude or behavior.
2. *Preventable conflict:* Tension that is preventable with the help of clear agreements and understandings. (Business draws up contracts to avoid this type of conflict).
3. *Negotiated compromise:* Conflict that requires negotiation to resolve.
4. *Complex conflict:* Arguments that trigger deep emotional wounds, requiring outside help or refined communication skills to resolve.

LET IT BEGIN WITH ME: WHAT YOU—ALONE—CAN DO TO RESOLVE CONFLICT WITH YOUR SPOUSE

Change Your Attitude, Not Your Spouse

We generally seek advice on conflict resolution for spousal transformation—how we can change our partners. We see ourselves as fair and reasonable and them as stubborn and irrational. Have you ever uttered, "If only my partner would...?" We need a great deal of self-discipline and self-awareness to stop pointing fingers and start looking inward at how we contribute to the problem. My practice is full of couples, entrepreneurs and small business owners who come with this agenda: "Please fix my spouse so that we can make this problem go away." Couples express a litany of grievances against their spouse and how they have been wronged. When asked what their contribution to the conflict is, I'm often met with deafening silence. We become so ingrained in seeing ourselves as victims and our partners as the perpetrator, we lose sight that conflict cannot exist within a vacuum; both partners are contributors (albeit willingly or unwillingly) to its development and continuation. Refusing to accept responsibility for conflict puts you in a powerless position to ameliorate it. This lack of personal responsibility contributes to a breakdown in trust and intimacy, which ultimately, if left unchecked, destroys the marital bond.

Rather than fretting over how we can change our partner's behavior, we might ponder how we can alter our attitude so that our partner's behavior no longer troubles us. A simple change in expression such as, "I would prefer if you..." (here you are stating a preference) rather than, "I need you to..." (here you are making more of a demand), can shift a destructive battle to a supportive discussion. The first step in resolving disagreement or tension is to examine how we can shift our own thinking or acting. As is often the case, change begins with a long hard look in the mirror.

Before going further on how to handle conflict it is essential to understand how we handle stress. Why? Because conflict inherently creates stress. The ability to manage stress directly impacts your ability to handle conflict. For effective conflict resolution you must be able to remain calm during stressful situations (whether in your business or your marriage). Difficulty handling stress interferes with your ability to effectively handle conflict in the following ways: it limits your ability to communicate clearly and effectively, to be cognizant of your own feelings, to be aware of your own deep rooted needs, to actively listen so you can hear what someone is *really* saying, and to accurately interpret someone's nonverbal and verbal messages. Remaining calm during stressful situations allows you to be in control of your emotions, rather than being ruled by them. This promotes effective communication in the absence of an intimidating, frightening and/or threatening manner. A demonstration of respect allows conflict to be resolved quicker and without hurtful words and deeds.

Resolving Conflict Through Acceptance and Positive Self-Talk

Sometimes the only resolution to a disagreement is for one of you to accept that the other will not or cannot alter a particular problematic behavior. Repeated confrontation proves only to be a waste of precious time and energy.

Ellen's husband, Steve, works hard during the day. By early evening he's exhausted and often falls asleep by 9:00 P.M.—sometimes in the middle of a conversation. Early in their life together, she felt insulted or angry when he fell asleep during an important discussion or dozed off as they tried to watch a movie together. The only real way for her to resolve the tension this often caused was to accept that Steve was not in conscious control of his fatigue and that he was doing the best he could; he was not intentionally doing anything "to" Ellen.

To change her attitude about Steve's sleep habits, she needed to change her internal monologue, without Steve's involvement at all.

"Should" self-talk: Steve shouldn't be so rude he falls asleep in the middle of an important conversation!

Positive self-talk: Steve is usually a courteous listener. Too bad he's too tired to listen to me now. I'll wait until a better time for him when he is not so exhausted.

"Always/Never" self-talk: Steve always falls asleep when we're watching a movie together. I don't know why we even bother to watch movies together anymore.

Positive self-talk: It's too bad Steve fell asleep. I enjoy watching the movie more when we watch it together.

"Hopeless" self-talk: Man, no matter how much sleep Steve gets, he's always tired. What's he going to be like when he gets old? He'll probably sleep half the day!

Positive self-talk: Maybe we should change the time of day we watch movies together. I will make a mental note to have a conversation with Steve about what works best for both of us, so we can truly enjoy the movie together.

"Character assassination" self-talk: He's just like his father, falling asleep in a chair halfway through the evening.

Positive self-talk: Poor guy does the same thing as his dad. It's hard for him to stay awake at night.

If you note those expressions that you say to yourself when your spouse irritates you, then your hostility might surprise you. No wonder a minor annoyance escalates to a major complaint. Your emotional and physical responses are natural manifestations of your internal thoughts and self-talk.

Changing the way you speak to yourself, especially about something that, as we say, "pushes your buttons" is not easy to do, and yet, if you really make the effort, you'll see real progress, and positive results. Changing our self-talk is a powerful way to change our internal dialogue—tantamount to changing ourselves. Check out this skill-building exercise to help you get a handle on how to influence positive change in your marriage through changing yourself, rather than your partner.

CLARIFICATION EXERCISE ONE: ACCEPTANCE OF DIFFERENCES— CHANGING YOUR SELF-TALK

Use this exercise while thinking about any member of your family or business associate.

- What ongoing conflicts in your life will you best resolve by accepting another person's behavior, rather than trying to change it? (This exercise is not appropriate for physical, sexual, or verbal abuse or violence.)

- Select a current conflict that introduces negative energy into your home or business. Start with annoying behavior—"He leaves the toilet seat up"—not severely problematic behavior— "He comes home at least two hours late all the time." For one week, practice accepting the behavior rather than trying to change it. When your urge to complain or advise arises, jot your inner dialogue down on a piece of paper instead of communicating aloud and directly to the person. Whenever possible, shift from destructive to positive self-talk.

- If you get positive results (more tolerance and less stress), then continue the exercise for another week with the same behavior or a new, more challenging one.

Many of us will recognize the well-known Serenity Prayer: "God grant me the serenity to accept the things that I cannot change, the courage to change the things I can, and the wisdom to know the difference." The prayer does not begin, God grant my husband or wife the ability to change...."

Starting with this week, choose Acceptance over Anger as your theme for communicating with your partner. When you catch yourself slipping into negative self-talk or engaging in a negative interaction with your spouse, repeat the relevant weekly affirmation silently to help you shift your mood. Relationship affirmations change our thinking and attitude towards our partner by focusing on their positive qualities and allowing us to accept them for who they are. If you are looking for an easy way to change your thinking and feelings about your partner and your relationship go to www.relationshiptoolbox.com/cards for a fun card game I created called Relationship Toolbox™ Affirmation Cards.

As mentioned in a previous chapter, neuroscience has taught us if we think negatively, over time we come to only see the negative. The exercise above has the added benefit of facilitating a shift from a negative mindset toward a positive mindset when thinking about your partner. Carol Dweck in her book, *Mindset: The New Psychology of Success*, talks about the difference between a fixed mindset and a growth mindset. A fixed mindset does not change; it is frozen and permanent. A growth mindset is flexible and evolves. In relationships, a fixed mindset gets stuck on revenge; a growth mindset is all about forgiveness.

> *"Mindsets frame the running account that's taking place in people's heads. They guide the whole interpretation process. The fixed mindset creates an internal monologue that is focused on judging: "This means I'm a loser." "This means I'm a better person than they are." This means I'm a bad husband." "This means my partner is selfish."*

> *"People with a growth mindset are also constantly monitoring what's going on, but their internal monologue is not about judging themselves and others in this way. Certainly they're sensitive to positive and negative information, but they're attuned to its implications for learning and constructive action: "What can I learn from this? How can I improve? How can I help my partner do this better?" (Dweck,* Mindset: The New Psychology of Success, *2006).*

The above discussion about mindset is designed to transition a fixed judgmental negative mindset into a growth non-judgmental positive mindset. This will create positive changes in how you view your partner, therefore creating positive changes in your marriage.

Resolving Conflict by Acknowledging Projection

Sometimes changing your inner dialogue isn't enough. Understanding where the dialogue originally came from is most important. Unwarranted criticism of your spouse can signal your judgment of yourself or another significant relationship from your past. Rather than pushing your spouse to change, you can identify and claim responsibility for the true source of tension. Sometimes other family members can help you see the projection(s) you aren't aware of yourself.

> Whenever my husband worked late, I would give him the cold shoulder or whine and complain. I felt guilty for not being more supportive, but I couldn't help being enraged with him. One day my sister pointed out to me that my dad, also an entrepreneur, was absent all the time too when we were growing up. Then it all made sense. I wasn't just furious with my husband—I was also angry with my dad for not being around when I was a child.
>
> *Supportive spouse of an international businessman*

> When my wife decided to start her own business, I thought it was going to be a little part-time thing that would bring in some extra cash and keep her busy. After a year she was suddenly running a big business. I started finding fault with everything about her and her company. Our marriage counselor pointed out to me that I was projecting onto my wife anger toward myself for not achieving my own goals. I got back to work on my own career and started feeling better about myself—and my wife—again.
>
> *Supportive husband of clothing manufacturer*

If you acknowledge your own projected anger, then your partner will likely work *with* you instead of against you. An apology for any undeserved hostility and discussion of its roots puts blame where you can address it more effectively—with yourself and not on your spouse! Often a relationship expert must help you through deep-seated projection. Projections also occur when we cannot or will not acknowledge unacceptable behavior or actions in ourselves that we blame or accuse our partner for demonstrating. When we have a strong negative reaction, or over-reaction to our partner's behavior, it is usually the result of a projection. We are projecting onto our partner feelings about our own unresolved issue(s) that we resist seeing in ourselves because we find them so unacceptable and painful. The greater the denial of the issue, the stronger the projection and the more difficult it is to resolve the issue in our marriage. We unconsciously and falsely believe it is easier for us to avoid our issues and project them onto our partner. When this occurs, professional help is recommended since we are all blind to our deep-seated projections—and we all have them.

Eliminating Trigger Points

All couples know how to press their partners "trigger points and hot buttons." Whatever name you want to use, we are all guilty of doing so from time to time. Greg knows how to make his wife Amy angry at him. Whenever Greg asks his wife to try to be on-time for their social engagements, Amy rolls her eyes to heaven and says, "Aye, aye sir," in an obnoxious manner, suggesting that he is bossing her around and giving her orders once again. Amy gets annoyed and feels spoken down to; Greg gets annoyed believing he is making a reasonable request. In this example, both husband and wife press each other's trigger points in a situation where a simple request, in fact, is trying to be communicated.

All of us discover our trigger points or hot buttons when a simple expression or behavior of our spouse hurts or enrages us in seconds. We may even use our partner's hot spots to punish or control when we feel vulnerable.

The cost of exploiting your spouse's vulnerability is lost intimacy and trust in the relationship. Eliminate the charged expressions and behaviors that hurt or annoy your spouse, and ask that your spouse do the same for you. In his research with married couples, Dr. John Gottman discovered that you need at least five times as many positive as negative moments together to stabilize your marriage (Gottman, *Why Marriages Succeed or Fail*). The following exercise helps eliminate such negative expressions and erosive habits.

Patty / Ann

CLARIFICATION EXERCISE TWO: ELIMINATING NEGATIVE BEHAVIORS THAT TRIGGER YOUR SPOUSE

Completion time: 15 minutes

The twenty expressions or behaviors below seem to have universal negative impact on communication. Here's how to use this exercise to help eliminate them.

1. Scan the list with your partner. Using a scale of 1 to 5, where 1=almost never and 5=frequently, first score your perception of how frequently you use these expressions or behaviors with your partner. Then score how often your partner uses these expressions or behaviors with you. Remember, you are rating your perception of the frequency, not taking an accurate count. If a particular behavior is a big problem for you, you may score its frequency higher than it actually occurs. Don't waste time arguing with your partner over frequency. For this exercise, perception is reality.

2. Using a scale of 1 to 5, where 1="no big deal" and 5="drives me crazy," rate how bothersome the behavior is for you.

3. Offer to eliminate or reduce for your partner any behaviors of yours that are a 3 or higher on his or her scale. Ask your partner to eliminate any of his or her behaviors that rank a 3 or higher for you.

4. Practice! You and your partner probably won't change these habits overnight. With due diligence, you can stop triggering your partner and decrease explosive conflict.

1 "No big deal"	2	3	4 "Drives me crazy" 5

Expressions and behaviors:	Frequency Score	Bothersome Score
1. Rolling eyes and saying "Yes, Dear" in an annoyed tone of voice when your partner makes a request.		
2. Yelling, using sarcasm, insults, or name-calling: "You selfish jerk!"		
3. Interrupting, not listening, eyes wandering, cutting off conversation.		
4. Mind reading, speaking for your partner, making assumptions about what your partner thinks or feels: "You're mad at me because…"		
5. Offering excuses, explanations, and defensiveness in response to complaints: "I'm late because of traffic—it's not my fault."		
6. Responding to criticism by changing the subject—"Well you do (fill in the blank), so my behavior isn't so bad."		
7. Using "always/never," exaggerating, blowing trivial issues out of proportion.		
8. Making vague general complaints instead of specifics: "You never help around here." "You always get in the way."		
9. Using character assassination instead of speaking directly about the behavior: "You are a (fill in the blank), just like your father."		
10. Threatening to exit the relationship, expressing hopelessness about the future.		
11. Agreeing to a compromise or solution, but then not following through.		

| 1 "No big deal" | 2 | 3 | 4 "Drives me crazy" 5 |

Expressions and behaviors:	Frequency Score	Bothersome Score
12. Asking questions instead of making statements—"Haven't we talked long enough?"		
13. Apologizing insincerely or refusing to apologize.		
14. Picking a fight at a bad time, when your partner is tired, distracted, depressed, overwhelmed, or angry—and you know it.		
15. Running on and on, overwhelming your partner with long-winded complaints.		
16. Digging up ancient history or a past issue that you didn't resolve.		
17. Leaving the room, the house, the restaurant, hanging up the phone, or abruptly ending the conversation when it gets uncomfortable for you.		
18. Complaining about and embarrassing your partner in front of other people.		
19. Using the expressions, "You should," or "You have to."		
20. Using the expression, "You make me feel (fill in the blank)."		

Add to this list any particular expressions or behaviors that you or your spouse engages in that irritate or trigger hot buttons in the other.

Releasing Negative Feelings and Returning to a Loving Space: The Love Letter Technique

No one, except perhaps our parents, can distress us as deeply as our spouses. The price we pay for intimacy is vulnerability. Our partners can hurt us deeply because we intentionally let our guard down and invite them closer than anyone else to us. If you want an emotionally-connected marriage, then your spouse will hurt you at times. Harville Hendrix believes that marriage is all about just that—the opportunity to heal old childhood wounds by working through the same wounding with our mates.

John Gray offers a technique called "The Love Letter" for returning to a loving space after you and your spouse argue (for more detail see Gray, *Men Are from Mars, Women Are from Venus*).

The Love Letter exercise has three parts and you can do one, two, or all three by yourself.

1. Write a love letter to your mate expressing your feelings of anger, sadness, fear, regret, and love.
2. Write a response letter expressing what you want to hear from your partner (optional).
3. Share your love letter and response letter with your partner (optional).

Address the letter to your partner, starting with your negative feelings and ending with loving ones, which rekindle by writing the letter. I recommend the love letter technique as a method for releasing angry, resentful, or fearful feelings, so that you can resume your conversation later, when you are calmer and emotionally centered. Barbara and Scott had a vile fight the Friday before Mother's Day while taking a walk.

Barbara: *So what are your plans for this weekend?* (They often discuss their plans for the weekend during their Friday morning walks, but Scott's mom had just moved into town so Barbara was testing him to see if he planned to spend Mother's Day with her or his mom).

Scott: *I'm going to spend Saturday going through all the paperwork piled high on my desk and then Sunday I'm going to visit my mom. I'm going to take her to lunch. What plans do you have in mind?* (Scott's use of the expression: "I'm going to" sounds like he's made firm plans without consulting Barbara.)

Barbara: *I have two problems with what you just said. One, your decision to spend Saturday going through paperwork means that I'm stuck taking care of the kids all by myself all day long. You didn't even bother to ask if that would work for me.* (Barbara feels taken for granted.) *Two, I'm also feeling disappointed that you didn't mention any plans to celebrate Mother's Day with me, only your mother.* (Barbara assumes that Scott has forgotten all about her and is focused on his mom now that she lives in town. Barbara feels hurt and rejected).

Scott rolls his eyes and groans. They walk separately around the golf course for awhile and when they return home Barbara asks Scott what's wrong. He reluctantly tells her what's on his mind.

Scott: *How can you not understand that my mom's health is failing and she is not getting any younger (she is 91)? I am not sure how many more years she will be around for me to spend Mother's Day with her.* (Scott is suggesting he cannot believe Barbara does not appreciate his mom's age and that he is worried about her declining health. He has a problem with his wife's insensitivity to his mother's situation. He is planning on buying his wife a card—isn't that good enough for her? What does she want from me?)

Barbara: (Scott's assumptions about what Barbara wants is inaccurate and she attempts to set him straight.) *I don't have a problem with that. I'm not asking that you spend a lot of time with me. I just felt disappointed that you didn't mention anything about celebrating Mother's Day with me when I asked you about the weekend.* (She felt as if she didn't matter when he made his weekend plans. She wanted some reassurance and some recognition.)

Scott: *We're just different about the way we treat holidays. You feel entitled to recognition, but when I have a birthday or it's Father's Day, I don't have any expectations.* (Her expectations make him feel controlled and frustrated. She should be open to whatever he may do this weekend for Mother's Day. If it's enough to make her happy, great. If it's not, too bad.)

Barbara: (Now she defends herself against his negative judgment.) *Just because I said I was feeling disappointed doesn't mean I feel entitled to a big deal on Mother's Day. A card and a gift, or even something as simple as bringing me coffee in bed, would have been fine. Now I don't want anything at all, not if it's coming from such a negative place.* (That's not true, she still wants him to recognize and appreciate her, but she doesn't want to beg for it. She wants him to give her his time or a gift because he loves her, not from obligation or because she told him to.)

This fight continued for another 20 minutes, with no resolution and a great deal of distance between them. Barbara went upstairs and cried. Scott ate his breakfast and went off to work feeling angry and frustrated. I suggested that Barbara try Dr. Gray's Love Letter technique during the day to calm herself while Scott was at work.

Dear Scott:

I am writing this letter to share my feelings with you.

Anger:

I don't like it when you make plans to work in the office on the weekend and I am stuck home to take care of the kids all by myself like I do during the weekdays.

I feel frustrated that the fight escalated this morning and now we're so distant.

I am angry that you think I am unempathic to your situation and your mom's age since I know you're really sensitive about anything having to do with your mom. You know I love your mom too.

I feel annoyed that you didn't simply hear my feelings of disappointment and apologize.

I want you to give me a hug, apologize, and tell me that you love me.

Sadness:

I feel disappointed that you didn't mention celebrating Mother's Day with me this weekend.

I am sad that you went off to work feeling angry and we are distant from each other now.

I feel hurt that you think of giving me a gift as an obligation, rather than a desire.

I wanted to have a special Mother's Day celebration. *I want you* and me to be back together again tonight.

Fear:

I feel worried that it will take us awhile to recover from this fight.

I am afraid that you think less of me because I want you to remember and acknowledge me.

I feel scared when we escalate so quickly into a fight.

I do not want you to give me anything out of duty or resentful obligation.

I need to know that you still love me.

I want you and me to make up.

Regret:

I feel embarrassed that I overreacted this morning. I should have trusted you.

I am sorry that I set you up from the beginning by asking you about the weekend, rather than just telling you that I hoped we would celebrate Mother's Day together.

I feel ashamed that I need so much reassurance and recognition.

I didn't want my telling you my feelings to turn into a fight.

I want you to forgive me.

Love:

I love you.

I want to trust you more.

I understand that you are doing the best you can with our busy schedule and that you are worried about your mom.

I forgive you for not mentioning me on Mother's Day and for accusing me of feeling entitled and unempathic.

I appreciate all the ways you show me that you love me.

I thank you for being the kind of guy who makes me one of your highest priorities.

I know that we will get over this and feel emotionally connected again and I hope it is soon.

I love you,

Barbara

P.S. The response I would like to hear from you includes a hug, a genuine apology for hurting me, acceptance of my need for you to recognize me, and your forgiveness, so that we can return to intimacy.

Barbara left this letter on Scott's pillow. When he read it before going to sleep, they hugged, and talked calmly about how they misunderstood one another that morning. The letter broke the ice, allowing them to let go of any resentment that was created and apologize with sincerity—reconfirming their bond of love, respect and intimacy to each other.

Getting Angry at the Problem, Not Your Spouse

Couples who thrive through the rigors of entrepreneurial life don't stay angry with one another for long. Whether working together in the same business, or partnering to manage the demands of family and self-employment, you need to resolve conflicts quickly. It isn't just the marriage that is at stake, but the health of the business as well. One of the simplest and most powerful shifts you can make as a couple is to focus your anger and frustration on the problems at hand, rather than each other. A small change of words can divert you from a nasty fight.

> My husband was explaining to me why he would have difficulty collecting his expected fee from a client. I felt upset when I heard we probably wouldn't see the money we were expecting. Rather than reflexively blaming him ("Why can't you...?"), I expressed in frustration, "God, I hate your business. First it's so difficult to get clients. Then when you finally get them, it's still hard to get paid." He just laughed and said, "I don't blame you for feeling that way." He didn't get defensive because I didn't attack him as the problem. I joined his side and empathized with how hard it was for him to collect the money he earned for his efforts.
>
> *Supportive spouse of struggling business consultant*

Under stressful circumstances, projecting our frustrations and anger on our spouse is easier but more destructive than directing the energy toward the problem itself. Watch for the pattern. If you find yourself growing hostile toward your spouse, ask yourself whether he or she deserves it. Would your anger energize you more productively if directed toward solving the problem or supporting your spouse in problem solving? Healthy conflict resolution is focused on solving the conflict not placing blame on your spouse for creating it.

PREVENTING CONFLICT: STRATEGIES YOU CAN DO TOGETHER

While you can do plenty to prevent or mitigate conflict without even interacting with your spouse, sometimes involving your spouse is critical to tackling a joint problem.

Preventing Conflict by Joining the Same Team

Many arguments escalate when a man invalidates a woman's feelings and when a woman responds to a man disapprovingly. A conflict escalates quickly from problem-solving to counterattacking when you start blaming each other, rather than joining forces to address a mutual problem. When you both cooperate, rather than try to win the argument, you will likely find a mutually satisfying solution. Which one of the following statements is more likely to solve a problem?

Husband: *You're always working and you're neglecting your family. Your job is more important to you than the kids or me.* (Attack)

Wife: *That's not true! You're just angry because I'm not here to wait on you hand and foot anymore. I'm not your maid!* (Defense)

or

Husband: *When you work so many hours the kids and I miss you.* (I statement)

Wife: *I miss you guys too. How can we find a way to spend more time together?* (Joint problem solving)

These couples solved stubborn problems by creatively implementing a joint solution, instead of continuing the blame/attack syndrome.

> I tried helping my husband in his store on weeknights and weekends after my full-time job. It drove me nuts trying to straighten out his office and the paperwork. I tried to convince him that if he kept his office organized he would be able to work fewer hours and be home more with the kids and me. He didn't see it that way. After six months, we knew we had to get me out of the store if we were going to stay married. We hired him a bookkeeper and payroll service to replace me. It was more expensive, but worth it!
>
> *Supportive spouse of store owner*

> My husband and I are business partners. I am always on time for my appointments but my husband prefers to be spontaneous and is always running late. Now we take separate cars even if we're going to the same event. He gets there when he gets there and I don't worry about him being late anymore—except when we need to go to the airport together!
>
> *Dog grooming business owner*

Preventing Conflict Through Clarifying Expectations

You enter your marriage and business with expectations of how people should treat you, based upon your upbringing, life experience, cultural and religious influences, media exposure, and other people's opinions. Some expectations of your spouse are clear and unquestioned, like fidelity or physical safety, but some are not clear until you discover how the wants and needs of each of you clash. Sharing your expectations makes for effective problem-solving, because you understand your starting point. These expectations couples had of each other, drawn from my research, could create conflict if not verbalized and agreed to ahead of time.

Bedtime

When I married my husband, I expected us to go to bed together every night. My husband expected the freedom to go to sleep whenever he felt tired. Often that was a few hours before me. I felt abandoned and lonely when we went to sleep separately, and my husband was resentful when he felt obliged to conform to my schedule for going to bed together.

Newlywed married to a real estate salesperson

Time and Intimacy

My husband and I have different ideas about balance. For me, if I work for three months, seven days a week, sixteen hours a day, and then we take a break and go to Australia for a month—that's balance. Balance doesn't have to be an everyday thing.

Author

Decision-Making

When I was growing up, my dad made all the major decisions for the family. My husband was raised in the same kind of family. I warned him that if he wants a silent sheep, like his mother or mine, he's marrying the wrong lady. I have my opinions, and I expect him to consider them.

Entrepreneur, running a business in the six-figures

Financial Goals

My husband had a small, established business when we married. I saw the business as an unpolished gem and planned to help him build the business to great success. I expected him to welcome my assistance. When he never implemented any of my ideas, I discovered we didn't have the same financial goals at all. Free time to play golf and tennis is more important to him than making money. I realized that if I wanted to make some money, I was better off starting my own business!

Home-based baking entrepreneur

Privacy

I had been living alone for seven years when my boyfriend moved in with me. Every morning when I was getting ready for work, he would watch me get dressed and put on my makeup. When I requested that he give me more privacy, he took it personally.

Female entrepreneur in her fifties

The extent of your dissatisfaction in a relationship can often be tied directly to unrealistic expectations along with expectations not being met. We often feel that our partner should somehow know exactly what we expect of him or her, and how to meet it, but this kind of mindreading gets a lot of couples in trouble. Here's an exercise you can do together that will help you avoid this trap.

Patty / Ann

CLARIFICATION EXERCISE THREE: CLARIFY YOUR EXPECTATIONS OF YOUR PARTNER

Completion time: 30 minutes

Record expectations of your partner which you have not yet verbalized. Your entries can be major expectations, like fidelity, or even small ones, like knocking on the bathroom door before entering, since the minor issues sometimes spark the biggest battles.

Write this sentence ten times, and complete it:

I expect that you will...

Examples: call if you are going to be late, spend Sunday with the family, stay monogamous when you are traveling, come home for dinner every night.

Write this sentence ten times, and complete it:

I expect that you will *not...*

Examples: criticize me in front of our employees, read my journal, go out with the boys on Friday nights, talk to your friends about our sex life, spend money we don't have.

Initial and sign off on the expectations to which you each agree 100 percent.

If your partner expects more than you can fulfill, use the skills that you've learned in this chapter to reach a mutually acceptable agreement. Many couples hold false expectations for their partners. These exercises should help couples avoid disappointment due to false expectations. Differing expectations once acknowledged do not necessarily lend themselves to mutual agreement; in these circumstances spouse's should accommodate by planning accordingly so they do not strain your marriage. For example, I have worked with an entrepreneurial couple whose wife is punctual for appointments and whose husband is usually late. After years of futile attempts from the wife to expect promptness from her husband, I suggested she accept her husband's tardiness not as anything being done to her, but as his issue. I further recommended she make the appropriate accommodation by taking her own car to functions and appointments. It was not the wife's preference to take two cars everywhere but it was the only way she could successfully come to terms with their differing expectations and still maintain intimacy in her marriage.

Preventing Conflict Through Clarifying Roles and Responsibilities

Most people need clearly defined roles, responsibilities, and areas of authority to minimize conflict and manage demanding businesses and family life. Couples may designate roles according to several different criteria:

- We each do what we are best at, at home and at work.

- I earn the money and my husband tends to all the details at home.

- We work different shifts so that we can share child-rearing equally.

- I handle my business, and my spouse takes care of hers. We share all family decisions equally.

- I manage the people end of the business and my spouse supervises operations.

- I act as a sounding board for my life partner, offering advice or emotional support.

It's advisable to delineate scopes of responsibility at home as well. List everything required weekly to keep your home neat and clean enough to meet both of your minimum standards—then divide the list in a fair and equal way.

> After years of fighting about how to divide household responsibilities fairly, we finally made enough money in our business to hire a full-time housekeeper and nanny. That's one of the best rewards we've received from working this hard to become successful.
>
> *President of multimillion-dollar company*

Job Descriptions

Corporations use job descriptions to clarify the company's expectations of employees. Job descriptions can get outdated quickly, encompass many unexpected tasks under "other duties as assigned," or prevent a willing employee from exceeding the basic requirements. Nonetheless, job descriptions provide good general outlines, so that both the supervisor and employee understand what the employer wants the employee to do, and how employees should interact with each other.

When we marry, or make a lifetime commitment, we implicitly agree to a loose job description called "husband" or "wife," or the equivalent thereof. If we work together as well, then we agree to "business partner or associate." The job description you imagine you have may differ from the one your partner expects of you. Significantly reduce both domestic and office tensions by forming a shared understanding of your roles and responsibilities at home and at work.

Joanne was raised in a home where her father was a firefighter. When working he would be away for three consecutive days and nights and then home for four straight days and nights. While home, Joanne's father cooked all the family meals and helped with household chores. When Joanne married her husband, Brian, she expected he would cook meals and help out with chores when he was home too. Fireworks erupted between this couple because Brian assumed no such thing. He wanted to spend his evenings and weekends relaxing after a stressful week of fourteen-hour-long days. Although many couples resist my suggestion to write up a job description listing roles and responsibilities for each partner, and then revisiting it when circumstances change, such as the birth of a child, etc., fights similar to the ones Joanne and Brian endured are easily avoided if clear responsibilities, roles and expectations between spouses are written down.

CLARIFICATION EXERCISE FOUR: DEFINE AREAS OF RESPONSIBILITIES THROUGH A JOB DESCRIPTION

Completion time: 30-60 minutes

The exercises below will help you avoid conflict by facilitating a well-written, carefully-orchestrated job description of roles and responsibility for each spouse.

If you work or plan to work together, write a job title and description for each of you that clearly defines intended job responsibilities. Your title might be more traditional (head of operations) or innovative (office mover-and-shaker or wife-in-chief). You might divide responsibilities by functions, expertise, working shift, products/services, client needs, or site of activity, in or outside the office. If your business has identical or interchangeable roles for each of you, then write one job description and add details where relevant.

For example: Each spouse is a musician who writes song lyrics. Karen's love is pop music and hip hop and Gary's love is classical music. In this situation both spouses are musicians but with different specialties. Therefore, Karen and Gary refer clients to each other according to their individual specialties.

If you are in the process of deciding whether to partner in business with your spouse or life partner, create a help-wanted advertisement and a job description of the ideal business partner. The written word acts as a much more powerful tool than a mere thought or idea. A written job description will help you decide objectively how your partner's skills and experience measure up to what you are looking for.

If you live together, create a job summary that clearly defines your separate duties at home.

You can detail your own job description as much or as little as you please, but plan to review and revise it at least once or twice a year or with the addition of children, pets, or any circumstance(s) which requires physical and emotional care or time and effort on your part, or your spouse's. If appropriate, create a job description for your kids, nanny, virtual assistants or any other person who shares the requisite tasks for running a profitable business and an efficient household. You'll quickly discover that events like the birth of a child, a relocation, or a financial setback all affect your roles at home and office dramatically.

Imagine playing a baseball game without an umpire who has the authority to call the plays. When you assign responsibilities, you determine how and when to share decisions, and where to draw boundaries of authority. Setting decision-making guidelines with your spouse ahead of time prevents daily and long-term conflict.

> In the beginning I would give a customer a refund and after the customer left the store my husband would complain I was giving away the store. We never argued in front of a customer, but you should have heard us in the back room! We finally got tired of fighting with each other. Twenty years ago we decided I take care of the customers and he takes care of the merchandise, and its still that way. We stay out of each other's hair.
>
> *Co-owners of a retail store for twenty five years*

Set the stage for productive negotiation and problem-solving by agreeing to the boundaries that will help guide your daily decisions. Each couple creates its own unique arrangement regarding who holds the authority to be the decision maker in a marriage. Authority in a marriage is influenced by many variables: cultural, religious, socio-economic, education, situational, etc. In modern society it is rare for one partner to "be the boss" and hold authority over all decisions made in one's marriage. Even the most geographically remote and patriarchal societies such as those found in some African and Middle Eastern countries have seen patriarchal authority shift due to the influence created by the internet and its ensuing ability to view socio-cultural norms different from your own.

Ideally, a healthy marriage and business sees authority shift between spouses and employees predicated upon specific areas of strengths, skills and interests. I made most of the academic decisions for our four children since I was the one who had the most consistent day-to-day, hands-on experience with our children's schools and teachers. Mitch made the investment decisions (although I was fully aware of them) since this was his expertise and I explicitly trust him.

The bottom line is every person has areas of strength and talent that are uniquely theirs. Any relationship that is to thrive, whether it be an intimate or business one, would be remiss not to tap into these areas of strength to capitalize on them for decision-making purposes. Managers who micro-manage kill creativity and innovation in their companies. Spouses who deny their partners' authority in an area of expertise kill respect and intimacy—creating resentment within the marriage.

Patty / Ann

CLARIFICATION EXERCISE FIVE: DECISION-MAKING AUTHORITY

Completion time: 15 minutes

The exercises below will reveal who has the authority to make decisions in your marriage (and your business too).

With your spouse, review the following methods for designating authority over decision-making in your marriage and business. Do your business rules differ from your marriage ones? Which of the following examples suit you the best for now?

- I am the decision-maker, and my partner is the follower. My partner relies on me to lead the way and trusts my judgment entirely.

- We don't operate with any set rules. The one who feels stronger makes the call. We fight only when we both feel really strongly about a decision. It evens out over time.

- We make major decisions that affect the whole company (or family) jointly by consensus. Otherwise, we make individual decisions for our agreed-upon areas of responsibility.

- We make virtually all business and home decisions together, striving for consensus every time.

- I decide everything for my business, and my partner decides everything for his (hers). We make most of our home decisions jointly.

- Our decisions in the business are collaborative, but since my mate knows so much more about the business than I do, his (her) voice is still the louder.

- Our business differs from our marriage. In our marriage, we decide everything as equals. In business, one of us is the employer and the other is an employee. The business owner takes full responsibility and makes all final decisions for the business, while respecting his/her partner's contribution to the process.

- In a tie or stalemate in a business decision, one of us is the tiebreaker. The other is the tiebreaker at home.

- Other: _____

Summarize with your partner your current perception of how you will ideally make decisions at home and at work. What changes need to happen from the way you make decisions today? The more detailed your agreements about how decisions should be made and what needs to change to support those agreements, the less confusion later on, but a simple statement of general understanding will do for many couples. Review this statement periodically as your marriage and your business evolve.

Conflict Resolved Through Negotiation Agreement

Later we will explore how to resolve conflict when one or both of you is too upset for a calm discussion. Now, we will focus on how to communicate effectively when you both are relatively calm and peaceful and need to resolve a difference of opinion. Effective communication is the most important relationship tool needed for conflict resolution in your marriage and your business. Reaching a satisfactory compromise in a productive way requires negotiation skills that accommodate both your needs—a win/win outcome.

You can tell if the discussion satisfies both of you. Even if you didn't get exactly what you requested initially, you both feel good about your exchange and closer to each other, with no negative residue or underlying resentment.

For many, the word compromise conjures up the unpleasant image of two people haggling for days and meeting somewhere between their needs, where neither person feels satisfied. The process can be so painful, the parties are simply relieved to be done. Sometimes compromise means that "I get my way now and you'll get yours later. We trade off." That works occasionally, but not in the long run because one of you is unhappy half the time. Secretly you keep score, and your partnership starts feeling like a competition.

Focus on Interests, Not Positions

The most appealing version of compromise is discovering a brand-new solution, better than what each originally sought and more satisfying to both. To reach such innovation, try what Fisher and Ury suggest in their bestseller, *Getting to Yes: Negotiating Agreement Without Giving In*—focus on interests, not positions. It is also imperative to honestly reveal differing positions as soon as possible before the conflict escalates to create resentment between spouses.

Most of us bargain with our spouses over positions, defending and arguing our points of view against attack and insisting upon the validity of our position, not theirs. It's a win/lose proposition. Even if we "win" the argument, we lose something more meaningful and precious: an intimate and loving relationship. If our partner concedes by sacrifice and deprivation, the conflict often recurs in another more noxious form. A bittersweet victory indeed—a true example of winning the battle only to lose the war.

Focus on the mutual interests behind your respective conflicting positions. Often we convince ourselves that our position is the only way to address our underlying interest. Not true! Usually several alternatives can satisfy you if you fully recognize your deepest concerns. You may discover shared, compatible, and even complementary interests behind seeming polarities. This fosters an understanding of your partner's position, even if you are not in agreement with them, increasing one's willingness to compromise.

This strategy works for Susie and Frieda, gay partners who operate a Midwestern floral shop together. Susie is the accountant and operations manager. Frieda is the floral designer.

Susie's position: "We've got to watch the bottom line. That means we can't keep giving away extra flowers in each assortment just to make them look better."

Frieda's position: "Our customers return to us because they know that we give them the best assortment possible. We shouldn't sacrifice quality and beauty just to save a few bucks."

Can you see how Susie and Frieda could argue these positions endlessly, without resolution? What interest lies behind each position?

Susie's is profitable business, and Frieda's is happy customers and high-quality product.

Their positions seem different, but both want happy customers and high-quality merchandise so they can have a profitable business. Susie and Frieda can step to the same side of the problem and plan together how to achieve their shared goal. Perhaps they can raise prices, charge extra for special arrangements, cut operation costs to afford extra flowers in each arrangement, or seek a better price on wholesale flowers. They can consider several alternatives to meet both of their interests, instead of bickering over seemingly incompatible positions.

Considering Several Alternatives

We can quickly lock into narrow, one-option thinking. Have you ever presented an exciting idea to your spouse or colleague, and he or she doesn't see the genius in it? Rather than looking for other options or listening to reasons why the idea won't work, you defend your suggestion and insist that you are right and he or she is wrong. Your original idea twists into a demand, which your partner hears as, "You jerk, anyone with intelligence would do this my way!" Naturally your partner defends him or herself and loses sight of shared interests.

The following ineffective dialogue between Diane and her husband Roger intensified into an argument. Look at how it might have turned out differently if they had both paid attention to shared interests:

Diane: *Let's go away for the weekend to a romantic bed and breakfast in Maine. We could really use the break from working and taking care of the kids.*

Roger: *I don't think that will work for me. I've got too much to do around here. The idea of driving five hours up and back in one weekend doesn't thrill me.*

Diane: *You've always got too much to do, and besides, five hours is no big deal. You like to drive in the mountains.* (He hears her saying that she is smarter about what he needs than he is.)

Roger: *My idea of relaxation isn't spending ten hours driving in a car. I'd rather relax here with you at home.* (Defending his position but still open to some intimate time.)

Diane: *Sure, that's what you say, but I know how it will be. You'll get distracted by all the things on your to-do list, and we won't spend any time relaxing together at all.* (Still maintaining that her original suggestion is a good one by making him wrong for his concerns.)

Roger: *That's not true! Last weekend we stayed here and we spent a whole evening together.* (Feeling exasperated—"Will he ever be able to satisfy this woman?")

Diane: *Going out for dinner is hardly the same thing as going away for an entire weekend. I want to get away for an entire weekend with you.* (She sees no other acceptable options other than the one she originally presented. If they don't go to Maine, she'll be unhappy.)

This dialogue spins further away from satisfying Diane's initial goal of spending romantic time away with Roger. She actually creates the opposite effect of her intention, argument instead of intimacy. Had Diane changed her response to Roger's initial resistance, the dialogue might have been as follows:

Version Two: Recognizing Shared Interests

Diane: *Let's go away for the weekend to a romantic bed and breakfast in Maine. We could really use the break from working and taking care of the kids.*

Roger: *I don't think that will work for me. I've got too much to do around here. The idea of driving five hours up and back in one weekend doesn't thrill me.*

Diane: *I can understand why you'd feel that way after commuting such a long distance to work each day. I know you're concerned about getting the house packed for our move. Can you think of any other way we could spend some romantic getaway time that would work for you? I really miss you.* (Focusing on her underlying interest—intimate time with her husband—rather than insisting on her original position.)

Roger: *I'd like to spend time together, but I'd rather relax here with you at home. That way we wouldn't have to spend half the weekend in the car. How about if we plan on all day Sunday together?* (Open to romantic time together, but not an entire weekend.)

Diane: *Maybe we can drive just an hour or two away and spend Sunday at the beach. I'd really like to get away, even if it's just for a day.* (Restating her interest but showing openness to another alternative.)

Roger: *If we spend Sunday together, is it OK with you if I work down in the basement on Saturday night, instead of going out for our regular Saturday night date? I'm really concerned about getting the basement packed up in time for our move.* (Negotiating so that he also cares for his interest in getting his work done.)

Diane: *Sure, I'll plan on getting some writing done too. That sounds like a good compromise. We'll have some time away together and be able to finish some work too.*

With version two, both partner's interests were satisfied. Even though Roger turned down Diane's original idea, their final solution still met each individual's primary need. Going to Maine wasn't Diane's actual need, just a means to the real need for intimate time with her husband. Keeping the primary desire in mind is key to negotiating beyond positions to the underlying interests.

Some couples are incredibly compatible sharing most of their passions and interests. These couples seem to do almost everything together and might be referred to as enmeshed with each other. Other couples appear to share few, if any interests, and do very little, if any activities together and may appear totally incompatible; if you ask these couples, however, they will state they are perfectly fine with being compatible only in the raising of their children. Other couples seem to share some interests and not others—which is the case for the majority of relationships. These couples are interdependent in how they relate to each other.

There is no mandate for couple compatibility. The goal is to be happy and content with your degree of compatibility and not fight about areas of incompatibility. Incompatibility in some areas of a marriage are not a problem if the couple acknowledges and comes to terms with them. For example, Joe loves to go ice climbing and does so with his buddies once a week annually; his wife Joan has no interest in this hobby and spends the weeks her husband ice climbs at a beach resort with her girlfriends—a win-win for this couple.

Patty / Ann

CLARIFICATION EXERCISE SIX: FINDING YOUR COMPATIBLE INTERESTS

Completion time: 30 minutes

This exercise can be done with your spouse, or any family member or coworker. Select a current scenario of incompatibilities, from any place in your work or family life. Write down your individual positions on a piece of paper. Separately, write down the immediate interest behind your stance. Then dig deeper for an interest behind the first. Keep digging until you find the core need or desire driving your overt request. Compare notes with your spouse or whoever you are joining with to do the exercise. Where are you compatible? Identify and write down a joint solution that meets both of your underlying interests when you find one. Repeat this exercise whenever you must negotiate a solution to seemingly incompatible positions.

Complex Conflicts: When Business And Personal Conflicts Merge

If only all conflict were simple enough to handle with straightforward negotiation and agreement upon compromise. Throughout your entrepreneurial journey, you will struggle to resolve complex issues in your relationship that require greater communication skill and technique, and sheer endurance. Such is the work of all married or long-term committed partnerships.

Complex conflicts are rooted in deep personal and emotional issues which act as barriers for the resolution of the conflict. Complex conflicts can occur in all relationships and produce the same effect if left unresolved: the demise of intimacy in the relationship and/or the demise of a project or a company (if a business). For entrepreneurs, unresolved complex conflicts from home can spill over into work, leaving critical business decisions unresolved due to home issues, potentially costing the loss of a significant amount of business revenue. In complex conflict, family issues tangle with business ones nonproductively and communication grows adversarial. Since many complex conflicts grow out of unresolved simple conflicts, the best way to avoid complex conflicts is to handle and resolve simple conflicts as soon as they appear on the horizon. Unresolved complex conflict leaves a couple fighting about an issue—which is not really the issue at all—rendering it impossible to reach a healthy conflict resolution.

Here is a classic example of complex conflict:

Fred and Joanne, a young couple who run an East Coast consulting agency together, held different opinions of how the new company brochure should appear. Fred preferred a slick, bold look, whereas Joanne wanted an elegant and classy presentation. They met twice with their graphic designer, fought with each other both times, and accomplished nothing. The graphic designer wisely refused to return a third time.

The brochure became the centerpiece of a much deeper unresolved problem: Joanne was furious at Fred for often making major business decisions unilaterally without consulting her. At home, Fred domineered and controlled and expected Joanne and their kids to respond promptly to him. Since Joanne lacked courage to complain about his ill-treatment of her and the family, she argued over the brochure. In effect, she picked a minor fight to avoid a much larger, more risky one. But neither the brochure nor their family benefits from her displaced self-assertion.

Here's another example that still resides in the recesses of Jacqueline's mind, after eighteen years of marriage. That's how strongly experienced these conflicts can be! Jacqueline recalls:

"I was seven months pregnant, and my husband and I were on our way to "baby" class. The car trip itself plus the class time gave us some time alone to enjoy each other's company and to focus on the upcoming baby. But I turned instead to my financial concerns about his business and asked when he expected to receive $5,000 from a client I knew he had billed several months ago. Worried about our finances, I needed my husband to reassure me that money was coming. He explained that, despite his efforts, the company wasn't paying, and he wouldn't waste any more time on it. How could he write this money off so easily? I was scared of running out of money and I fired back.

On the surface, I criticized his handling of an accounts receivable problem. At a deeper level, I was attacking our relationship and my husband as a man. He wasn't caring for me financially the way I had hoped for as a married woman, and I resented his business' drain on our savings account and relationship. My venomous words and angry tone of voice hurt him deeply, because he felt as if he was failing me as a husband. I had reached my limit of being a "supportive spouse" to a business I no longer supported. It took a long while for us to recover from that argument.

Amidst tears later that night, Jacqueline realized that she needed to stop trying to fix her husband's business and to put her energies into the next chapter in her life—becoming a mother.

If destructive futile conflict erodes your relationship, and begins to wear you down, then seek professional help. If you experience accounting troubles in your business, you find a trustworthy accountant to advise you. When unraveling a tricky legal matter related to your business requires a competent lawyer, you find one. Hire the right professional, if necessary, to guide you through your interpersonal disputes. Consider going to www.relationshiptoolbox.com where you can get all the proven relationship skills needed for reaching a successful conflict resolution in your relationship.

Role Reversal

When a couple is at an impasse, I frequently engage the role reversal method of conflict resolution: each partner switches roles to take on their partner's position in a conflict. This technique puts each spouse in the other's shoes, which acts as a catalyst for developing a deeper emotional understanding of their partner's position. Once the switched positions are clearly understood, spouses not only "argue" their partner's factual side of the conflict, they are also encouraged to take on their partner's manner, tone and attitude when conversing. Role reversal, when properly done, helps partner's actually feel their partner's position. This promotes empathy between spouses and a tolerance for the opposing position. It also provides a safe space for each spouse to see flaws in their own position and attitude—creating change within themselves. It eliminates the futile question: "Why can't you just see it *my* way?"

Role Reversal Example

Original conversation:

Eric: *The guys are coming over for a poker game this Friday. Can you pick up some food and beer for us?* (Eric likes to unwind by playing cards with his buddies after a long week.)

Mary: *You're playing cards again? Every Friday night for the past six months you've been playing cards and I now have to worry about feeding your friends? It's bad enough I have to wait on you and the kids all week long. Now I have to add Friday night snacks and drinks to my already long list of "to-do's?"* (Mary is exhausted from a busy week too and she would like to unwind at home on Friday with just she and Eric.)

Eric: *Oh my God, Mary! What's the big deal? Is it too much to ask for you to pick up a bag of chips and a six-pack when you are at the store? Never mind, I will get the snacks and beer myself. Wouldn't want to put you out.* (Eric doesn't see why his request is such a big deal and he feels angry Mary can't just throw in a bag of chips and beer when she is already at the store shopping.)

Mary: *You are so dramatic! I'll get the stuff already—stop being such a baby.* (It is not that Mary doesn't want to do what Eric is asking of her as much as she resents not being able to spend Friday evenings with him anymore. She feels he is choosing to spend time with his friends over her and she feels rejected.)

Role Reversal Conversation

Mary speaking as Eric: *The guys are coming over for a poker game Friday night, hon. Would you mind picking up some chips and beer for us? Playing cards with the boys really helps me unwind after a long week and gets me ready for the weekend with you and the kids.*

Eric speaking as Mary: *Eric, I am exhausted from spending all week with the kids and now you want me to go shopping for your Friday night card game? I used*

	to look forward to unwinding and getting ready for the weekend with you on Friday nights. If you really want to play cards with the guys, maybe you can play every other Friday night instead of every single week? I want you to be able to unwind, but I would like to be able to unwind with you too.
Mary speaking as Eric:	*Oh, I didn't realize that. I will tell the guys tonight they can count me in every other Friday night and that opens up the off weeks for us to be alone and relax. Is that okay with you?*
Eric speaking as Mary:	*Yes! I would love that, thanks.*
Mary speaking as Eric:	*I don't want you to make a special trip to the store to get the chips and beer, so I will pick the stuff up on my way home from work Friday night.*
Eric speaking as Mary:	*That's okay. I can get the food and beer when I am already shopping. I don't really mind picking up the stuff for you and I don't want to take you away from your friends. I just wanted some relaxing time with you too. You are pretty much gone all week and I miss you—I look forward to the weekends to catch up. Don't worry about the beer and chips—I can pick them up for you. Is their anything else you think you will need since I will already be at the store?*

You can see from this role reversal conversation how the couple begins to appreciate the other one's position. They both feel the need to unwind and relax after a long week at work and with the kids. They were just choosing a different manner in which to do this. Eric is not rejecting Mary; he just wants to relax by playing cards with the guys. Mary doesn't really resent his card playing as much as she doesn't want the card game to monopolize all of their Friday nights. The role reversal technique allows each partner to appreciate and develop a deeper understanding of the other one's position.

The Speaker—Listener Technique

Drs. Markman, Stanley, and Blumberg, seasoned researchers and couples therapists, recommend the "Speaker—Listener" technique (Markman, Stanley, and Blumberg, *Fighting for Your Marriage*) to help couples communicate more effectively on hot issues. Many variations of this technique exist, but the basic premise remains the same. The technique involves structured conversation, paraphrasing, and giving one partner the floor to speak uninterruptedly until that person feels heard. These three therapists suggest assigning an object to signify who has the floor. For example, whoever is holding the paperweight is having their turn to speak while his/her partner listens. Using this technique helps liberate couples from the following patterns that normally destroy, rather than create, intimacy:

Escalation. The act of paraphrasing everything, though tedious at times, slows the dialogue, reduces the reactive tendency toward escalation, and with enough practice, spares you both a nasty fight. It also insures the listener has correctly heard the speaker's intended message.

Invalidation. By not listening to our partners or instantly attacking their point of view, we invalidate them and spark a combative dialogue, rather than a calm conversation in which both partners feel heard. Paraphrasing promotes the latter. Once we feel heard, we are more inclined to listen to what our partner has to say.

Withdrawal and pursuit. When one partner withdraws from conflict, the other usually pursues the conflict even harder (also referred to as the distancer vs. pursuer). The Speaker–Listener technique affords the withdrawn person safety, since the discourse is less likely to escalate. When the withdrawer sticks around, the chasing partner gets a chance to voice the issues and feel heard, thus diminishing the need to pursue.

Filters. Internal and external filters (the way that we hear and interpret what is being said to us) interfere with straightforward communication with our partners. The Speaker–Listener technique gives each partner the opportunity to say, "That's not quite what I mean." You can then clarify and modify the message until your partner understands.

Let's look at how the Speaker–Listener technique could have been helpful to Armand and Kirsten, an entrepreneurial couple who manage an office supply business. When Kirsten was fired from her job, she joined Armand in his established business as his new business partner. Not long after, this dialogue took place:

Kirsten: *I'm sick of doing all the copying and filing around here. What do you think I am, your secretary?*

Armand: *Don't be ridiculous. I didn't tell you to do it; you just started filing one day, so I let you.*

Kirsten: *Someone has to file around here. If I didn't do it, it would never get done. You do all the fun work and you leave the crappy work to me. I thought we were going to be business partners. I feel more like your unpaid servant.*

Armand: *That's your problem. Ever since you lost your job, you've been really touchy. Your feelings about our business are all in your imagination.*

What did Armand and Kirsten accomplish in this conversation? Both partners angered and alienated each other, and Kirsten got no satisfaction. Let's revisit the same dialogue using the Speaker—Listener technique.

Kirsten has the floor:

Kirsten: *I'm sick of doing all the copying and filing around here. What do you think I am, your secretary?*

Armand: *You're tired of doing secretarial work. You want me to do it instead?*

Kirsten: *No, that's not true. I don't want you to do all of it. I just want you to share some of the responsibilities with me. It seems as if all I do all day is copy and file and you get to do the fun work.*

Armand: *You want me to help you with some of the copying and filing?*

Kirsten: *That's right. Ever since I started doing it, it seems like I do all of it.*

Armand asks for the floor:

Armand: *I appreciate the copying and filing that you do to make our business work. It's true that I don't do much of it. The truth is, I can't stand doing the paperwork part of our business. I'd rather hire someone than do it myself.*

Kirsten: *You don't want to help me since you hate paperwork.*

Armand: *It's not true that I don't want to help you. I feel bad that you're so unhappy. I think we should consider hiring someone part-time to help you rather than expecting me to help. I probably won't follow through on my promise to help and that will just make you madder.*

Kirsten: *You're suggesting we hire someone to help me since you don't want to do the work, and you agree that I need help.*

Kirsten asks for the floor.

Kirsten: *The problem is not really that I need help; but that I feel unappreciated for the work I do. You never thank me and the clients never thank me. You have all the glamorous work and I have the behind-the-scenes work that everyone takes for granted.*

Armand: *You feel unappreciated and you would like to work more with the clients.*

Kirsten: *I think it would help a lot if you thanked me occasionally for doing the work that I do. Maybe if I didn't feel taken for granted, I wouldn't mind it so much. You know I'm still a little raw from being fired. I need some extra reassurance that I'm useful to the business.*

Armand: *You would like me to thank you more often so you feel appreciated. You also mentioned earlier that you want to work more with the clients.*

Kirsten: *That's right. I know that sales and marketing is your forte, but I wish I could have a bit more interaction with the clients. I want to go on sales calls with you, rather than being stuck at the office all day while you're out on the road.*

Armand: *You'd like to go out on the road with me.*

Kirsten: *Not all the time, just once in a while to help me get to know the clients and to get out of the office.*

At this point Armand and Kirsten can stop the structured dialogue and move into joint problem solving. Using the Speaker—Listener technique, Armand heard Kirsten's complaint without invalidating her or defending himself. Kirsten clarified the underlying reasons for her feelings so that they could find a mutually pleasing solution. Without a full discussion, they may have prematurely agreed to hire additional help, which didn't solve her real issue about being underappreciated and wanting more client interaction.

The most common objection to using methods like Speaker—Listener is, "It's too contrived." Most couples overcome that objection when they get results and can talk about a hot issue without a blow-up. Some couples need the safe environment of a professional office, with a third party present, to get through this technique. Structuring your dialogue gives you the power to discuss an otherwise volatile topic with uncharacteristic serenity. Perhaps one of the most valuable benefits of this technique is taking your partner's words and repeating them as your own. This is more powerful than just listening to what your partner is saying. Words delivered from your own mouth allows you to feel them from an emotional, not just a cognitive perspective—minimizing the temptation to intellectualize and/or rationalize your position.

CLARIFICATION EXERCISE SEVEN: USING THE SPEAKER—LISTENER TECHNIQUE TO RESOLVE A COMPLEX CONFLICT

Completion time: 30-60 minutes

Try the Speaker-Listener technique to reach a compromise on a highly charged issue—business, personal, or a combination—that you and your spouse have been unable to resolve satisfactorily. You might practice the technique on comparatively minor problems before you tackle your most difficult issues. Schedule quiet, private time for this exercise. Don't give up if your first attempts don't go perfectly, or you don't get ideal results. Like learning any new language, you need time and practice to become fluent.

Slow It Down and Take the Time You Need

Most couples try to solve their problems before they have a full, clear discussion of the issues. It's no wonder that the solutions don't stick, or that the problem escalates instead of dissipates. If you combine a fast-paced overloaded day with an aversion to conflict, you often get quick-fix decisions that aren't really solutions in the long run. There is no shortcut; communicating well takes time, effort and concentration.

When you come to your partner at a bad time—right before an important client meeting or while helping a child with homework—to address a problem you feel needs immediate resolution, *you take a hostage rather than find a listener.* Timing is critical for resolving conflict. You need to be sensitive to your partner's mood and what they are doing when you approach them if you are seeking an effective, long-term solution to a problem. You achieve your primary goal better if you wait for a time when both of you are cognitively and emotionally present and attentive.

You may be telling yourself now: "Wait a minute! We don't have the time to negotiate everything at length. We grab moments when we can." Couples skilled in negotiation and problem-solving find that planned business or couple meetings, even if they are short, are more effective for solving some problems than ill-timed conversations on the fly. For couples who prefer spontaneous meetings, it is still recommended you start these conversations by asking: "Hon, is now a good time to talk?"

Couple Meetings

Partners who handle conflict well speak highly of regular couple meetings, which all relationship experts unanimously endorse. These meetings—scheduled times for the couple to concentrate on speaking with each other without interruption or distraction—need not be long because you can get a lot accomplished when you are focused. Come to these meetings with a clear written agenda—and stick to the agenda. Err on the side of having too little as opposed to too many issues to discuss, leaving sufficient time for an open, honest and thorough conversation. Some couples meet at the start or end of every day. Others prefer meeting once a week, biweekly, or monthly.

> My husband and I tried having regular business meetings in the morning to start off the day but it didn't work. Charlie is a night owl, and he can stay up all night working. I do my best work from six to eleven in the morning but Charlie is usually too tired then to have a productive meeting. We compromised and now we talk over business or personal concerns at lunch twice a week. If something comes up on a day we're not having lunch together, we save it until our lunch meeting unless it's urgent.
>
> *Newspaper publisher*

> My partner and I meet at a local Starbucks one evening every two weeks. We've created a list together of our values and goals as individuals, as a couple, and for our businesses. The first hour and half of the meeting we go over each goal and value and talk about how we're each doing, measured against that list. We encourage and congratulate each other, as well as give feedback and acknowledge where we've fallen short. Then we set goals for the next two weeks. We've been meeting like this for five years. I think it's the most important thing we do for our relationship.
> *Lawyer and corporate consultant*

Since every relationship is unique there is not one "correct" way to approach and/or solve conflicts. A key to successful conflict resolution is not to avoid conflict but to acknowledge and address it before a simple conflict escalates into an out of control disaster. In either situation, contain the conflict so marriage conflicts do not permeate your business and visa versa. The goal is to resolve conflicts in a healthy productive manner that strengths the marital relationship.

The Power of an Apology

Never underestimate the power of a sincere apology. Why is offering an apology to our partner during or after a conflict so difficult? Like the word compromise, apology carries a lot of negative baggage. When we compete habitually with one another for the superior position, apologizing feels like surrender or admission that our partner is right and that we are wrong, implying we have been defeated. Apologies tap into our Achilles Heel; by apologizing we are acknowledging our vulnerabilities, weaknesses and mistakes (not easy to admit to ourselves, let alone our spouse). If your marriage is a true partnership, however, you are on the same team. A mistake corrected makes the team, and partnership, stronger. But if your marriage is a competition, apologizing indicates you did something wrong; therefore, you "lost" and your partner "won." In this case, an apology, in essence, admits defeat and weakens the team and the relationship, which is already vulnerable due to the adversarial nature of the relationship.

Properly timed, an apology can prevent a disagreement from becoming a volatile argument. An apology is a sincere expression of regret that your partner feels hurt, angry, sad, or otherwise upset by your actions even if you don't agree with his or her point of view.

If you say "I'm sorry" insincerely just because your partner wants to hear it, or if your "I'm sorry" is followed immediately by a defense of your actions, the effect is negligible. On the other hand, demanding an apology from your spouse will get you little except defiance. If your spouse thinks he or she deserves an apology, hear this demand as a clue that he or she is feeling invalidated and needs acknowledgment of his or her point of view. When emotions are running high, it is important to remember we are vulnerable to our partner because we have put our trust in them; nobody wants to feel their trust has been violated.

An apology is the catalyst needed for forgiveness. Forgiveness following an argument prevents the build up of resentment of real or perceived hurts by our partner. Resentment is the single most influential variable which destroys intimacy in our relationship and is to be avoided at all costs; a sincere apology will go along way in doing just that.

Childhood Wounds

Complex conflicts trigger emotional outbursts when they re-open childhood wounds. Dr. Harville Hendrix is renowned for his development of the Imago Relationship Theory, which can be enormously helpful to all couples seeking more introspection and understanding of the dynamics in their relationship, and how to heal one another from childhood trauma. Imago Relationship Theory asserts how individuals experience childhood partially determines their choice of partners in adulthood and how they will behave with their partners. When a controversial issue arises, conflict becomes calamitous because couples tune out, interrupt, criticize, give unwanted advice, or attempt to fix the problem. When a fight reopens childhood wounds, couples react defensively to each other. Criticism becomes the adult equivalent of the screaming child. Couples must look behind the criticism for the underlying childhood frustration, hurt, fear, abandonment, or other emotion.

Understanding childhood wounds helped Ed and Julia, co-owners of a multimillion-dollar manufacturing company. Before counseling, they had this typical hurtful argument:

Ed: *I'm sick and tired of having a business partner who isn't pulling her weight. The clients are very demanding and you don't offer any help.*

Julia: *That's ridiculous! I'm in the office plenty, but you never take my suggestions anyway. You're sick and tired of me not pulling my weight? I'm always the one who takes care of the house and kids— besides working at least forty hours a week.*

Ed: *I'm never home because I have to work all the time to make up for the fact that you sit on your butt all day and talk to your friends. If I had a real working partner maybe I could come home more often. Someone has to keep this business afloat!*

Julia: *Just because I'm not a social hermit like you doesn't mean I don't pull my fair share.*

This fight led Ed and Julia to seek counseling, where they talked about their early childhood experiences. Ed came from a family of six kids; as the oldest, he was often left in charge of his siblings without much support from his parents. His perception that Julia also left him responsible for the business without adequately supporting him instigated his childhood rage. In contrast, Julia's family communicated, "Children are better seen than heard." Her overworked and inattentive parents largely ignored Julia's opinions, feelings, and needs. Her perception that Ed ignored her contribution to the business sparked her childhood hurt and frustration.

A replay of the former dialogue, redrafted with an understanding of childhood wounds, illustrates more effective communication:

Ed: *I'm sick and tired of having a business partner who isn't pulling her weight. The clients are so demanding and you're never there to help.*

Julia: *You think I'm not doing enough.*

Ed: *I know you're very busy with the kids and the house and the office. It's just that I'm exhausted. Some days I just want to walk away from the whole damn thing. It feels just like when I was growing up as the oldest kid, responsible for taking care of my brothers and sisters.*

Julia: *I bet you would give anything for some time off. May I speak? I'm feeling really frustrated. You say you are overwhelmed and that I don't help you enough, but you don't listen to my opinions and you make your own decisions anyway, no matter what I say.*

Ed: *You think I don't take your advice when you give it?*

Julia: *You make decisions on your own and then get mad at me for not helping you. You say you want a business partner, but you also want total control. It really pushes my buttons because my parents were always making decisions without involving me, just like you do.*

Ed: *I've spent time with your parents so I know what you mean about them. May I speak? I didn't mean to exclude you. I'm used to doing everything myself, and I thought you wanted it that way too. Why don't we start having regular business meetings first thing in the morning, before the clients start calling? Maybe you can take over some of the problems that have been weighing me down. I would really appreciate your help.*

Julia: *That sounds good to me. I'd like you to involve me more. Let's try eight tomorrow morning. And one more thing: can we get a babysitter this weekend so we can go out for a date? I miss having fun together.*

Ed: *Sure, that sounds good.*

Childhood wounds represent unresolved childhood issues; as we mature, they are scabbed over. When we marry, the slightest provocation by our partner may rip open these scabs, revealing deep and raw wounds of complicated and often times confusing emotions. Left unattended, these wounds which were formed in our childhood negatively impact our marriage and other relationships. It is akin to being overweight and getting angry at the scale for telling us our weight.

Although difficult, once revealed and addressed, childhood wounds often leave you with improved self-esteem and increased self-confidence, making you a healthier, more loving and mature partner. Keeping those benefits in mind, do the exercises of self-reflection below and some childhood wounds might be revealed. Although these exercises may be difficult, you and your relationship will gain tremendously from your efforts.

DISCOVERY EXERCISE EIGHT: RECOGNIZING CHILDHOOD WOUNDS

Completion time: 30-60 minutes

While you should seriously consider seeking professional help for resolving deep emotional pain from childhood, you and your partner can still consider how your most troubling conflicts may be rooted in childhood trauma. Set aside a period of uninterrupted time to share your insights with each other. Use a structured dialogue technique if it helps you to communicate with each other. You may find your hostility diminish afterward and be able to empathize more tenderly. With increased awareness, you will be less apt to blame your partner for not giving you what you needed, but never got, as a child.

Patty / Ann

CONCLUSION

Relationship techniques or counseling will never eliminate conflict entirely between a husband and wife or two intimate partners. You may benefit from developing self-awareness and greater insight through individual therapy to take the charge out of your vulnerable "hot buttons." Every action to prevent, reduce, or resolve conflict between you will enrich your relationship and strengthen your business partnership as well. You may eventually welcome the opportunity to work through some of your differences. Focus on the process and be satisfied with small accomplishments along the way.

Progress, not perfection, is a worthy goal. View conflict as an opportunity for growth through the lens of a growth mindset. This will go a long way towards keeping your marriage solid and your business sustainable and profitable. All success begins with relationships and all relationships experience conflict. The skills and techniques learned in this chapter will directly and greatly improve your chances for success in both areas of your life.

VIP Couples Days, workshops, and seminars like the ones I offer on conflict resolution skills and communication will instruct you on shifting from destructive to constructive communication. Reading some of the outstanding books for couples (including this one!) is an inexpensive way to invest in your relationship.

Wondering where your mindset stands when dealing with conflict in your relationship? Take this Conflict Resolution Quiz by going to
www.relationshiptoolbox.com/mindsetquiz.pdf

Consider going to www.relationshiptoolbox.com
where you can get all the proven relationship skills needed for reaching a successful conflict resolution in your relationships.

VII
KEEPING IT HOT, INTIMATE & FUN

Creative Ways to Keep You Close
and Feeling Sexy

After working together for a number of years, we filed for divorce. We endured the heartbreak of not only losing our marriage, but also the businesses we had worked so hard to create. We were always working and never took any personal or relationship time away from the business. Instead of being lovers, we became only business partners.

Divorced entrepreneurial couple

After 35 years of marriage I have deepened my love for the lady I married. Before we began working together, she was a trophy wife, a beautiful woman who took care of my kids and stood at my arm when we went to business functions. I never discussed my business with her because I didn't know she had anything to contribute. When my wife came to work with me in my business, I discovered a brilliant, creative woman and I fell in love with her in a whole new way.

Professional speaker and consultant

When you hear the word romance, what comes to mind? Images of giving or receiving candy, flowers, and expensive gifts? Whatever the image, the allure of romance is universal. Romantic love is the seductress that brought you together and compelled you, for better or worse, to spend the rest of your lives together. Romance naturally fades with time and the pressures of daily life. When you are struggling to manage both business and family affairs, sustaining romance in your marriage may fall low on your list of priorities.

This chapter will help you find ways to express love amidst the stress of entrepreneurial life and child-rearing. You'll learn how to cultivate romance in both attitude and action and how to overcome the most common obstacles to preserving a loving, romantic relationship.

WHAT IS A ROMANTIC MARRIAGE?

Romance may include buying gifts, sending flowers, and leaving love notes for each other, all traditional modes of romantic expression. But it is far more than that. "Keeping the romance alive" means maintaining a relationship with each other in such a way that you both feel loved, appreciated, cherished, and admired daily. Your love for each other will change and mature over time. Your heart may not palpitate the way it used to when your spouse walks into the room, yet your love for each other can deepen into an even more satisfying feeling over the years.

Paying bills, raising children, maintaining a household, responding to medical crises, and, of course, starting a business, zaps your energy and thwarts intimate connection. Sustaining the expression of love in your marriage is one of the most essential skills you can develop to protect and enrich your marriage. Without romantic rituals, every day passes like all the others. Without expressions of love, spouses and soul mates become merely roommates and business associates.

THE TEN CHARACTERISTICS OF
A ROMANTIC MARRIAGE

How romantic is your marriage in terms of the following checklist of qualities normally found in a romantic, passionate, thriving marriage?

1. You express reverence and respect for the other's abilities and accept each other for who you are.

2. You often focus your attention on how to please your spouse and regularly go the extra distance to help your spouse feel cherished and loved.

3. You delight in the companionship of your mate. You can experience togetherness side by side, even when doing different activities at the same time.

4. You have developed joint hobbies or pursuits such as raising kids, grandchildren, travel, business, antiques, religion, music and the arts, or sports.

5. You carry in your heart a constant gratitude and appreciation for your spouse and express these feelings often.

6. You usually look for the good in your mate and focus on the positive in your relationship and life together.

7. You have fun, laugh together, and savor spontaneous, creative romantic activities from time to time.

8. Your relationship fulfills you on many levels: recreational, sexual, intellectual, emotional, and spiritual. You regularly share activities in each of these spheres of life.

9. You have learned over time how to accept each other's weaknesses and to release resentment.

10. You have learned how to say "I am sorry," forgive each other, and give each other grace.

DEVELOPING A ROMANTIC MARRIAGE

What if you spent only one half-hour a week taking care of your customers, developing your marketing plan, or collecting your receivables? Your business would die of neglect. The same goes for marriage. The first step toward a romantic marriage is to focus on keeping the romance alive in your marriage a priority in your life. Yet, as several experts report, most couples spend fewer than thirty minutes a week sharing intimate feelings or private time. No wonder the divorce rate now exceeds 50 percent. In my practice, I regularly see the disastrous results of neglect. Couples with young children often put romance on the backburner assuming they will get back to it once the kids are grown; entrepreneurs wait until their businesses turns a profit, then they will worry about passion in their marriage; corporate people insist once they get that next promotion—then they will wine and dine their spouse again. The problem with all these case scenarios is these couples often do not have a marriage or relationship to get back to, a passionate flame to rekindle or anyone home to wine and dine—since the romance, and very often the relationship itself, has been left for dead a long time ago.

Give Your Relationship Regular Attention

"Romance is the environment in which love flourishes," according to Greg Godek, author and romance expert. Romance is the garden where our relationship can bloom with great beauty, or wither from inattention. Jennifer's husband, Charlie, is a gardening aficionado. He nourishes their lawn and garden with only the highest quality organic fertilizers, high-quality soil, and regular attention to weeding. If Charlie only spent thirty minutes a week on the garden, or waited until June and put his hands in the soil for forty hours, the garden wouldn't flourish. Charlie makes time to mow and weed during an extraordinarily busy work week because he prioritizes the health and beauty of their yard above many other items on his to-do list. Just as gardening results are in direct proportion to the effort he puts in, the same is true for marriage. Reaping what you sow is as true for your relationship as it is for your garden (and for parenting as well).

Treat Your Spouse Like Your Best Client

If you work hard to acquire a client who becomes your biggest income producer, you provide the best service and consideration possible. Imagine if after a few years you decide that you now need to pay more attention to your newer clients, so you stop giving that client your best service. Your prize client will become dissatisfied and take the business elsewhere.

Your mate is your most important life client. Satisfying this person with high-quality attention requires a major investment of your time and energy. For many couples, a marriage license becomes permission to relegate their relationship to the lowest priority on the never-ending "to-do" list. If you are a married entrepreneur, or if you married an entrepreneur, you must make the time needed to romance your intimate partner. If your business depends on getting clients, you create the time to get clients—or you go out of business very soon. If you don't make romance a priority, then you may find your marriage going emotionally bankrupt as well. There is a reason nobody ever said at the end of their life, "I wish I spent more time at the office." Instead, people consistently express regret with the lack of time devoted to their marriage and family. Many people do not realize the true value of their relationships until they are lost to either death or divorce, yet everyone gives lip service to their importance. Over a decade ago, the tragic events of 9/11 sparked a resurgence in the world-wide conversation about the value of relationships and family life. People changed careers motivated by the desire to spend more time with their spouse and children. It is unfortunate that tragedies like 9/11 have to occur to remind people that relationships are what life is really all about. If you are in an intimate relationship, this is the most important relationship in your life, bar none.

If you are thinking, *Hey, I'm a mom. Isn't my relationship with my children the most important relationship in my life?* Don't worry, we'll address that later in this chapter.

Keep Business in Perspective

Entrepreneurial life can absorb all of your physical and mental energy. Entrepreneurs who value their marriages and family life learn how to leave their business worries at the office and return in the morning with a fresh mind and heart. Transition rituals can help you make the transition from work to home so that you can be fully present for your spouse and kids when you are home. Take a half-hour to surf the web or read an ebook before joining the family, work out at the local gym, or take a quick shower before starting dinner to get your second wind after a long workday. Ease into the transition, and then be as fully present as possible.

Abigail has learned that when her husband, Ricardo, gets off the train after a 12-hour workday, plus a 3-hour train commute, he needs "chill time." Not only does she have dinner waiting for him every night without fail, but he also looks forward to his end of the day ritual—a drink of scotch or bourbon and the daily paper. This reliable ritual helps ground him back into family life, and separate him from his stressful job.

Mitch and I both respect each other's need to change gears. When working in my office outside our home, I like to come home and go upstairs to change out of my work clothes and put on casual clothes, and just take a minute or two to transition myself for my role as wife and mother. (Well—the mother role is transitioning for me now since my youngest child just went off to college). Mitch likes to come home, go through the mail and change his clothes, which allows him to transition from worker to husband and father. Although our children are now young adults, for years we did not have the luxury of time to transition from one role to the next. We took the little time we had and made the best of it, transitioning our mindset more than anything else.

How much of your personal time in the evenings will you devote to discussing work, working on the business, taking care of kids, or sharing intimate time with your spouse? Every couple needs different amounts of daily intimate contact. Some guard their evening time together carefully and leave work entirely at the office. Others live, eat, and breathe the business day and night, by choice. Although some outsiders label this behavior as unhealthy, these couples remain happy, excited, and connected passionately to one another. For them, co-creating the business is as good as sex, because working toward a common goal is as romantic an activity as they can imagine.

If you suffer from workaholic tendencies and your spouse is complaining, however, you may need to curtail your incessant devotion to work in exchange for attending to your spouse's intimacy needs.

When his or her needs for romance and connection are fulfilled, they will be a lot more supportive of whatever you need to make your business work. If you neglect your spouse because of the business, your spouse can't help but resent the business for taking you away from them like a mistress. When this happens and your spouse believes your business is the most important thing in your life, consuming all of your time, passion and energy, taking precedence over your marriage, looking for their support will be an exercise in futility. Would you support something you believe facilitates your spouse's emotional and physically disengagement from you? Probably not!

Communicating What You Need

What makes you feel loved, respected, and connected to your partner? "If I have to ask for it, it doesn't count" is a defeating attitude that guarantees your needs will go unmet. I run into this all the time in my practice, a pouting wife who says, "I shouldn't have to tell him what I need. He should know!" I advise couples that their spouse does not have a crystal ball. If asked to do something, many people say their spouse will gladly do it—whatever "it" is—and quickly add, "But I shouldn't have to ask." Long-term intimate relationships do not have the luxury of standing on ceremony. If all you have to do to get your needs met is to make them known, and your spouse is willing to accommodate your request, consider yourself lucky.

The expectation for your spouse to be able to read your mind is nowhere more prevalent than with gift-giving, especially with women thinking their husbands should just know what they want for their birthdays, anniversaries, holidays, etc. When a wife with this mindset does not get the gift she assumed her husband "knew" she wanted, even though she *never told* him, she is disappointed and may become angry or resentful.

If you do not tell your spouse what your desires are for gifts, or anything else, you have a pretty good chance of not having them met. This might sound harsh but it is true; not verbalizing your needs in marriage sets you up for a lifetime of disappointment. Here Lilly and David show us how this plays out in a marriage:

Lilly: *For crying out loud David, why are these dishes still in the sink? And why is all this food left out on the counter and not put in the refrigerator? Would it kill you to clean up the kitchen and put the food away after dinner instead of being glued to the TV watching the baseball game all night long?*

David: *Lilly, I didn't know you wanted me to clean up the kitchen. I just sat down five minutes ago to watch the game. I left the food on the counter in case you were hungry when you came home and felt like eating something. I can clean up the kitchen—it's not a big deal. I just didn't know you wanted me to.*

Lilly: *When do I ever leave the kitchen a mess after dinner? I always clean up right after we eat, but if I am not home I thought you would just do it. Now I'm not even hungry anymore.*

David: *I didn't know what time you were coming home so I thought I would leave everything out for you. I wasn't even thinking about the dishes—I was just trying to make sure you had some food to eat if you were hungry. And I know you don't leave the kitchen a mess; I can clean up now—it really isn't a big deal. Just ask me instead of acting all pissed off. I can't read your mind, hon.*

Lilly: *I shouldn't have to ask you—you should know. You look like you were ready to hunker down with your drink and watch the game for the next few hours and leave the dirty dishes for me.*

David: *Lilly, if you ask me to do something I am more than willing to do it, but I've told you a hundred times that I can't read your mind. Just ask already.*

It is childish and immature to stand in the kitchen annoyed, with your hands on your hips, bent all out of shape like Lilly did when she came home to dirty dishes in the sink. Lilly never asked David to clean up the kitchen, yet she acts as if he didn't do something she asked. Lilly assumed David knew he wanted her to clean the kitchen. But as you read the above case scenario, it is absurd for Lilly to assume this. If you don't verbally ask your spouse to do something, how will they know?

Don't expect your spouse to be a mind reader. Give him or her specific guidance on how to make you happy. Ask for what you need to feel loved by your partner. You may want your spouse home at 6:00 P.M. for dinner every night, but your expectation may be entirely unrealistic given your spouse's business. You can at least ask when to expect your spouse home, and if you want your spouse to he home for dinner earlier or more often, say it.

As discussed previously, neuroscience provides some organic understanding of why men and women communicate differently. Many continue referring to John Gray's bestselling book, *Men are From Mars, Women are From Venus,* which discusses how couples can fall into a vicious cycle of dissatisfaction related to gender-based communication style differences. A significant difference in the way each gender values or "rates" a gift provides some perspective. For a woman, no matter how big or small a gift is, it scores one point; each gift has equal value. A spontaneous hug and an "I love you" are equal in romance value to an expensive dinner at a romantic restaurant. In contrast, men measure gifts by their perception of how much it costs or how much effort went into creating it. A man thinks he earns one point for a small gift and thirty points for a big one, so he focuses on giving one or two big gifts which "last" in value. The problem is, a woman usually prefers ongoing steady gifts, no matter how small.

In a relationship, women need many expressions of love to feel loved. Dr. Gray equates women to a gas tank that needs repeated filling. When a woman doesn't appropriately recognize a man for his big romantic gifts, he stops giving. "Why should I bother?" he asks himself. When he starts giving less, her resentment grows and the vicious cycle begins. Women must learn how to give men adequate appreciation for their romantic gifts, and men must learn how to prime the pump more regularly. Couples who ignore these differences run the risk of misinterpreting gestures of good faith.

Patty / Ann

DISCOVERY EXERCISE ONE:
WHAT MAKES ME FEEL LOVED

Completion time: 30 minutes

Write this sentence on a piece of paper: "I feel loved, cherished, and appreciated when you_____." Fill in the blanks and share your list with your spouse. For example:

- Feel loved when you offer to take the babies for a few hours so that I can get some work done or enjoy some private time.

- Feel loved when you spontaneously give me a hug—just because you feel like it.

- Feel loved when you look at me admiringly and tell me I look beautiful.

- Feel loved when you leave me a love note before you go to work.

- Feel loved when you make us a special dinner.

- Feel loved when you watch the kids so I can go work-out.

- Feel loved when you watch my TV show instead of the one I know you want to watch,

- Feel loved when you automatically get up and help me bring in groceries from the car.

- Feel loved when you see I am tired and you take the kids off my hands so I can sleep or just relax by myself.

Commit to doing something loving for your spouse every day, weekly, or monthly. Post the list on the wall by your bed, in the bathroom, on the refrigerator, or on your desk at work. Carry it around in your wallet, refer to it often, and add to it whenever an idea comes to mind. Create and share new lists every six months. Make random acts of kindness and expressions of love a consistent aspect of your relationship.

Schedule Intimacy

"It's not romantic to schedule sex." "My whole life is planned for me; I don't want to have to plan intimacy with my spouse too." "We keep saying were going to spend some time together, but the day just disappears before you know it." Do you recognize any of these common complaints of entrepreneurial couples? Couples thriving in the midst of entrepreneurial demands often schedule intimacy as a priority. Dates, even sex, with your spouse gets put on the agenda, with baby-sitters hired on retainer to ensure a regular date night. Couples become creative and insist upon new ways to spend time together.

Scheduling intimate time doesn't preclude spontaneous closeness when time allows, but it ensures a baseline of connection to hedge against a hectic business schedule. The main resistance I meet when I tell couples to schedule sex is that scheduled sex isn't romantic. If you don't schedule sex you might very well not have any sex at all—and how romantic can that possibly be? Making the effort to schedule dates and sex sends the message that your relationship is a priority, so important you schedule it into your life. You would not think twice about scheduling an important work meeting with a client or Friday nights out with your friends, why should your marriage be any different? We schedule what is important to us in other areas of our lives; romantic time and sex in our marriage deserves no less.

DISCOVERY EXERCISE TWO: SCHEDULING INTIMACY

Completion time: 30 minutes

Create a system with your spouse to schedule intimacy. Refer to the previous exercise, "What Makes Me Feel Loved," for ideas. Your scheduled activities may include:

- private dates
- celebrating special days
- daily connection
- sex
- walks
- bike rides
- play board games or card games together
- go out for drinks
- go out for coffee
- teach your partner something new
- make a scrapbook of the history of your relationship
- vacations

Buy a special calendar, use Google, Outlook, or any other computer program you prefer just for planning your relationship activities, or put the ideas directly into your daily agenda. Plan your calendar for the following month or as far out as you can possibly go and repeat this exercise monthly. I have my professional and personal calendars combined to avoid scheduling conflicts between these areas of my life.

ROMANCE KILLERS—THE EMOTIONAL WEEDS OF THE ENTREPRENEURIAL ROMANCE GARDEN

Even planting heirloom seeds purchased from the best source won't guarantee an abundant flower and vegetable garden without rich fertilization and careful pruning. Entrepreneurial life has its own weeds and slugs that overrun the garden of romantic love first planted during courtship. The next section of this chapter looks at the negativity, "the weeds" that you need to eradicate so that your relationship can flourish. We will examine five common business-related causes for boredom or distance in your marriage, followed by concrete ways to rise above these challenges.

During a difficult time in their marriage, Gina complained to her husband, Barry, about the perceptible lack of intimacy and romance between them. Barry, in a decidedly unromantic mood for several weeks, used the following metaphor to explain his feelings:

Picture a delicate bud vase holding a single red rose. The rose represents romance and intimacy; the vase our marriage. Now imagine dropping a pebble in the vase. The pebble represents disapproval, resentment, demands, or my beating myself up. That first pebble in the vase may displace some water, but the rose can still live. But pebble upon pebble in the vase eventually displaces all the water so that the rose withers and dies. With so much negativity between us lately, too many pebbles crowd the rose for me to feel romantic.

The next section explores how to protect your marriage garden from being overrun by the following weeds:

1. anger and resentment
2. depression and melancholy
3. fatigue and feeling overwhelmed
4. disappointment or disillusionment
5. boredom or being in a rut
6. lack of personal space
7. worries about money

Anger and Resentment

> Driving home from my job as a critical care nurse, I was exhausted by the demands of a 50-hour workweek, terminally ill patients, and demanding families. I wanted to work part-time but I couldn't as long as my husband's business wasn't earning any money. I was furious when I drove up the driveway and saw him polishing his car. "Why isn't he in his office making business calls and getting some clients?" I ranted to myself.
>
> *Critical care nurse*

The Pebbles

I'm exhausted and it's all her fault.

He doesn't deserve to have fun while I'm working so hard.

He isn't doing what it takes to make the business work. He's incompetent.

I deserve to be taken care of. This isn't what I bargained for when we got married.

Why can't he get a real job, with benefits and perks?

How long am I supposed to be the only one in the family making any money?

He works more hours now than he ever did before—with absolutely nothing to show for it.

Shifting Attitude

When anger clouds the picture, romance is the farthest idea from your mind. Rather than wanting to give to your spouse in a generous and loving way, you want to punish and withdraw from your spouse in anger and resentment. If you express your hostility inappropriately, then your partner may retaliate. If you swallow your feelings and numb yourself out, then you choke the positive, passionate feelings as well, so that your loving connection frays anyway.

Lack of effective communication kills romance and passion and is at the root of many problems in marriage. Passion is created by effectively communicating intense feelings. Denying or suppressing your true feelings eventually inhibits your ability to feel anything, including passion. The inability to feel passion is the precursor for an inability to love. A relationship begins to wither once a couple becomes apathetic to each other. When couples say they really just don't have the energy or the desire anymore to argue, or that they really don't care, it can be a sign that the passion and intimacy has been lost and the relationship is over.

To tell the truth to yourself and to your partner in a loving way, the key is to peel back and examine all your feelings about the issue, not just the outermost layer. For example, when you react with anger as your primary defense, you may also discover hurt, fear, frustration and regret beneath the rage. If you communicate only the angry message, you sound unloving and your partner may react defensively. If you learn to express the range of emotions, then you uncover loving feelings behind the angrier hurt ones, and your partner will be better able to hear you. Locating deeper feelings isn't easy because the intensity of the first layer blocks our feelings. Like all skills and positive habits, slowing down the process and looking for hidden emotion takes practice and determination. For many people the easiest emotion to demonstrate is anger—when it is often hurt that underlies the anger and is the emotion that really needs to be addressed.

Consider the wife who finds her entrepreneurial husband polishing his car. She feels rage instantly upon seeing him caring for his car instead of working. But she also feels hurt: "He doesn't love me enough to protect me and make sure I don't have to work this hard when I'm exhausted." She feels fear: "If he doesn't make any money, then I'm going to have to keep working this killer schedule. I don't know how I will manage that." She feels remorse: "I wish I could be more compassionate and forgiving about his difficulties getting clients." Beneath all of these emotions she feels love: "I love my husband and I want to feel reconnected to him again instead of feeling angry."

With intention you can learn to pause in the middle of anger and tell yourself the whole truth about your feelings. In a calm voice, perhaps after a cool-down time, use "I" statements to communicate your feelings and needs to your spouse. Try the Love Letter technique (Chapter 6) for a structured way to write all your feelings when speaking is too difficult. With this new awareness, the critical care nurse returning home from work might he able to communicate the following to her husband:

"I am exhausted and overwhelmed today and I'm feeling angry that you aren't contributing more income to the family. It's hard for me to continue to be supportive of you starting your own business when I'm so scared of running out of money at the end of this month. I love you, and I want you to be happy. What can you say that would reassure me?"

If the timing wasn't right to tell the truth to her husband as she pulls in the driveway, then she could request a couple's meeting, wait until she has calmed down and he is in a receptive mode, or at least tell herself the whole truth. By doing so, she opens the door for intimacy.

I once helped an entrepreneurial couple get back on track when they both arrived in my office seething with anger.

Sarah: *We are in such a deep hole financially. After twenty years I have finally tapped out of the money I saved from Wall Street—money meant for our retirement, that we now have to use to pay the bills. My family was never in debt growing up and my mother would be mortified if she knew how little money your business makes. I am so furious I could scream.*

Carl: *You are screaming and you are always so angry and focused on money. We have been in this situation before and we have always managed to come out okay. Getting angry doesn't solve anything. After twenty years we haven't had to close up shop and we've been in worse financial situations before. Can you please just calm down?!*

Sarah: *Calm down? Yeah, we've come out of worse financial situations before because I keep tapping into our retirement money. Now we are all maxed out on credit cards, we used up all our equity in the house and I am scared that we won't be able to pay the kids college tuition—which is due in six weeks. What are we going to retire on? Who is going to take care of me like I take care of my mom?*

Carl: *Sarah, I know you worry about money but I didn't realize you were so worried about our retirement. What makes you think you will have no one to take care of when you get older? I'm not going anywhere. Your mom spent your entire childhood harping about money. I know she had it rough after your dad died but you have to remember I am still here and you are not in the same situation as your mom. The business isn't doing well now but that is not the same as me not being here for you, Sarah.*

Sarah: *I know I am not my mom but she drilled it into my head growing up to never go into debt, never spend more money than you have, etc. Whenever the business is slow I get scared to death we will have no money and have to go bankrupt. What will happen then?*

Carl: *We are not going to go bankrupt, even though money is tight now. We will pull back on our expenses and save more. Will that make you feel better, Sarah? And you are not your mom. I don't plan on leaving you alone to fend for yourself and you know I have taken out an insurance policy in case anything ever happens to me.*

Sarah: *I know, Carl, but I still worry when business gets slow and the money is tight.*

This couple was able to defuse Sarah's anger once it was revealed what it really represented. Sarah's anger was an expression of her worry and fear about her financial future and being left alone. Her dad died when she was a young child and her mom struggled to make ends meet, expressing financial concerns to Sarah throughout her childhood. As an adult, whenever finances become tight Sarah's childhood fears were reactivated. Carl reassured her that although things had been financially tight over the last two decades, they always managed to survive—and in some years even thrive. He also addressed Sarah's fear of being abandoned, insisting he was not going to leave her alone to struggle with finances like her mom had to for most of her adult life.

Depression and Melancholy

When my husband declared bankruptcy and closed his business, he moped around the house for six months in a deep depression. He didn't shower, hardly ate, didn't want to be near the kids or me, and wouldn't socialize with any of our friends. Our sex life was nonexistent. I didn't mind losing the business or our money as much as I mourned losing my husband.

Spouse of former clothing store owner

The Pebbles

I lost everything we worked so hard to save. I'm a loser.

I'm so ashamed of myself. I can barely face my wife or kids.

I'm sure my wife doesn't even want to make love with me anymore.

My wife and kids would be better off without me.

Romance as Unconditional Love

One entrepreneur referred to the state of mind of the gentleman above as "mental knots." When our spouses are depressed, we hurt too, and want to "unknot" the twisted thinking behind their depression so they can forgive themselves and again enjoy life as our partner. We move from compassion to impatience, through fear to anger as we wait for time to heal our partner's wounds—and our own. Most entrepreneurs are resilient, but even six months of depression and disconnection can feel like an eternity. When your mate suffers and your life together loses virtually all expression of love and romance, your relationship becomes predicated upon a conscious decision to weather the storm; for better or worse. Most marriages go through phases when partners make a conscious decision to stay together, unconditionally, even though things might feel pretty bleak for long periods of time. Staying married is often a conscious decision and choice firmly grounded in the belief that although the relationship might not feel so great at this point in time, it is only a matter of time before it will get better, and that this, too, shall pass.

When our partner is depressed, unattractive, (or feels that way), and unavailable, we learn about real love. For a time, the relationship is neither balanced nor fair. We give more than we get, suffer from a lack of intimacy, and fear that our partner will never be loving toward him- or herself or us again. During this time, romance rises above flowers and cute little gifts. If your partner is depressed, then express your ongoing and unconditional love for your spouse often, even if your spouse does not reciprocate. As mentioned previously, a healthy marriage is a partnership that is rarely a 50/50 give and take proposition. At times one partner might give 75% and the other gives 25%. At the end of a lifetime together the give and take of a relationship often evens out in the wash. If it doesn't, partners either don't know because they have not been keeping score or they don't really care.

The most romantic gesture that you can make for your depressed spouse is to be there unconditionally, with compassion, acceptance, and a whole lot of patience. Be persistent in your efforts to reassure and love. Eventually your spouse's wounds are likely to heal. Find unique ways to express your love daily, even if your spouse has difficulty receiving it, or doesn't know how to thank you. Eventually the interminable winter blossoms into spring, and your lover will warm to your gestures and receive again. Partnership is as much about cycles as it is about constant growth; it ebbs and flows with the tide.

> I was a bear to live with when my restaurant went under. My husband kept on taking care of the kids, making dinner, rubbing my back, and reassuring me that he still loved me. I don't know how he put up with me. One day he arranged for the kids to spend the weekend at their grandmother's. He booked us for a three-day weekend at the cabin we honeymooned in. At first I didn't want to go, but he insisted. Getting away really helped. I have never forgotten how he was there for me during my lowest point.
> *Bankrupt restaurant owner*

Fatigue and Feeling Overwhelmed

> My husband got the ax and decided to go out on his own as a consultant just when my home business was getting started and wasn't bringing in much money yet. We both tried to work out of our home offices during the day with two toddlers running around. It was nuts! Sex, intimacy, personal time with my husband? You've got to be kidding. All either of us wanted to do when we had some free time was sleep!
>
> *Business owner whose husband also started a business at the same time*

The Pebbles

We're going to lose the house if we don't make some money quick.

The kids have got to come first.

I can survive without sex.

Who's got time for romance? I'd rather sleep.

Staying Anchored

When you combine entrepreneurship, children, and financial worries, you may easily feel overwhelmed and exhausted. Creative romantic ideas usually take a back burner. When you've little time and energy to invent new romantic rituals, then identify the anchors in your marriage that sustain your commitment and connection. Like an anchor which secures a ship through inclement weather, emotional anchors are the expression or demonstration of behavior which emotionally secures partners to each other. Anchors are reminders of your love for each other on a daily basis since they act like little ties that bind you to each other. Whatever else might be going on during your day, the anchors in your relationship allow you to feel connected to your partner. They require little effort yet play a huge role in reminding us of our love and commitment to our partner.

Every day you find a way to eat, bathe, and get dressed. You decide to prioritize the essentials, even when you have too much to do in too little time. Put on your priority list the anchoring rituals you share with your spouse. Anchoring rituals may seem intimidating at first. Who has time to add more responsibilities to the day? Anchoring rituals may be as simple as:

- We say "I love you" every day.
- We hug before we leave the house.
- We take a walk together on weekends.
- We talk over breakfast about the day.
- We have dinner together every evening.
- We go to religious services every week.
- We text at least once a day while at work.

When you find yourself saying, "All the romance is gone in our marriage," remember to count those daily rituals taken for granted. Look for and acknowledge the simple daily routines and habits you have developed together that demonstrate your ongoing love and connection with each other. Financial professionals teach when you take care of the pennies, the dollars take care of themselves. The same is true for romance in our relationship. Perform little routines in your marriage to encourage romance and the flames of passion will not burn out.

DISCOVERY EXERCISE THREE: ANCHORING RITUALS

Completion time: 20 minutes

Complete the following sentence with your mate by writing down 10 activities you do daily as anchoring rituals for your relationship:

Amidst these crazy times, it's important that, as a minimum, we do the following with and for each other, every day or week. We commit to each other that no matter how busy we get, we will make the time for those activities that center us and sustain our marriage during difficult times. (Sign your names at the end of the sentence.)

With four children to support and two busy careers, Mitch and I could easily have gone into the ditch with our marriage. Instead, we have excelled in keeping anchoring rituals an everyday part of our relationship. Here are some of those actions that infuse our marriage with stability and strength:

Our marriage is anchored in a commitment to health and wellness. When our children were young, we would take turns on the weekends watching the kids so we could each exercise. Sure, it took up a couple of hours in the morning, but we started really early and sacrificed sleep. This physical activity anchored our relationship because it kept us feeling healthy as individuals and committed to our belief in health and wellness as a couple and a young family. Currently, with busy travel schedules, we make it a point to call each other at the end of the day to say, "I love you" and "good night" when either one is on the road. If we don't reach each other, we leave a voice message and/or send a text. Our relationship is anchored in the very act of trying to reach each other, regardless of whether we actually connect or not, and health and wellness now permeates our children's relationships as well as our own.

Disappointment or Disillusionment

When I first married my wife, I thought I had found the perfect woman. She was beautiful, she wanted to stay home and raise my kids, she was intelligent enough to converse with my clients, and she was a great cook. But after the second baby came, she wasn't the same woman anymore. She started her own business that took her away practically every night of the week to one client or networking meeting or another. Instead of coming home to dinner on the table, I usually cooked the meal and put the kids to bed by myself. When she came home from her meetings she wanted to tell me all about it, but I didn't really want to hear it. I wanted my old wife back.

Husband of a blossoming business owner

The Pebbles

If I wanted to marry a businesswoman I could have done so.

My wife belongs back home with the kids.

I'm sick of handling the kids every night while she's out having fun at her client meetings.

Why doesn't she lose weight? She's gotten so fat and unattractive.

Romantic Illusions Versus Mature Love

When our romantic illusions fade and we realize that our partner lacks certain personal qualities we wish they had, it's called "disillusionment." Many people come into marriage with holes in their heart hoping their partners will fill them. They want to be made complete. When their spouse fails to complete them, they become disillusioned with the partner and their relationship. The truth is no one can complete you, only you can complete yourself. Your partner can complement you, but that is not the same. There is a Chinese proverb that states: "A candle loses nothing by lighting another candle." If you do not have enough light within yourself to shine, another person cannot light the way for you. If we expect them to, and they don't, we become disillusioned with them. As stated in Bugen's book, *Love and Renewal, a Couple's Guide to Commitment:*

301

Young love has an element of infatuation tied to it. As our love matures, disillusionment is part of the maturity process where we are no longer blinded to the flaws of our partner. Infatuation is replaced with disillusionment. Mature love works through this disillusionment to include acceptance for who our partner really is—truly taking the good with the bad and appreciating what they bring to our lives.

Going into business together or dealing with the strains of self-employment accelerates the disillusionment phase of your marriage. Working in close quarters, you will see aspects of your spouse's character that may irritate you. The frustrations associated with a demanding business speed the transition from lighthearted courtship and romance to unpleasant realities that will test your marriage.

You can transform romantic love into a more rewarding and deeper love by learning how to do the following:

- Transform intense passion into real intimacy and genuine loving affection.

- Exchange your blindness to your spouse's imperfections and flaws with the discovery and acceptance of who they really are.

- Develop a tolerance towards your partner that nurtures and supports a safe, loving environment.

- Carpe diem—seize the day, and live in the present. Enjoy the moments you create in a world where we seem to have an excess of everything except time. Spend quality time with your partner and cherish the little expressions of love and appreciation. Be realistic, understanding every week cannot include dinner at a five star restaurant.

- Understand all things new lose their luster, including the glow of early romantic love where the world felt as if it revolved around you and your relationship. Take pleasure in the security of knowing your relationship has faced challenges and your love and romance is still present while your dedication and commitment to each other remained strong even in the face of adversity.

- Treasure your commitment to a life journey together; remember it is taking the journey together that counts.

Your marriage is more of a marathon than a sprint; persistence and an unyielding commitment towards the marriage, rather than personal selfishness will help your relationship endure. Persevere and keep your eye toward the future as you travel one step at time on your journey together.

Entrepreneurial couples with a strong commitment to a lifelong partnership convert the hardships of business ownership into bedrock for building a greater, more dependable relationship. Mature and lasting love replaces the idealized infatuation of your dating.

Boredom and Being in a Rut

> I remember how excited my husband and I were many years ago when we opened our first store. As newlyweds, every day was different and exhilarating. Even though we have plenty of money now and our first store has turned into twenty stores, I miss the struggling years—in a way, they were more fun.
> *Franchise owner*

The Pebbles

My marriage has become dull and boring. Life isn't any fun anymore.

I miss the earlier years when our marriage was more exciting.

Working together as business partners has killed our sex life.

I don't know if we have what it takes to turn each other on anymore.

Fighting Inertia

Even though a long-term, stable marriage lets you relax and be yourself around your spouse, putting no effort into being attractive, sexy or interesting to your spouse will result in a dull, distant marriage. Even if your marriage is like a perennial garden that needs little daily care, you should still attend regularly to it or the flowers will eventually die.

Boredom and/or being in a rut is best eradicated with mutual commitment and energy to shake up the status quo. Enroll your spouse on the mission or start making a few changes yourself. Begin by being as objective and honest with the responsibility you bring to the boredom you are feeling. There is a good chance you are not the only one who is bored and whose needs are left unsatisfied. Your partner might find you and your marriage to be just as boring as you do. It is always best to begin making changes to yourself and your routine and your spouse will eventually respond. Romance is contagious. Alexa and Dan were able to break through the boredom cycle by working on their relationship with my help:

Alexa was getting ready to leave for work in the morning and she noticed her husband Dan left a note on the kitchen table reminding himself to pick up a birthday present for their friend's party over the upcoming weekend. During her lunch hour that day, Alexa bought the present and then called her husband and told him what she did. Dan was so surprised by Alexa's actions he couldn't wait to see her that evening and give her a huge hug and kiss. This one little act of kindness meant so much to Dan. It told him Alexa was thinking about him and he was worth her taking the time and effort to take a "to-do" off his list and put it on her own. This act promoted a sense of goodwill between this couple who had been bored with each other and in a rut; it was a catalyst for more acts of random kindness between Dan and Alexa. That weekend Dan surprised Alexa and cooked her favorite dinner, fostering more positive feelings. Kindness, like romance, is contagious and this couple went on surprising each other with unexpected niceties that broke them out of their rut while simultaneously increasing romance in their relationship.

Other suggestions for getting your relationship out of boredom and a rut:

- Turn off your laptop, TV and all other electronic devices for an hour each evening so you can really be "present" and give your partner your undivided attention.

- Schedule a date to a "no-tell" motel for a few hours—anytime of the day or evening.

- Spend a spontaneous weekend alone and do not speak about work, kids or the bills—anything else goes.

- Take long walks together.

- Reminisce about when you first fell in love and tell each other why—out of all the people in the world—you choose to spend the rest of your life with them. In other words, tell your partner what made them special to you.

- Repeat your marriage vows to one another. (Some couples write their own marriage vows and during rough patches in their relationship, I encourage them to say them to each other again.).

Just like a marathon runner, anyone in a long-term committed relationship cannot go the distance without preparation. Like a marathon, there are times when it is really difficult and you want to quit; there are times when you hit your stride and it feels effortless. There are good times and bad times, flat, smooth surfaces and stretches marked with potholes and pitfalls. There are times when the monotony of the journey makes watching paint dry seem exciting. But once you have negotiated these rough patches you can look back and feel an overwhelming sense of pride and accomplishment. You will feel a tremendous sense of love, gratitude and appreciation for sticking with it—even when you thought you couldn't last one more day together or take one more step in the race. But you did—and you now reap the unmitigated rewards of your persistence, perseverance and unwillingness to give into doubt. Your commitment to your relationship will get your marriage through the inevitable phases of boredom and the humdrum of life.

Lack of Personal Space

I get up at six o'clock in the morning, help get my kids ready for school, and then leave for the office. I work in a cubicle all day, surrounded by hundreds of other employees. When I get home at night, my family is waiting with dinner. After helping the kids with their homework and cleaning up the kitchen, it's time for bed. The only moment I've been alone all day was in my car. I have no opportunity to unwind and recharge my batteries so that I can be available for, or even interested in, intimacy with my wife. She's got her own business operating out of the house, so she takes care of her need for space all day long, and she gives me a hard time because I'm not so into connecting with her when I get home.

Corporate accountant

The Pebbles

I want to get away from everyone and be by myself.

I wish I could have a drink and read the newspaper without interruption.

Sometimes I wish I was single and coming home to an empty house.

Every day it's the same old routine. I'm trapped in all my obligations.

Finding Personal Space

A lifestyle that deprives you of personal space will limit your desire for romance with your spouse. Without minimum privacy, you may seek solitude rather than togetherness, common behavior of men and women who work in a full-time job, returning home to their families burned out. After interacting with people all day, you quite naturally crave at least an hour alone (which may be unrealistic if you have young children,) and may sacrifice intimate relationship time in favor of some solitude. Without your own personal space you will feel physically and emotionally suffocated. Just as time spent together has many benefits for your marriage, so too does time spent alone. Personal space naturally promotes alone time to grow and realize your own potential as an individual. It is important that you do not get consumed by your identity as a spouse or parent. These roles define functions and aspects of who you are but they should not be how you are exclusively defined—to yourself and others. Personal space allows you to regroup and just breathe, to do whatever you choose to do, including nothing at all. It allows you the space to put an argument between you and your spouse or the general stressors of life in proper perspective.

When you marry you are deciding to spend your entire life together paying bills, raising kids, problem solving, etc. It is not only okay to have personal space; it is a requisite for all happy couples. Couples who do not have personal space from each other will create it, sometimes in ways detrimental to their relationship. Consistent, countless hours every night on Facebook, video chat, playing solitaire, etc., are examples of inappropriately creating personal space from your spouse with the unintended consequence of emotional estrangement. Modern technology may create personal space in a relationship in very destructive ways.

If you do not find ways to get your necessary space, then you both may unconsciously create it for yourselves in destructive ways, by distancing emotionally, starting an argument, turning on the laptop or TV, sleeping, or other habits that annoy your spouse. Sacrifice together time with your spouse to give one another needed alone time, and you will create greater passion and intimacy as a couple over the long term.

Successful entrepreneurial couples create strategies to provide both partners with replenishing private time. Sometimes one partner must sacrifice—babysitting the kids, postponing dinner, forfeiting conversation or sex, or even spending weekends apart occasionally—to make private time available for the other partner.

Worries About Money

We were barely scraping by on my teaching salary while my husband started his own high-tech company when quite unexpectedly I got pregnant. Next thing I know I was in and out of the hospital with a high risk pregnancy, so I had to stop teaching. Financially, this was really bad timing. Looking back, I don't know how we made it, except I know this: the most expensive thing we did all year was rent DVD movies!

Schoolteacher married to an entrepreneur

The Pebbles

We don't have enough money to even think of doing anything romantic.

If my husband wasn't chasing this foolish dream of his, we'd have the money to have some fun together.

Laura is so lucky. Her husband takes her out to a nice restaurant every week.

I have no idea what to give my wife for her birthday since we're so short on cash.

Romantic Gifts that Don't Cost Money

One of the fallacies about romance is that it has to cost a lot of money. Some of the most romantic experiences shared by couples require no money and only a little time. In fact, many report deeper satisfaction with a personal and creative gift, than with an ostentatious one. The first step toward weeding the garden of money worries that are keeping you from being romantic is to seek out creative non-cash gestures for keeping the romance alive. Here are some ideas I have recommended to clients to light the flame without draining the bank account. They work! I know, because I use these myself!

Love notes. Leave each other love notes in unexpected places—on the dashboard, on the computer desktop, on the bathroom mirror written in soap, on your pillow, in the car, or in a briefcase or backpack.

Doing chores. As a surprise, do one of your spouse's chores for him or her. Fill up your spouse's gas tank without him or her even asking. Lighten the daily load just a bit.

The gift of time. Designate a period of time on the weekend when your spouse can consider him or herself completely free of childcare and household responsibility, to spend the time as he or she chooses. I refer to this jokingly as a "get out of jail free" card.

Flowers. Place a single flower from the garden on your spouse's car seat, pillow, or in the bathroom, just to let your spouse know you were thinking of him or her.

Prepare a meal. Create and serve a delicious dish that took some time and effort to prepare. You don't need to go out to a restaurant for a fine-dining experience.

Massage. Give your spouse a neck, back, foot, or hand massage for twenty minutes.

Napkin notes. Make your spouse lunch for work and include a special poem or love note written on a napkin as an extra-unexpected surprise.

Phone call, text, or email. Call your spouse at an unexpected time just to say, "I love you and appreciate you." Depending on your mood and your spouse's, the phone call could even be erotic. Better to keep the erotic for the phone, than the text.... You never know where that text message could go!

Compliment. Take a moment to compliment how your spouse dresses, cooks, takes care of the children or the house, or brings home a paycheck.

Kiss and a hug. A no-cost and practically no-time way of saying "I love you." Give your spouse a sign of affection at an unexpected moment with some heartfelt enthusiasm! According to recent research, a hug that lasts at least twenty seconds raises the oxytocin levels (also known as the love hormone) in your bloodstream, so establish a ritual of an oxytocin hug every morning!

Sex. This may be one of the most direct ways to your spouse's heart, and it won't cost you a dime.

Listen. Give your spouse the gift of your undivided attention and support when he or she needs it most.

Shower. After your shower, write "I love you" in the fogged up mirror so your partner sees it when they go into the bathroom after you.

Draw a fake tatoo. Use your lipstick or eyeliner and draw a fake heart with you and your partner's initials inside of it on a private part of your body.

Treasure hunt. Leave a trail of post-it notes throughout your home leading to a special treat—or even you—in the bedroom.

Brag. Brag about your partner to your friends and family about how much you love something your partner says or does. Be complimentary but not unbearable.

Preference. Let your partner decide which movie he or she wants to go to or restaurant to eat in. Instead of you getting your preference, willingly give your partner his preference without him asking for it.

Picture. Put your picture on your husband's cell phone and make the ringer a special love song.

Music. Call your husband when you hear a love song that reminds you of him.

KEEPING THE ROMANCE ALIVE
WHEN YOU ARE RAISING KIDS

It's hard to think about being romantic with my husband when I've got three kids crawling all over me, a house to keep up, and a demanding business.
Restaurant owner

Setting Boundaries

When the kids and your careers are so demanding, (and whose aren't?) it takes real creativity and commitment to keep the romance alive in your marriage. One of the secrets to sustaining a vital couple connection is the ability to set and maintain boundaries, refusing to give yourselves entirely to the incessant demands of business or children. The best gift you can offer to your children is a solid intimate marriage that energizes and supports you.

With children around, you learn to grab intimacy when you can, in the middle of the night or at dawn if necessary. You no longer hope to spend entire weekends together in romantic privacy. Children get sick, need your attention, and take much of your time. You become grateful for an occasional night out, rather than a weekly date. You are happy for sex twice a month, instead of twice a week.

If your children are old enough, put that 'Do Not Disturb' sign on your bedroom door, and teach your children to respect your privacy. If your children are young, then put them on a regular bedtime schedule so that you get some adult time together in the evenings. When you spend most of your time as "Mom and Dad," feeling or acting like lovers takes effort. If you tell yourselves that the romance will end once the children come, then it probably will. When you commit to keeping romance alive despite family pressures, you can sustain a satisfactory level of intimacy. But you will have to work hard to achieve it. Remember, nothing worthwhile comes easy.

Give your spouse the gift of freedom from child-care for a while so that he or she can recharge and be more emotionally and sexually available to you. Take turns allowing one of you to sleep late on the weekend or hire a teenager to entertain the kids during a weekend afternoon so you have the time to read in bed or take an extra long shower. If your spouse usually gets up in the middle of the night to take care of the baby, offer to take over for a night or two.

The key is balance. Hold reasonable expectations of each other; yes, children do change things substantially, but don't give up entirely on keeping romance alive! As long as you keep the embers burning, the hot flames of passion are still within your reach when the time and mood are right. Let the fire grow cold between you, and when the children are raised and out of the house, the fire will be much harder to start again.

COMMUNICATING ABOUT SEX

How often have you heard "he wants sex and she wants romance"? A more accurate statement is, 'If you ask a man what his number one favorite romantic and intimate activity is, he'll tell you it's sex. If you ask a woman what her favorite romantic and intimate activity is, she'll tell you it's talking and cuddling with her mate." Does that mean that a woman doesn't want sex or a man doesn't want romance? Absolutely not! Most men and women want and appreciate both expressions of love and intimacy, but they prioritize specific activities differently. Couples who thrive learn how to meet the sexual and romantic needs of both individuals, so that there is a natural flow of goodwill between them. He's enjoying plenty of good sex so he naturally expresses love and romance to her in a way that encourages her to want to make love to him (or vice versa).

Never mind what a "normal" sex life is for a married couple. Throw out the stereotypes and discover what really turns on your mate. Perhaps great sex monthly satisfies you, or maybe you need sex every other day to feel connected, or ten minutes of cuddling to get warmed up. Can you enjoy quick sex when the opportunity arises, or do you need more time? Do you prefer to make love in the morning or the evening? Do you need a certain amount of emotional closeness in your relationship to be in the mood, or a certain amount of sleep?

I am continually asked by couples what is appropriate sexual activity between partners. My answer is always the same—any sexual activity which is mutually agreed upon between partners is appropriate. Sex should be a natural extension of intimacy between a couple; the end goal is not to have an orgasm but to feel emotionally and physically connected in body and soul. For all the talking and marketing about sex, misinformation and confusion prevails about this important and sensitive topic. In the midst of the 21st century, sex still remains a forbidden topic in many cultural and religious communities and double standards prevail. Like it or not, let's be honest, a guy who sleeps around is considered a stud and a girl who sleeps around is considered a slut. We maintain a double standard regarding sexual activity for our sons than for our daughters—and this carries over into their marriages. If good girls "don't," then what happens when these good girls marry and become wives, still harboring these good girls "don't" virtues? Is there any wonder that sex, along with money, is at the top of the list for why couples have marital troubles and/or divorce?

From an historical perspective, romantic love is a relatively new concept. It was not long ago people married to procreate, sex before marriage was taboo, and romantic love was virtually unheard of. (Throughout most of history marriages were arranged for political and social agendas.) The invention of the birth control pill in the 1960's revolutionized our sexual activity, allowing people to engage in premarital sex free from the fear of pregnancy, altering the rules of sexual engagement forever. But what the birth control pill did not change was how we perceived the sexual activities of men versus women, along with how men and women think about sex—and, wow, do men think differently about sex than women! Therefore it is imperative you have a frank discussion with your spouse about sex and your sexual preferences to keep your sex life alive and well.

What prevents women from sharing their sexual needs with their partners? Modesty, shyness and perhaps most importantly fear of rejection and ridicule often keep women silent in the bedroom. This jeopardizes our sexual relationship with our spouse by *hoping* our partner will figure out what we like, and/or prefer. To avoid the wide chasm this lack of communication can create, maximize and strengthen the romantic time you spend with your partner by sharing your specific sexual preferences with them (verbally and/or non-verbally). As mentioned in earlier chapters, assuming your partner knows what you want and need in your relationship is a prescription for disaster; your sex life is way too tantamount to your happiness and intimacy to leave to chance.

Patty / Ann

DISCOVERY EXERCISE FOUR:
SEXUAL AWARENESS

Completion time: 30 minutes

Following are some questions you should ask yourself and your partner to gain an understanding of your views on sex and sexuality. Write down your answers to these questions and discuss them with your spouse. They will reveal areas of sexual compatibility and incompatibility that must to be worked out to avoid sexual conflict within your marriage. These questions are by no means exhaustive, rather they provide an excellent starting point for what is usually a sensitive, and at times difficult, discussion.

1. Do you feel comfortable initiating sex? Why or why not?
2. What sexual activities do you prefer and/or enjoy? Be very specific and list them in order of preference and/or enjoyment.
3. What sexual activities do you refuse to engage in? Be as specific and comprehensive as possible.
4. What puts you in the mood for sex?
5. What turns you off and kills any desire for sex?
6. Who taught you about sex and were you taught accurate information?
7. Where do you get your sexual information (ie, the Internet, magazines, self-help books, etc.)?
8. What are your views on pornography? Do you, or are you willing to use it as a sexual prop to turn you on? If so, how do you access it?
9. What was your family's attitude about sex growing up? Was sex ever talked about in your home or was it a forbidden topic?
10. Have you ever been sexually molested or abused?
11. How often do you want or expect sex?
12. Are you comfortable telling your partner "no" if you do not want to engage in a specific sexual activity or with having sex at all?

13. How comfortable are you telling or showing your partner what you like and don't like sexually?
14. Has sex, or lack of it, ever contributed to the breakup of a previous relationship?
15. What is your attitude about sex toys like vibrators?

A discussion of these questions and answers will begin to promote an understanding between you and your spouse regarding sexual expectations, limitations and desires. The point of the exercise is to begin an open, honest dialogue between you and your partner to enrich your sexual life.

It is very difficult to enjoy a completely fulfilling marriage in the absence of a healthy sex life, one which provides both physical and emotional benefits. Couples who enjoy a satisfying sex life report feeling more connected to each other and according to current research, suffer less physical and emotional conditions such as depression, heart problems, anxiety and other medical conditions. Lack of a healthy sexual life is often a barometer for other serious emotional issues in a relationship and suggests a major warning sign for the viability of the marriage.

It is important to note there may be some physical barriers to an active sex life. Current research shows impotence, historically thought to be a psychological issue, may very well be an organic problem, often due to circulatory or vascular disease known as Erectile Dysfunction. If impotence is impairing your sex life, get a full medical checkup to rule out any medical disease before assuming it is a reflection of the emotional health of one's marriage.

It is my hope that the information provided above will shed light on how you and your partner view and enjoy sex. Sexual activity is a prime indicator of the health of your marriage. Take a no-excuses approach for creating a satisfying sex life, since it is the cornerstone for promoting happiness and romance in your relationship.

KEEPING THE ROMANCE ALIVE
WHEN YOU WORK TOGETHER

Sustaining an active intimate sex life with your business partner is tricky business. Can you allow your spouse to be your lover as well as your business partner? Sometimes it is hard enough to live with your spouse, let alone work with them too. There is often a period of adjustment when you begin to professionally partner with your spouse, to say the least.

> I love working with my wife, but for a while it ruined our sex life. I wasn't sure it was worth the trade. In bed, instead of making love, we discussed our clients or the mailing we had to get out. We had to learn how to be business partners at the office and lovers at home.
> *Business Development Consultants*

Romance arises from feelings of goodwill and love, and the desire to give a gift to your lover. But when tension exists between both of you at the office and you carry it home, it'll kill any romantic energy between you. Communicate early with each other about the issue. Discriminatingly bring the romance of your relationship into the office if that helps keep you intimately connected. Leave your mate a steamy email or love note on his desk or seduce your husband at lunch if you share a home office. Try changing into sexy clothes at the end of the work day to transition from co-worker to wife. Give your spouse a hug, a high five or tickets to the baseball game or even flowers (its not illegal for guys to get flowers, is it?), when you land a great deal. Use your imagination. Check out your partner's mood so you don't offend them by trying to make love or be flirtatious while he or she is in work mode.

The key to keeping romance alive in your relationship while working with your spouse is summed up in one word: boundaries. It is imperative you have clear boundaries in specific areas of your life if you do not want the romance to be a casualty of your work together or visa versa.

Working with your spouse from home makes it imperative to create a clearly defined boundary for your office, your home and each other's workspace. A merged work/life space is a romance killer, especially if your bedroom masquerades as an office. Don't allow your home office to become an oil spill, taking over your entire living area with papers on the kitchen table, work magazines in the bathroom, work-related books in the family room, the computer in your bedroom and your car acting as a library on wheels. Oil spills are very difficult to contain; a lack of boundaries around your home office is toxic to intimacy in your relationship. Keep your home office as just that—an office within your home. If you have space limitations, be sure each partner has, at the very least, individual space for their own computers. My husband and I would kill each other if we had to share a computer or desk!

Like the Grinch who stole Christmas, entrepreneurial work can steal most, if not all, of a couple's intimate time together. Set clear boundaries around your work hours. On your way out the door to dinner, it is easy to send out "just one more email" that ends up being fifteen more emails—making you late for your dinner date. Avoid this by setting time constraints on your work hours and stay disciplined and honor these hours.

Entrepreneurs who work together can easily have their "out of the office" conversations monopolized by talking about work-related issues. Avoid this temptation, difficult as it may be, so your business relationship does not eventually eclipse your relationship as lovers. At whatever time the "whistle blows" to signal the end of your work day, transition your mindset to transform yourself from co-worker to spouse. This segues into the final boundary entrepreneurial couples must create, and that is to be totally present in the role you are fulfilling at any given time. Many people, and women specifically, try to be all things to all people all the time. Not happening! Being an entrepreneurial working mom made me feel unsuccessful as an entrepreneur, a mom, and as a spouse when I tried to perform all three roles simultaneously, failing miserably. When you are working, give work your full effort and concentration; when you are with your kids, be totally present and give them your undivided attention and when you are with your spouse outside work hours, be a spouse. Do not talk about work issues and curb your incessant desire to check your blackberry, droid, iPhone, etc. for work messages.

Each couple needs a different degree of separation from work to maintain a desirable level of sexual and romantic intimacy. On the bright side, working together may improve your romantic and sexual life considerably. Flexible work hours allows you to make love, share a dream, and develop a renewed respect and admiration for each other, and spending more time together can fan or rekindle the flames of passion.

The first time I saw my wife give a presentation to our board of directors, I was stunned by her beauty and power. It was a real turn on for me to see her in the role of Executive VP of Operations, not just Susie, my wife. I appreciated her in a whole new way, and it increased my desire for her.

President of multimillion-dollar sales organization

CLARIFICATION EXERCISE FOUR: MAINTAINING ROMANCE WHEN YOU WORK TOGETHER

Completion time: 20 minutes

Write the following on a piece of paper:

"It is important that we maintain a healthy romantic and sexual relationship while working together as business partners. To that end, I would like you to:

1.
2.
3.
4.
5.

And I would like you to refrain from:

1.
2.
3.
4.
5.

List at least five ideas in each blank, and share your requests with your spouse. Update these lists quarterly.

Patty / Ann

CONCLUSION

Many choose the entrepreneurial path to overcome banality and complacency. For women, it is often the only realistic way to create a life that fulfills our dream of prospering in business while enriching our marriage and family life. Even in the aftermath of the financial meltdown, and despite technology that makes work flexibility more possible than ever, most corporations are as unforgiving as ever, maintaining rigid expectations that frustrate women (and men) who want to lead a fulfilling balanced life. Corporate professional women are still advised to tell their bosses when they are late for work, or need to be absent, any reason other than they need to be home with a sick kid or they are participating in a school activity. The concept of "face time"—being seen in the office just for the sake of being seen, whether productively working or not—is still the norm in most organizations in which one wants to climb the corporate ladder.

Entrepreneurial couples experience the joy of achieving a shared dream, the creativity, spontaneity and rewards of struggling together to forge a thriving business and a rewarding marriage. Every entrepreneur I've worked with acknowledges that when his or her marriage is vibrant, strong, and loving, the business performs better and life in general is more fun and rewarding. There is great synergy between romantic fulfillment at home and entrepreneurial achievement. Current research proves people in happy relationships are more successful and make more money. Therefore, romance is good for your marriage and good for your business.

Entrepreneurs want to go for it, to create it all: passion, accomplishment, prosperity, fame, and meaningful contribution in both work and marriage. Keeping romance alive is hard work (and great fun too), and will make the difference between a boring, vulnerable marriage or a stupendous, dependable one. You can have a marriage without romance, but why would you want to?

Start making immediate moves toward keeping romance alive in your marriage. Select a new and different way to express your love for your spouse and implement it—NOW! The rewards will be bountiful.

—⟋ℳ⟍—

To download the Ten Characteristics of a Romantic Marriage, go to
www.relationshiptoolbox.com/romanticmarriage.pdf

—⟋ℳ⟍—

VIII
BENDING WITHOUT BREAKING

Meeting Hard Times with Strength,
Courage, and Commitment

> It was bad enough when my husband, Bill, lost his job. Then he invested all our savings in a small business that went bankrupt two years later. I don't know what was worse, losing all our money or losing Bill for two years while he was working ninety hours a week trying to make the business successful. Sometimes the only thing that kept me from walking out the door was the commitment I made to him on our wedding day.
>
> *Supportive spouse of bankrupt entrepreneur*

The incessant demands of entrepreneurship and the ever-present risk of business failure can jeopardize or strengthen your marriage. If you battle together against difficult circumstances, rather than fight each other, then you improve your chances of surviving as a couple. When you are constantly overworked, deprived of sleep, or worried about finances, you might find yourself really struggling to stay happily married or even in a relationship.

Although waterbeds are not as popular as they were years ago, they offer a perfect metaphor for entrepreneurial couples. Before you buy a waterbed, you consider how "wave-free" the mattress should be. You could choose one extreme, where one person's movement sets the other side rolling dramatically, or complete wave reduction, where one sleeper scarcely knows the other is there. In entrepreneurial life, some partners can cope with waves, but others completely lose their peace of mind. If every action your partner takes in his or her business—or in your business together—ruins your serenity, it's like sleeping on a waterbed with no wave control. This chapter doesn't guarantee complete wave reduction, but its eight strategies can help you to maintain some stability in your relationship while riding out the rocky waves of entrepreneurial life together.

DIFFERENT PERCEPTIONS OF STRESS

Krysten is not the brave, athletic sort. Many years ago, when a friend pressured her into white-water rafting, she responded to turbulent waters as if she were going to die. She was in crisis until that dreadful trip ended and her feet were ashore! To her thrill-seeking friend, the river lacked enough white-water action to stimulate her, so she experienced virtually no stress.

I, on the other hand am quite a thrill-seeking adventuresome sportswoman. Having never been on a pair of skis before, my friends took me to the top of a mountain on a zero visibility day. They told me to point my skis straight down, keep my legs together and just take off. They assured me there was nothing else to "it" and I would be fine. Well, I knew nothing about skiing at the time, and I was instructed on how to parallel ski, the fastest way to get down a mountain. On a zero visibility day, with icy patches all over the Vermont mountain, I took off. I loved the feel of the cold air and wind in my face as I picked up speed. At some point it dawned on me that I had no clue how to stop, so I decided to just fall down, laughing hysterical at how out of control I was. It wasn't until I actually learned how to ski that I understood what a dangerous thing I had done, but I had a blast. To me, it was a great adventure. Krysten wouldn't take a million dollars to do what I did!

If you approach business ownership as Krysten did white-water rafting, where the slightest turbulence threatens your feeling of safety, the entrepreneurial journey will terrify and exhaust you. If you approach entrepreneurship as I did when skiing for the first time, the sense of not quite knowing what lies ahead will feel exhilarating, even if it is a little scary. For all entrepreneurs, a smooth, calm entrepreneurial journey is an unrealistic expectation; a snowball has a better chance of survival in hell.

Most of us can distinguish between a daily frustration, like traffic, and a devastating tragedy, like a fatal car crash. However, your idea of crisis may be your partner's notion of disappointment. When financial difficulties prevented one entrepreneur from paying for his daughter's college education, he considered suicide for a short time, as he confronted his feelings of failure as a father. Since his wife didn't measure her success as a mother by her ability to financially provide for their family, she coped better with their financial circumstances than her husband did.

What unsettles one of you may actually excite the other at any given time. Financial uncertainty of a husband's self-employment gave his wife many sleepless nights and anxiety attacks. The challenge excited him. In fact, he enjoyed the adrenaline rush of the game—until they faced bankruptcy and losing the company. Then he crashed. His wife, on the other hand, calmed down, faced the worst, and accepted that business failure wasn't so bad after all. This husband and wife, on the journey together, each experienced personal crisis at different times and managed to keep their relationship together by supporting each other when the chips were down.

CLARIFICATION EXERCISE ONE: DEFINING THE LEVEL OF CRISIS

Completion time: 15 minutes

Consider the following questions and share your responses with your partner. How do you differ? Where do you agree? Refrain from judging your partner's response as wrong if it differs from yours. Answers to these questions will help you understand how you and your partner differ in response to stressful events in your life together.

- The top five daily frustrations of my (our) business:

- The top five daily frustrations of my (our) personal and family life:

- The current business problem I find the most distressing:

- The current relationship/family problem I find the most distressing:

- I am feeling devastated by (if applicable):

- I would be devastated by:

COMMON STRESS RESPONSES TO ENTREPRENEURIAL LIFE

Throughout your life, uninvited circumstances may precipitate crisis in your relationship, family, business, health, or other aspects of your life. Following are four examples from my practice of these types of unanticipated situations. One couple lost everything they owned in a house fire a week after they opened their new business. Another couple lost their business in a California earthquake, and they were totally uninsured. A third couple lost an adult son in a car accident, while they negotiated a deal to sell their business. A fourth couple dealt with the wife's breast cancer and their subsequent inability to find affordable health insurance. All of these couples were resilient enough to survive, and even thrive, in the midst of crisis and adversity. In this chapter you will learn the secrets to finding strength through adversity for your marriage when your business does not go according to plan.

Entrepreneurial couples who have met with business failure or struggled with the hardships of building a business frequently report the following:

- Depression, anxiety, loss of self-esteem

- Guilt, inability to forgive oneself or partner

- Anger or rage at self or partner

- Loss of sex drive, exhaustion

- Health problems

- Addictive behaviors—overeating, smoking, drinking, gambling

- Financial difficulties

- Emotionally unavailable for relationship or children

- Disintegration of intimate relationship

If you are plagued by any items on this list, then your relationship or personal well-being may be severely impaired. Seek professional help immediately—a trained relationship expert, financial consultant, or clergy may be necessary to guide you through these difficult times. Do not wait until the crisis becomes unbearable; seek help the moment you feel yourself losing control. It is easier to rescue someone from drowning while their head is still above water. Remember, it is a sign of strength to ask for help.

Patty / Ann

EIGHT STRATEGIES FOR MEETING CHALLENGES SUCCESSFULLY AS A COUPLE

Strategy One: The Importance of Flexibility

To survive hard times, you must shift gears to meet changing conditions. Dr. Al Siebert, an expert on the survivor personality, found that life's best survivors are highly adaptable, with a wide range of responses to any given situation. Not fixed on one emotional state or personality characteristic, a survivor can seemingly contradict him or herself at any one time, selfish and unselfish, cooperative and rebellious, whatever the situation requires. A survivor may appear paradoxical and unpredictable, but that flexibility protects the survivor in crisis. Similar to animals who camouflage themselves by changing colors to blend into their surroundings, resilient entrepreneurs change to survive and accommodate unfavorable business conditions. Entrepreneurs must act like a willow tree, bending with the direction of the winds of change, rather than standing strong and inflexible like an oak tree.

I see this in my practice all the time. Thinking outside the box is an invaluable asset for couples who successfully survive and thrive during challenging moments. Those couples who come to me with rigid ideas about the way that everything must be, are often the ones who end up in divorce court. As John Steinbeck famously wrote: "the best laid plans of mice and men have often gone astray". We have two choices when our business and relationships do not proceed as planned (and there is a good chance they won't). We can lament our situation, play the martyr and sing the "woe is me song" or we can be creative and innovative, interpreting the twists and turns of life as an opportunity and a challenge. Instead of continuing to bang your head against a wall, (remembering the definition of insanity is doing the same thing over and over again expecting different results), turn your head around and look for a window of opportunity, or create one. Nothing is impossible unless we think it is.

As mentioned earlier, individuals with a fixed mindset will be judgmental and unforgiving while those with growth mindsets will see challenges as an opportunity to learn and grow. Thriving couples avoid fixed ideas and mindsets of what must be and accommodate each other by changing their expectations predicated upon the reality of the situation. These couples are not bound by preconceived expectations. Flexibility is evident daily and in the big picture as well. Flourishing entrepreneurial couples make decisions based on the desired outcome for everyone in the family, not just the entrepreneur's need. Each member of the family may sacrifice to support the entrepreneur to reap long-term rewards for the family. When the entrepreneur ignores family needs, is unyielding and rigid, trouble is on the horizon.

> My wife refused to accept that her business was unprofitable, after seven years of working it hard. Here I am, working two jobs to support the family while she refuses to face the music. I begged her to get a part-time job, but she refused. We finally separated. I feel that she chose the business over me.
> *Burnt-Out Entrepreneur*

If this couple had come into couples counseling with me before they landed in divorce court I might have suggested they sit down and create a family plan as discussed in Chapter 1. They would be asked to draw up and sign a family contract that was negotiated in good faith, which both could adhere to. This contract would include their deal breakers—what they were and were not willing to tolerate and sacrifice during the startup phase of the wife's business. This couple would have annually revisited, (at the bare minimum), this contract and re-negotiated it as necessary. Doing this would have allowed them to avoid hitting a point of no return in their relationship because the expectations would have been communicated from the start. The wife would not have felt her husband was unjustifiably pulling his support for her business. Clear expectations, rather than non-verbalized assumptions, would have helped this couple traverse the wife's entrepreneurial path together, instead of it pulling them apart.

The family plan, not just the business plan, drives successful entrepreneurial couples. They willingly make personal sacrifices, like the following, in response to family circumstances.

> When my daughter was born, I wanted to quit my job and stay home with her full-time. My job was pulling in $70,000 a year for our family, so that was no easy decision. My husband took a second job, we moved to a smaller house, and we quit our membership to the golf club. It wasn't easy, but my husband was totally behind my decision. Then, I started a home-based business so that I could take care of my daughter and still bring in some income, and it ended up pulling in more than the salary I quit!
>
> *Former marketing executive turned entrepreneur*

Daily flexibility is as important as a willingness to make major life changes. If you must have dinner at six every night, and a predictable cash flow every month, don't marry or become a business owner! Successful entrepreneurial couples are like a pair of willow trees—strong at the roots, but bending with the weather.

Strategy Two: Find Outside Support

Your intimate partner may be your best friend and confidant, but make sure he or she isn't your only one. A healthy relationship requires two kinds of outside assistance: objective advice and emotional support provided by friends.

Jim and Suzanne, partners in a troubled business, lost money at a frightening rate and fought constantly about how to remedy the situation. Each blamed the other for the company's decline. Their marriage, like their business, was almost bankrupt. They credit their marriage being saved by their joint decision to call upon an outside third party, a seasoned businessman who could advise them on restructuring their company. Since the consultant had no bias or loyalty to either Jim or Suzanne, the couple could hear constructive criticism from him more easily than from each other. Whether you work with your spouse or use your partner as an unpaid business adviser, you will still need occasional objective and neutral input, as from a board of directors, a strategic planner, consultant or business partner. You may invite or even encourage your partner's opinions, but not as your only source.

Find support outside your marriage to help you navigate the twists and turns of entrepreneurial life. As much as you might love your partner, he or she cannot be all things to you all the time. Your spouse can certainly be your best friend, cheerleader and confidant, but should not be your only friend.

> I joined a businesswomen's association that meets once a month at a local restaurant. I've met some terrific women who I confide in when I'm having a hard time. After going to so many business meetings where I focus on putting my best foot forward to attract business, I appreciate the opportunity to be honest front time to time.
> *Graphic artist*

> I found it very difficult to talk about the emotional problems I was having in my business. I didn't want another colleague to think I was a wimp. One day, over lunch, I mentioned to a business colleague that I was having a lot of trouble prospecting new clients. She admitted she was having the same trouble, and we talked openly about it. We agreed to check in with each other once a week. Connecting with a "buddy" to bounce things off was critical to building my business.
> *Business consultant*

> My business coach is as essential to my business success as my investors. Once a week my coach listens to my problems and helps me find solutions. She helps me think creatively and keep my spirits up when I get discouraged. It's great to have a cheerleader other than my husband.
> *Independent IT consultant*

Isolation and emotional hardship can lead the business owner either to bottle everything up (and eventually explode, usually at the most inopportune times) or to flood his or her intimate partner with troubles. Neither response leads to a healthy relationship. Channeling some of the need to complain, brainstorm, or get reassurance will protect your significant other from burnout. Connecting to a spiritual source, a group of like-minded people, or even just one good friend or a journal, can save your marriage during challenging times.

Strategy Three: It's All How You Think About It

You can convert even the worst disasters into good fortune, with the right perspective and enough time. How you cope with unexpected and unwelcomed turns of events directly affects how you explain the meaning of the events to yourself. Are you basically an optimist or a pessimist? Do you have a fixed mindset or a growth mindset?

Pessimists dwell on the worst possibilities, blame themselves for the problem, expect bad events to persist forever, and let problems in one area spill over to all aspects of their life. Depressed pessimists can stay depressed for a long time. They exude negative, heavy energy and bring everyone around them down. Misery enjoys company.

A pessimist might respond to business failure, "It's all my fault. We're never going to recover from this and it's going to ruin every aspect of our life." They take a fatalistic approach as if everything is lost and out of their control.

A disaster to a pessimist is a mere setback to an optimist who sees sad events as temporary and surmountable. Optimists, ever-resilient, rarely get down for long and can contain worries about one issue of their life without spreading them to all aspects of their life. An optimist understands many variables and circumstances play a role in a failure; they do not just blame themselves. Because optimists have a growth mindset, they see difficulties as an opportunity for growth and learning. During trying times they think, "What confluence of events created this situation? What do I need to do differently to avoid it in the future? How do I get out of it?" There is no blame-taking place for optimists; their thoughts and energy are solely directed toward problem-solving activities.

An optimist might say, "The business failed because of my limitations, the economy, and circumstances beyond my control. We'll bounce back from this. I'm not going to let a business disappointment ruin our lives."

The main difference between an optimist and a pessimist is the amount of hope brought to a difficult situation. Thriving entrepreneurial couples maintain an optimistic long-term outlook, always converting lemons to lemonade and reframing life events to see the positive. All situations can be reframed from the negative to the positive if you are willing to create the necessary mindset shift. You can choose to be defeated or you can choose to change course and redirect your actions toward success. In the final analysis, when you are presented with the unanticipated, you make a choice. Winston Churchill famously said at the beginning of WWII, "We have nothing to fear but fear itself."

No one seeks out adversity. If you can avoid hard times, all the better. But reframing your circumstances in a more optimistic light is a skill that you can learn, even if you are of a more pessimistic nature. You can train your mind to shift from negative to positive thinking. After all, worry is simply imagining over and over again the worst happening. Praying for the positive repeatedly is much more productive. Research shows the futility in worrying, since more than 90% of our worries never materialize. Therefore, worrying only serves to drain your time and energy. Instead of worrying, use strategies to shift your mindset—replace negative self-talk with positive, dispute catastrophic thinking, and distract yourself when negative thoughts overwhelm or consume you. Say daily meditations and/or positive affirmations which directly influence the creation of a positive mindset shift.

Following are examples of how you can alter your mindset by choosing your words to shift your thinking from the negative to the positive.

Pessimistic thought: "I'm a real jerk. We're going to lose everything. My wife will probably leave me, and my kids are going to have no respect for me."

Refrained positive thought: "It's too bad that the business didn't make it. It's a good thing that my wife is sticking by me. I guess the kids are going to get a lesson on what the business world is really like."

Catastrophic thinking: "Running a company together is much harder than I expected. We'll probably be divorced in a year."

Refrained positive thought: "Everyone says we'll be a stronger business team because we don't always think alike. I hope that we can learn how to accept our differences."

CLARIFICATION EXERCISE TWO: REFRAMING UNWELCOME CIRCUMSTANCES

Completion time: 30 minutes

Take a few moments with your partner to review your lives together. Select three unwelcomed events since you met, and answer the following questions about each.

1. What good has come of that difficult circumstance?
2. What lessons can you now apply to the future?
3. What strengths have you developed individually and as a couple as a result?
4. What are you thankful for?

Sample event: Miriam was hospitalized for depression and anxiety after she lost her job. Kevin's business performance improved when Miriam's hospitalization forced him to be the sole provider for their family for a year. Miriam opened up emotionally to Kevin after her hospitalization, and they are closer now as a result. They've learned that they can survive tough times together. Miriam has learned how to stop some of her negative thinking, and how to lean on Kevin for support when she needs it. Kevin has learned how to focus on his business productively, even when his personal life is in upheaval. They are thankful that their relationship has survived and that they are still able to live in the house they love.

When You Are Upbeat and Your Partner Is Not

When you can view circumstances brightly, but your partner remains entrenched in toxic thinking, try some of the following approaches:

- Listen without reacting to any negative statements. Give your partner a chance to vent without arguing about his or her right to that point of view.

- Listen for a few moments, and then change the subject. Don't participate in your partner's ruminations beyond what is productive.

- Don't dismiss everything your partner says. You may discover an element of realism worth your attention and immediate acknowledgment.

- Set limits. When you can't handle hearing negative talk, ask your partner to respect your request and explain carefully why you need to keep your positive frame of mind.

- Ask your partner how you can help ease his or her mind or remedy the situation. A simple action like a hug, or a non-action such as not leaving the room when your partner starts to cry, can make a huge difference.

- Be patient and kindhearted. See the world through your partner's eyes and feel compassion for his or her suffering. Walk a mile in his or her shoes to feel the burden, making it easier to relate to. This is not the same as owning it, but feeling it will create empathy for your partner's point of view. Accept his or her negativity as what's true for your partner and hope that in time he or she will come around.

- Reward your partner with affection and positive reinforcement when you spot any signs of optimism.

I am always amazed at how my husband Mitch remains unscathed regardless of the curve balls business and life may throw. He views every problem as a challenge to "think outside the box," and to create innovative solutions—traits which make him an excellent leader and strategic planner. Fatalistic thinking never enters his mind, so he does not have to waste energy minimizing or eradicating it—it just doesn't present itself. Mitch is the calm in the eye of the storm. He helps keep me focused on problem-solving strategies, minimizing my tendency to waste my resources or worry about the "what ifs" while shifting to the "let's think" or "let's try" orientation.

Strategy Four: Take Action and Celebrate Your Progress

When you are overwhelmed and discouraged, you are particularly prone to paralyzing depression and inertia. A downward spiral takes you further from a solution and toward a more monumental problem.

If one is depressed, the other may take the lead. Suggest that the two of you picnic in the park, clean out the garage, or go for a bicycle ride. Action can break a depressive cycle. Respecting your partner's mood and need for solitude, you can coax him or her gently into a change of scenery.

> My wife and I had a business in our basement. Sales weren't coming in, and I was having panic attacks throughout the day. One beautiful spring day my wife demanded that we get out of the house and go to the local park. I protested taking time off from the business during the day, but by getting out of that dark basement I was able to relax and gain a more optimistic perspective. Now, whenever I start to have a panic attack, I go for a walk and it helps me calm down.
>
> *Toymaker*

When Lucinda was in labor with her first daughter, her midwife coached her to get through it one contraction at a time, viewing each contraction as an accomplishment in itself. She assured her that after a finite number of contractions, her daughter would be born. By focusing on the moment and experiencing the progress of labor, she kept Lucinda's fear and frustration to a manageable level.

Couples in any kind of crisis need analogous concentration in the moment. Break your largest challenges into manageable steps and celebrate the small victories along the way. Recognize your partner's progress toward personal and business goals and don't wait until the big moment at the end. When your partner overcomes even one obstacle, express your excitement in a tangible way.

While writing this book, I felt at times the end would never come. For anyone who has ever written a book, or a thesis or a dissertation, there are moments where it feels as if you will never be finished. The task can seem overwhelming and daunting. With every completed chapter however, Mitch would congratulate me and cheer me on saying, "Terrific, every week you get closer to your goal of being a published author. I am so proud of you. I am amazed with how hard you work. You should be proud of yourself." This support and encouragement was exactly what was needed to get me through the frustrations of writing, re-writing, editing and re-editing that a book requires. When I couldn't see the end in sight, Mitch could. If you have ever run a marathon, you understand how the support and cheers of the crowd encourage you to take the next step that you weren't so sure you could take. Yes, there truly is strength in numbers; a couple working in harmony can accomplish so much more than a couple that fights each other every step of the way. The whole is greater than the sum of its parts—this is why a good player might win a game, but a cohesive team can win a championship.

Patty Ann

CLARIFICATION EXERCISE THREE: SMALL ACTIONS WE CAN TAKE TO RESTORE HOPE AND BALANCE

Take a moment to write down—alone or with your partner—ten simple daily actions you can take when you are depressed or overwhelmed that have a history of making you feel better. For example: taking a walk, exercising, going for a drive, walking the dog, cooking a meal, buying flowers, petting the cat. Keep it simple. Think of activities you can do by yourself or with your partner.

Strategy Five: Shift from Dwelling on the Past to Focusing on the Future

Studying the past to learn something, rather than dwelling on it regretfully, is a productive use of energy. Couples who thrive during hard times shift their mindset and emotional attention to building a new future. The entrepreneurial phoenix rises from the ashes of failure and flies toward the couple's new vision.

> We originally had big dreams for a nationwide franchise, at least twenty stores, when my husband and I were childless and driven by ambition. Then I got pregnant unexpectedly with twins. Due to complications, I spent four months of my pregnancy in bed. Our franchise plans went on hold. Once the twins were born, devoting the same level of energy to our business was impossible. We refocused on making our one store the best it could be and raising our family. We aren't as wealthy now as we had hoped we could be, but our decision was the right one for us, and we're happy.
>
> *Gift store owner*

My wife and I moved our family to a new state and bought a small business where we hoped to retire. Six months later, my wife was diagnosed with multiple sclerosis. There we were, in the middle of nowhere, far from decent medical care. We sold the business, moved back to a metropolitan area where she could receive the finest care, and took in a foster child, whom we have since adopted. Our daughter would never have become part of our family had the diagnosis not forced us to move. God had different plans for us than we had for ourselves.

Midwest entrepreneur

CLARIFICATION EXERCISE FOUR: CREATING A NEW VISION

Completion time: 30-60 minutes

Consider your short-term and long-term goals, as an individual and as a couple. Write down, or articulate to each other, a new vision of your future in the next six months, year, and five years. Get the children involved and encourage some family brainstorming, where all ideas, no matter how fantastic or outrageous, are put on the table.

Goals	6 mo	1 yr	5 yrs
Financial Career			
Business direction			
Relationship			
Children			
Social			
Community			
Spiritual Health			
Education			
Health & Wellness			

Revise these goals when new circumstances have entered the picture.

Strategy Six: Solidify Commitment to Your Relationship

People and events will repeatedly test your commitment to your significant other over your lifetime together. In crisis, you may re-evaluate your relationship, question your belonging together, even intensely dislike each other temporarily when hard times bring out the worst in your partner. No, you never bargained for such unpleasant times, but it's what you've got for the time being. Will you walk away when it isn't fun anymore, or will you remain committed to your partner?

Some breakups, precipitated by business crisis, are inevitable. You discover that you have completely incompatible life goals, or you or your partner becomes an uncontrolled alcoholic, adulterer, or workaholic who is never home. I don't assume that every couple that comes into my practice are destined to remain together. Abuse and many addictions should not be tolerated in any relationship. The rise in prescription drug abuse has seen people who would never think of taking illegal substances become drug addicts. Anyone who is an addict, or married to one, must seek help to maintain the viability of their marriage, or their marriage will turn into nothing less than a living hell. When an addict refuses to seek help, these marriages are often doomed. Addictions such as alcoholism, gambling, etc., may have a genetic origin; however, until we can isolate these genes and discover medications that effectively treat these conditions, current treatment for addictions have an incredibly high failure rate. Addictions are a game changer that puts relationships in jeopardy. You are put at risk, emotionally and/or physically when you are married to or you become an addict. Yes we should help our partner if they struggle with addiction; however if an addict refuses to seek help, not only is your business at risk but so is your self esteem, health and that of your children. The dissolution of your relationship may be a necessary, though painful, part of your journey.

Dr. Scott Stanley, a national expert on commitment, distinguishes between two kinds of commitment between couples: constraint commitment and dedication commitment. Constraint commitment rests on obligation and responsibility or the perceived negative consequences of breaking up. If you run a business with your spouse, then you may stay married because dividing the business is too much of a hassle or too costly. These are the main reasons I hear in my work with couples who are miserable yet stay together; they have an overwhelming sense of obligation to their business together and/or their children and they can't afford to get divorced. Your children's well-being may concern you, or you may question your ability to support yourself on your own. A divorce would compromise your family's lifestyle too much. These thoughts constrain you to stay in relationship.

During hard times, you may rely on constraint commitment to pull you through. A deeper form of commitment, however, is that of dedication. You have dedication commitment when you devote yourself to your partner's well-being, growing old together, and developing a healthy, nourishing, and mature relationship. Your marriage is one of your highest priorities and you willingly devote your life to it through the good times and the bad.

When you commit strongly to each other, you sustain your long-term vision toward being in a relationship with your partner. When you experience periods of relationship dissatisfaction, (periods that may last for months or even years) you don't leave; over the long haul, life with your partner is truly satisfying.

When you feel the least in love with your partner you may need to express your lifelong commitment even more. Say to your mate something as simple as, "We're going to stay together through these difficult times, no matter what," or "I'm having trouble expressing affection to you right now, but I still love you," or "Never in a million years did I think we would be dealing with this crap; I love you a lot, but this is really hard for me right now, so don't expect me to fall all over you when you walk in the room." Pull out your marriage vows and reread them to each other. Give your spouse a card that conveys your commitment. Pray for the ability to live up to your commitment that you struggle to keep. Keep your sense of humor, remembering "this too shall pass;" it might just take longer than you would prefer!

In difficult times, a man in financial trouble needs frequent reassurance that his wife won't leave him for a better provider. A woman, when she's not at her best, needs to feel loved, cherished, and reassured that she won't be abandoned. When you are in a crisis or struggle to stay connected, frequently reaffirm your ongoing love and commitment and ask yourself—are we together only because of constraints, or are we still fully dedicated to one another, for a lifetime?

CLARIFICATION EXERCISE FIVE: REMINDERS OF YOUR STRENGTH

Completion time: 30 minutes

This difficult time in your relationship is probably not the first. Yet, you are still together. Rejuvenate your commitment and optimism by reminding yourself of your history as a couple, and your success in overcoming previous obstacles. What previous obstacles have you overcome and with what unwelcome circumstances have you managed to cope? How has your relationship grown and thrived as a result of challenge?

What five challenges have you met as a couple?

What strengths have you developed individually and as a couple as a result?

How has your previous experience together prepared you for your current challenge?

Strategy Seven: Accept and Appreciate Differences in Coping Styles

When Carol faces crisis, she tends to grin and bear it, keep her feelings to herself and act as if everything is fine. Paul deals with his intense anger by immersing himself in distracting activity. Suzanna prays a lot and seeks out a good friend to talk to. Jeffrey analyzes all the different components of the problem and searches for a logical solution. Each has a unique coping style, one no better than another.

From a distance, we can forgive total strangers for their response to crisis. But what about our own partners? When we fear, despair, or fume we may demand that our partners respond the same way that we do. If they don't, we criticize them. "He's in denial." "When will he deal with his real feelings?" "She's so damn hysterical all the time." "Why can't she control herself?"

When we hurt, we want our partners to validate and comfort us, not reject or judge us incompetent. The greatest gift you can give your partner is what he or she needs, not what you think they need. As you each move through stages of denial, anger, depression, and acceptance, you advance at different paces and use different coping strategies. One partner may prefer solitude, another companionship. One partner may need to talk about the problem repeatedly, the other only a little. One partner may rush to solution, while the other deliberates and weighs the possibilities for a long while.

Regardless, expending all your energy to convert or coerce your partner into your way of healing loses a valuable opportunity to support your partner. You likely alienate, rather than comfort, them. Reach out your hand, stretch yourself, and be there for your partner as he or she needs you to be.

Supporting your partner's emotional process is not incompatible with helping them reframe their perceptions when their view of reality has become distorted. Describe to your partner your more hopeful vision and show them a more optimistic way of looking at the same situation without invalidating their feelings. The key is to reframe rather than criticize. Take a look at how the couples below process real fears that have entered their marriages, and how one spouse is able to help the other reframe.

Preston: We're going down the tubes and we're going to lose the house. What a disaster!

Kim: You're right, the business may be closing. That doesn't mean we'll lose the house. We have enough in savings until we find jobs, and in the meantime, my parents will help. We'll be okay.

Cheryl: All of our employees hate me. I'm a lousy boss. I should never have agreed to supervise operations.

Phil: Sure, some employees are angry with you because of our new work rules. But being the boss is tough sometimes. Come on, how many people love their boss? I still think you're doing a great job.

Georgie: That damn insurance company is making our lives miserable ever since the fire. Why do I even bother trying to be a nice guy?

Fred: The employees in data entry wrote a thank you letter about how much they appreciate not being laid off after the fire. They really appreciate you. Here, let me show you that letter—it might cheer you up.

When expectations are not met and one spouse develops a negative mindset, his or her partner can help shift this mindset to a positive one. Acknowledge the difficulty and disappointment of the situation and then remind your partner of the choice they have to change their situation and learn from the experience. When we are afraid, we often express feelings of anger rather than fear; this is especially true for men. The thought of losing a business or a job is very frightening, but it needs to be kept in perspective. Sure, it is scary, yet it is nowhere near the same as facing a life-threatening illness.

Just as partners might have different mindsets borne out of the same circumstance, spouses may also respond differently to the same levels of stress inherent in life. Turning to athletic performance under stress helps illustrate how different people react differently to the same stress levels. A certain level of anxiety is necessary for an athlete to perform at their optimum level and rise to the occasion. Once their anxiety surpasses this level, the athlete can no longer perform optimally. This failure to perform is referred to very derogatively as "choking."

Know what level of anxiety you and your partner can tolerate in your marriage and your business. The ability to tolerate different levels of stress between partners helps stabilize the relationship. This is similar to John Maxwell's concept of "The Law of the Lid," as described in his best-selling book *The 21 Irrefutable Laws of Leadership*, illustrates how an organization can only perform to the level of its leader. We all have our breaking point; when one partner is reaching or at this point, the other partner can play a significant role in reducing the anxiety and fear to enable his or her partner to re-group, re-focus, and create a positive mindset necessary for moving forward. Great advances are often made when businesses have been forced to change courses in the face of adversity and unmet expectations.

Patty / Ann

CLARIFICATION EXERCISE SIX: DEFINE YOUR COPING STYLE

Completion time: 15 minutes

You may assume that your partner knows exactly what you want or need when you are in distress. Explain these needs clearly so that your partner can better support you as you desire. Complete the following sentences with your partner:

- When I am tired, or overwhelmed, I need you to…

- When I am angry at circumstances or other people, I need…

- When I am depressed, I need you to…

- When you (blank) I usually feel so much better.

Strategy Eight: Forgive Your Partner and Yourself

What if you struggle because your partner made a serious error in judgment or did something entirely wrong in your estimation? Now you must live with the consequences. Can you forgive your partner? What if you yourself messed up? Can you forgive yourself and move on?

Forgiveness is a process and a choice; it takes time. It does not happen overnight. Forgiveness begins with a desire to forgive, even if you can't do so right away. To forgive does not mean to condone the hurtful experience. To forgive is to let go of prolonged guilt, regret, or resentment that poisons your ability to move beyond unfortunate circumstances. A business or personal crisis can capsize some of your cherished beliefs. If you always believed that your husband would provide for you, how will you respond when your husband's business fails? Couples who work through these disillusions emerge with a more impenetrable love and a stronger relationship, but disillusionment can be the most painful experience of your marriage. It shatters any illusions you brought into your marriage based on preconceived notions of how you thought your marriage was going to play out. It is a bitter pill to swallow and you might find yourself bitterly saying, "This is not what I signed up for when I got married." If you are at this crossroads in your marriage, seek the help of a relationship expert.

If you forgive your partner, make sure your partner knows this and clearly communicate your forgiveness directly and often. Put it in writing. Partners may need to hear it, or read it, several times and experience you behaving as if its true, before they trust you. Remember: If your spouse cannot forgive him or herself, it will be difficult for him or her to believe in your forgiveness. As you both get on with your lives, and positive directions emerge, your partner may only then be able to see his or her actions in a brighter light.

If your partner is angry at you, a simple and direct "I'm sorry," goes a long way to healing the relationship. Refrain from either of two extremes—denying your responsibility or exaggerating the magnitude of your sins. An error in judgment is not a failure in life. Nobody is perfect; those who think they are tend to most vigorously deny their imperfections. Above all, be patient with yourself and your partner. This too shall pass, though perhaps not as quickly as you would like.

KEEP PERSPECTIVE AND
REMEMBER YOUR PRIORITIES

When business challenges throw us off center, we may take actions inconsistent with our deepest values or concerns. Although many entrepreneurs describe a stable, satisfying marriage with healthy and happy children as a higher priority than having business success, many admit being locked into daily business routines that preclude time with their families. Long hours, emotional absenteeism, and money pressures all contribute to temporary amnesia. Some entrepreneurs lose perspective and forget their deepest priorities until a family, health, or business crisis forces them to reorient themselves.

We learned a big lesson seven years ago. My father died, and we had to bury him within twenty-four hours because he was Jewish. My husband and I were working on three tight deadlines, but we wanted to go to the funeral. One client threatened to sue us if we didn't stick with our original commitment. We were so scared of being sued and losing everything in the business, we didn't go to the funeral. Now we regret our decision.

Husband and wife business partners

On the worst days, what helps most is knowing that the alternative is working for someone else in a job. When I think about that, I make a conscious choice again to keep struggling in my own business.

Home based graphic artist

Some entrepreneurs rise to the top, acquire material wealth, and then lose all of their assets in a subsequent humiliating business failure. After rebounding, they never look at business success or prosperity in quite the same way. Those who kept their sense of humor and connection as a team coped best.

In 2011, the bank that financed me ran into big trouble and demanded payment for my loan, due in full immediately. I knew I hit bottom when I traded in my Porsche for a 1994 minivan.

Business consultant

Patty / Ann

CONCLUSION:
BROKEN BONES OR SHATTERED GLASS?

A client once described her previous marriage as a crystal pitcher that shattered into thousands of pieces when her husband had an affair. She felt that no amount of effort or love could glue those pieces back again, and that her marriage was destroyed. Some crises hit so deep, you have no way to recover and you lose the relationship forever, but in my experience as a relationship expert and therapist, I have seen tremendous healing in relationships, and I dare say, although an affair is never a welcomed event in a marriage, some marriages have to go really far down, before they come back up stronger and closer than ever.

I prefer the broken bone analogy for any crises in a long committed marriage. A broken bone heals stronger at the break and so can your relationship with optimism, reflection and relationship skills that can be learned.

Dr. Mihaly Csikszentmihalyi counsels, "Adversity, unfortunately, is a fact of life. It will always be present in one form or the other. The question is, are you going to let it destroy the quality of your life, or are you going to find ways of making it a springboard for some new adventure or growth? One way or another, you have to cope with it. You might as well find a way that will make life richer."

What is life really all about? This has not been a book about the philosophy of life, yet I hope it has been a book which has demonstrated the answer to this question. Life is all about relationships. The way to successfully chart a course which leads to an enriched marriage and a prosperous business is through the relationship skills discussed in this book. At lightning speed, more and more people seek to create a life on their own terms. These women and men, the next generation of business leaders, wives, husbands, mothers and fathers want to live a meaningful life with happy marriages, successful careers and deep friendships. The goal of this book has been to provide you with proven strategies and tools that allow you to do just that.

Flexibility is essential for any entrepreneurial journey. The Japanese observe how, during a heavy snowfall, the resilient bamboo bends but the unyielding oak breaks. May you and your partner celebrate your successes, learn from your mistakes, and thrive as a couple on your entrepreneurial adventure.

For a list of my products and services go to:
www.relationshiptoolbox/products and/or
www.relationshiptoolbox/services
for proven strategies and tools created for successfully
resolving business and relationship challenges.

RESOURCES

Relationship Tools for Success in Business and Life are available on my website: www.relationshiptoolbox.com

For more information on Marriage and Intimate Relationship topics, please refer to the following website and books:

www.drpattyann.com—My website dedicated to couples who are looking to save their marriage from infidelity, lack of effective communication, money fights and other relationship problems.

The Seven Principles for Making Marriage Work by John Gottman—a relationship book based on scientific research that outlines seven principles that guides couples on a path of harmonious and long-lasting relationships (2000,Three Rivers Press).

10 Lessons to Transform Your Marriage by John M. Gottman and Julie Schwartz Gottman—another book by the award winning author John Gottman, a leading authority on relationships where he provides tools and proven strategies to regain affection and romance through effective communication skills (June 26, 2007, Three Rivers Press).

The Divorce Remedy: The Proven 7-Step Program for Saving Your Marriage by Michele Weiner-Davis—a practical guide with proven strategies and tools to save your marriage from divorce (2002, Fireside).

For more information on How to Become a Successful Entrepreneur, consider the following books:

Shark Tales: How I Turned $1000.00 into a Billion Dollar Business by Barbara Corcoran and Bruce Littlefield (February 9, 2011, Portfolio/Penguin). In this book Barbara Corcoran shares her personal story on how she built a real estate empire in New York based on gut, determination and an indomitable spirit.

The Boss of You: Everything A Woman Needs to Know to Start, Run and Maintain Her Own Business by Lauren Bacon and Emira Mears (2008, Seal Press). This book walks you through the process of turning your hobby into a money making business.

The Startup Owner's Manual, the Step-by-Step guide to Build a Great Company by Steve Blank and Bob Dorf. This manual is an indispensable reference guide for entrepreneurs on "how to" build a successful, scalable startup company.

For more information on Leadership, any book by John C. Maxwell is a must read. Below are two of my favorites by this author:

The 21 Irrefutable Laws of Leadership. Follow Them and People Will Follow You (10th Anniversary Edition) by John C. Maxwell (2007, Thomas Nelson, Inc).

The 5 Levels of Leadership. Proven Steps to Maximize Your Potential by John C. Maxwell (2011, Thomas Nelson, Inc).

For more information on Mindset and Positive Psychology consider the following books:

Authentic Happiness: Using the New Positive Psychology to Realize Your Potential for Lasting Fulfillment, by Martin Seligman. (January 5, 2006, Free Press).

Mindset: The New Psychology of Success, How We Can Learn To Fulfill Our Potential by Carol S. Dweck, Ph.D (2006, Ballantine Books).

Spontaneous Happiness (Kindle Edition) by Andrew Weil, MD.

For more information on Personal Self Development, consider the following books:

Awaken the Giant Within: How to Take Immediate Control of Your Mental, Emotional, Physical, and Financial Destiny! by Anthony Robbins (November 1, 1992, Free Press).

Living an Extraordinary Life. Unlocking Your Potential for Success, Joy and Fulfillment by Robert White, (2004, Balance Point International).

Unlimited: How to Build an Exceptional Life by Jillian Michaels (2011, Crown Archetype).

For more information on Women and Wealth, consider the following books:

A Purse of Your Own: An Easy Guide to Financial Security by Deborah Owens and Brenda Lane Richardson (December 29, 2009, Simon and Schuster).

Emotional Currency: A Woman's Guide to Building a Healthy Relationship with Money by Kate Levinson, Ph.D., (April 12, 2011, Crown Publishing House).

The Money Class: Learn to Create Your New American Dream, by Suze Orman ((March 8, 2011, Spiegel & Grau).

Self Publish Today! by Cindy Tyler (July 21, 2011, Vervante), For more information visit www.vervante.com.

For more information about Emotional Intelligence and Success, consider the following books:

Emotional Intelligence, 10th Anniversary Edition, Why It Can Matter More than IQ by Daniel Goleman, (September 26, 2006, Bantam Books).

The 7 Habits of Highly Effective People. Powerful Lessons in Personal Change by Stephen R. Covey (1989, Free Press).

The 10 Laws of Enduring Success by Maria Bartiromo and Catherine Whitney (March 30, 2010, Crown Business).

Dr. Patty Ann's Product Links

Dr. Patty Ann's Relationship Toolbox™
Rekindle Romance & Happiness in Your Relationship
Go to: www.relationshiptoolbox.com/toolbox

Stop Fighting and Bring Back the Romance in Your Relationship with this revolutionary one-of-a-kind product! This product reveals secrets and proven strategies & tools that will *dramatically renew love & happiness in your intimate relationship* while tremendously improving the overall quality of your life. Bonus exercises and other extras! Want to fall in love all over again? Don't delay – Order your copy now.

Dr. Patty Ann's Relationship Toolbox™
Quick Start Program
Go to: www.relationshiptoolbox.com/quickstart

Are you *really serious* about learning effective communication skills to enrich your relationship? Don't miss out on these *secret, proven communication skills and techniques* practically guaranteed to *dramatically* improve your verbal and non-verbal communication skills so you stop having the same old arguments - once and for all. Take the first step - Buy your copy now.

Relationship Toolbox™
Affirmation Cards
Go to: www.relationshiptoolbox.com/cards

Affirmation Cards - An A-Z guide to increase romance & happiness in your relationship by playing a matching card game using *never before revealed* relationship affirmations. Buy a few – The perfect gift!

Relationship Affirmation Playing Cards – enjoy playing any regular card game with the one you love. The added fun is every card has an affirmation for you to read out aloud, say to yourself or make it part of the game. Be creative! These make great gifts!

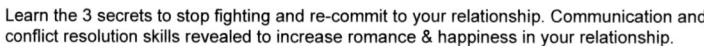

E-BOOK: The 3 Secrets to Increase Romance & Happiness In Your Relationship
Go to: www.relationshiptoolbox.com/products/ebook

Learn the 3 secrets to stop fighting and re-commit to your relationship. Communication and conflict resolution skills revealed to increase romance & happiness in your relationship.

Love.Money.Freedom.
Go to: www.relationshiptoolbox.com/lmf

Proven strategies for successfully resolving business and relationship challenges. This product is specifically designed for entrepreneurs and small business owners who want to create the best of both worlds – a thriving profitable business and a healthy, happy relationship.

How to Have an Organized Home Even With a Disorganized Spouse (or Partner, Significant Other, Roommate, Whatever)
Go to: www.relationshiptoolbox.com/organized

Does your spouse's mess and/or clutter drive you crazy? Dr. Patty Ann has teamed up with an organization expert to offer tools, strategies & great gadgets to get your home or office organized just the way you love it!

Patty / Ann

SERVICES AVAILABLE
FROM DR. PATTY ANN

Dr. Patty Ann is available for speaking engagements, workshops, seminars and corporate retreats. To book these events contact info@relationshiptoolbox.com or call 1-877-456-7230

In addition to her relationship work with individuals, Dr. Patty Ann offers exclusive work with couples and/or individuals in powerful, transformational VIP Couple Days, VIP Couples Weekend, Individual and Couple Consultations in-person or remotely via skype, or phone. To schedule these exclusive offerings contact us at: info@relationshiptoolbox.com or call 1-877-456-7230

Patty Ann

**GET READY FOR
DR. PATTY ANN TUBLIN'S
NEXT BOOK:**

Not Tonight Dear, I Saw Who You Are "Friends" with on Facebook

Save your Marriage from the Cheating, Lies, and Devastation of Infidelity

Infidelity is no longer a tragedy that happens to someone else you heard about, or even, your best girlfriend. It could hit closer to home than you ever thought possible. In fact, you might be the one cheating on your spouse or you may be married to someone who has cheated on you. Record numbers of very successful entrepreneurial and corporate women are drawn into affairs, or been the victim of an affair, and whether they are emotional or sexual, the damage to their marriage, and often themselves, is devastating.

Not Tonight Dear, I Saw Who You Are "Friends" with on Facebook is the next book in the *Not Tonight Dear* series. This book focuses on the lessons learned from my years of helping high profile, successful, wealthy entrepreneurial and corporate women who might appear to their neighbors and friends like they "have it all," but behind closed doors, their marriages are crumbling, and they are too. These marriages can not only be saved but they can also thrive, and even better, the devastation of infidelity can be avoided all together!

Be the first to own and have this relationship saving advice to prevent an affair or heal from its traumatic aftermath! Email Dr. Patty Ann at: info@relationshiptoolbox.com.